333.79 HAL
Hallett, Steve, 1966-
Life without oil

P9-CAD-529

EAGLE VALLEY LIBRARY DISTRICT
P.O. BOX 240 600 BROADWAY
EAGLE, CO 81631 / 328-8800

EAGLE VALLEY LIBRARY DISTRICT

1 06 0004934981

LIFE
WITHOUT
OIL

Moai of Manhattan. Image courtesy of Steve Hallett.

STEVE HALLETT WITH JOHN WRIGHT

LIFE

WHY WE MUST SHIFT

WITHOUT

TO A NEW ENERGY FUTURE

OIL

Prometheus Books

59 John Glenn Drive
Amherst, New York 14228–2119

Published 2011 by Prometheus Books

Life without Oil: Why We Must Shift to a New Energy Future. Copyright © 2011 by Steve Hallett and John Wright. All rights reserved. No part of this publication may be reproduced, stored
in a retrieval system, or transmitted in any form or by any means, digital, electronic, mechanical,
photocopying, recording, or otherwise, or conveyed via the Internet or a website without prior
written permission of the publisher, except in the case of brief quotations embodied in critical
articles and reviews.

Cover image © 2011 Media Bakery, Inc.
Jacket design by Grace M. Conti-Zilsberger

Inquiries should be addressed to
Prometheus Books
59 John Glenn Drive
Amherst, New York 14228–2119
VOICE: 716–691–0133
FAX: 716–691–0137
WWW.PROMETHEUSBOOKS.COM

15 14 13 12 11   5 4 3 2 1

Library of Congress Cataloging-in-Publication Data

Hallett, Steve, 1966–
    Life without oil : why we must shift to a new energy future / by Steve Hallett and John
Wright.
        p. cm.
    Includes bibliographical references and index.
    ISBN 978–1–61614–401–2 (cloth : alk. paper)
    1. Energy policy—Social aspects. 2. Energy consumption—Social aspects. 3. Energy
development—Social aspects. 4. Social change—Forecasting. 5. Technology and
civilization. 6. Human ecology. 7. Fossil fuels. I. Wright, John, 1952– II. Title.

HD9502.A2H2425 2011
333.79—dc22

2010048463

Printed in the United States of America on acid-free paper

EAGLE VALLEY LIBRARY DISTRICT
P.O. BOX 240 600 BROADWAY
EAGLE, CO 81631 / 328-8800

To

Dan, Pat, Sami, Juliana, and Joseph

CONTENTS

THE INVISIBLE HAND

We live in a society absolutely dependent on science and technology and yet have cleverly arranged things so that almost no one understands science and technology.

Carl Sagan[1]

There is a fascinating group of religions unique to the South Pacific and Papua New Guinea known as cargo cults. These religions arose independently on a number of islands when Japanese and American forces set up bases during the Second World War. The islanders were struck by the huge volumes of "cargo" these strange new people repeatedly received. Planes that appeared to have been summoned from the skies flew down to land on flattened strips beside mysterious towers. They watched their odd new neighbors perform even stranger rituals: marching in step, carrying weapons, saluting one another, wearing matching clothing, and the like. And the cargo kept coming, in great volumes, delivered by an invisible hand.

The islanders concluded that the strangers had summoned the cargo from their gods with these rituals, and so they set out to summon their own cargo. They prepared landing strips in clearings in the jungle and erected replica control towers and even mock planes. They marched carrying sticks and waited for the gods to deliver. That the cargo never arrived proved only that their rituals were inadequate and their faith imperfect, and so they persisted.

Cargo cults exist to this day, and there are a number of variations on the theme. The largest cult awaits the return of the prophet John Frum, who was probably an American airman posted on the island of Tanna, Vanuatu, during the war. Another group on Tanna reveres Prince Phillip (yes, Queen Elizabeth's bloke). The honored greeting he received as he descended from his plane on a royal visit in 1974 made it abundantly clear that he was a prophet of high standing.[2]

It's tempting to giggle, but lacking knowledge of the outside world, the concept of divinely supplied cargo is not completely unreasonable. That it is flat wrong is only clear to those who presume to know how the world works. But ask your average American or Brit where their last meal came from. When they flick on a light switch, ask them who or what supplied the electricity. Where does the water come from that fills your glass? And what about the glass? These questions are surprisingly difficult to answer in full. The modern world has become so complex that most of us have a very limited understanding of how it works. Every time I hear somebody "say grace" to thank God for a meal, I secretly hope they don't really mean it.

None of this may matter as long as there is food in the grocery, electricity at the flick of a switch, and clean freshwater to pour into a waiting glass. The problem comes when things start to go wrong. When they do, we will need to try harder, have more faith, and convince the gods to send more cargo.

EXISTENTIAL THREAT, ROOT CAUSE, CORE PROBLEM

We seem to have quite a few problems: global climate change, peak oil, overpopulation, collapsing fisheries, desertification, wealth inequality, species extinctions, freshwater shortages, hapless governments, deforestation, disease epidemics, and agricultural failures top the list. These problems are occurring either globally or regionally, and each is severe in its own right. The fact that they are all accumulating at the same time makes them significantly more dangerous. They represent a serious challenge—but do they represent an existential threat?

The threat is real, imminent, and largely unavoidable. It is not a threat to the existence of our species, but it is a threat to our societies. What's more, our civilizations have been in similar situations before. Facing rising populations, environmental degradation, and resource depletion, a long list of civilizations from the Maya to the Romans all collapsed. The precedent is set—and it is not an encouraging one.

The problems we face interact in many different ways, making analysis of the potential outcomes confusing. Declining rainfall can threaten forests, and this might be one consequence of global climate change. Deforestation, meanwhile, can inhibit cloud formation and decrease rainfall, magnifying the impacts of climate change. Desertification and freshwater depletion are accelerated by overpopulation, and the pressure on collapsing fisheries is exacerbated by agricultural failures. Disease epidemics are closely linked with poverty, and biodiversity loss is linked to urbanization and deforestation. The massive collection of problems we face appears to paint a picture too complex to fully comprehend, but, in many ways, the situation is rather simple, and a few rules render analysis more straightforward. As complex as the dangerous, interacting impacts may be, they are all connected to a recent change in the ways societies function—a root cause—and an inherent failing in human societies—a core problem.

Humans have trodden the pathway of development since we chipped our first stone tools out of the rocks of Olduvai Gorge millions of years ago. For the first million years or so, progress was painstakingly slow: better tools and the taming of fire were our great accomplishments. We shifted up a gear when we began to farm about ten thousand years ago. Thousands of years of grand experiments in civilization followed, leaving some of the most enduring monuments to the power of our innovation—the Moai of Easter Island, the Great Pyramid at Giza, the hieroglyphic stairway at Copán, and the Roman Colosseum—but all those civilizations failed. But then, little more than two centuries ago, the pathway of civilization took a sudden turn, and who would have guessed that it would happen on a rather small, cold island at the western edge of the known world?[3]

A dramatic chain of events was set in motion when the British Empire began to burn coal. Coal was the catalyst for the Industrial Revolution, and the Industrial Revolution launched the modern world. We tend to think of the Industrial Revolution as an era of machines, and it was, but it was much more fundamentally the era of coal. Coal was the fuel for a new type of machine that ran on a new, external power source, and none of these machines could have been invented and developed until this new energy-dense fuel was tapped.

The importance of coal is hard to overstate: its adoption did nothing less than change the thermodynamics of civilization. Here, suddenly, was not just a powerful new fuel but a fuel that did not need to be made. Coal did not need to be planted and grown. It could be simply dug out of the ground and burned, and there were vast reserves. A source of energy that had been stored underground for millions of years could now be unleashed, and civilization embarked on a new energy-input model.

While the first fossil fuel propelled us along our path toward this glittering modern world, it also propelled our environmental decline. This new energy source spewed pollutants and spawned polluting industries. Forests could be logged faster, goods could be transported more rapidly, and more and better steel could be smelted. Populations began to grow, and societies were reorganized under industrialization.

And then, while the coal era was in full swing, another energy input eclipsed it. The second fossil fuel was more energy-dense than coal and much more versatile. Its power to create and destroy was even greater than coal's, and so, barely a century ago, the Industrial Revolution morphed into the petroleum interval. We have spent the last two centuries building a civilization on coal and the last century building it bigger still on oil. Fossil fuels have been the wellspring of this massive, complex, glorious modern world. Fossil fuels are also the root cause of the biggest problems we face.

But coal and oil are finite resources, and they will run out. This is very dangerous because our civilization is highly dependent on them. On the other hand, it may also be viewed as encouraging because our destruction of the natural world has been accelerated by the use of fossil fuels. We don't know exactly when our fossil fuels will run out, but we can predict it to within a few decades. By the end of this century, our oil and natural gas supplies will be virtually nonexistent, and limited coal supplies will be restricted to only a handful of countries.

Even more important than the end of oil is the point at which its production goes into decline, and this peak of oil production is upon us. Our supply of fossil fuels—oil first, then natural gas, and then coal—will go into decline over the next few decades. We are at the peak of a remarkable two-hundred-year glitch in the history of civilization and are about to embark on the descent. The coming changes will be earth-shattering.

But it's foolish to blame fossil fuels for all this—they are rocks, oils, and gases. We are to blame. We have chosen to burn these fuels to power our civilization, and so, beyond this root cause, the core problem is our failure to see that this model of civilization would lead us into danger and then, when we can see, it is our failure to act.

FAILURE TO SEE, FAILURE TO ACT

"What you see is what you get" is a favorite truism, but, like most truisms, as an Ames room at any decent children's museum will ably demonstrate, it's not entirely true. An Ames room is misshapen room with misshapen furnishings adjusted to match. When we look into the room from the outside, our brains recalibrate the scene so that we "see" a regular room that has square tiles on the floor, a round clock face, and a normal-looking sofa in front of a rectangular television. Nothing seems strange until two people walk in. Although the two people may be of equal stature, the person standing at one end of the room looks tiny and the other looks huge. Our brain tells us that the room should be a set of regular geometries, and we therefore conclude that the people must be different sizes. Wow, that is one *big* guy, we say, but he's simply standing at the end of the room with a five-foot ceiling. The little midget at the other end of the room is no such thing; he's simply under a fifteen-foot ceiling. As the two subjects look at the clock face from inside the room, they see that it's not round at all but oval, and they no longer want to sit on the crazy-looking sofa or watch anything on the rhomboid television.

This doesn't mean that we can't trust what we see at all. Trees look as though they grow upward because they do, and elephants look bigger then mice because they are; but the example of the Ames room is a good way of reminding us just how reliant we are on our sight. It's also a good reminder that while we can depend on most of what we see, we can't trust it entirely. What you see is not always what you get.

The dominance of our sense of sight enables us to respond rapidly to our environment, and this has been entirely adequate for millions of years. However, it is no longer adequate. There has been little need to plan more than a year into the future through virtually the entire history of our species, but there is a great need for planning now. Our brains have perceived and processed the environment in the same way since our hunter-gatherer days.

A key part of the brain responding to fear is the amygdala, which responds quickly to potential danger before more cognitive parts of the brain can add reason. A sudden noise might be an onrushing predator; a movement in the grass might be a snake. In these cases, a rapid response is essential, and so we have evolved an extremely efficient mechanism for coping with immediate dangers. Evolution under response to environments that are visible and immediate, such as an attack by a lion, are use-less for understanding the depletion of an underground aquifer or the enrichment of the atmosphere with an invisible gas that creeps up on you and is impossible to "see." Our mechanism for coping with abstract, slow-developing dangers is not hardwired. We need to learn and then teach it.

Another way to consider this is through the eyes of Louis Pasteur. In the middle of the nineteenth century, people still believed that food spoilage and disease were caused by the spontaneous alteration of the nature of materials—a classic nonscientific phenomenological explana-tion. It had entered the human psyche as fact simply because it seemed to fit with what people could see. A glass of milk is liquid, white, and has little smell. Leave it a while, and it transforms into something more solid, colorful, and stinky.

Pasteur disproved the theory of spontaneous generation in a simple and elegant experiment. He put broth in flasks, sterilized them, and then drew out the necks of the flasks into a long curve. Microbes could not pass the curve in the neck to contaminate the broth, so it remained sterile: it never spontaneously altered. Tipping the broth into the curved neck brought it into contact with microbes, and it spoiled. The spoilage was no mysterious phenomenon. It was caused by living things too small to see. What was particularly brilliant about Pasteur's experiment was that he was able to expand people's vision through science. Suddenly, microbiology had a scientific basis on which to operate, and it developed by leaps and bounds.

The intuitive, obvious-seeming explanation for a particular phe-nomenon is not always the right one. Science methodically unravels counterintuitive phenomena, finds ways to understand the workings of the natural world, and draws back the curtain on the invisible hand of nature.

At the beginning of the Industrial Revolution, nobody could have predicted that there would be cheap transatlantic flights, that their great-grandchildren would be buying their toys from China, or that a population of seven billion would be inhabiting what is now a warming world. We see it now, however, and so we have made a major step. But seeing a problem and acting on it are two very different things.

The sirens have been blaring for years, and yet change does not seem to be coming. There has been a substantial change in awareness and attitude, and many people have responded in small ways, but the roller coaster surges forward. Populations still climb, the destruction of natural systems continues unabated, the planet warms, and coal and oil continue to be sought and burned. In fact, despite our professed concern and protestations, our consumption of resources and our destruction of the environment have not only failed to stabilize but have continued to accelerate. The willingness to act is not translated from individuals to groups of people. It is becoming clear that what is needed is not only motivated people but also motivated communities.

The failure of communities to motivate and enable people to live up to their capabilities comes in a number of forms. One is explained by social psychologists such as Stanley Milgram and Phil Zimbardo, who demonstrated that individuals can be very weak-minded in coercive social settings.[4] Another is the tragedy of the commons, explained by Garrett Hardin, which shows how nonfunctional communities can rapidly destroy their own resource base.[5]

Milgram demonstrated the horrendous things that regular people can do in their unthinking obedience to authority. He led Yale University students to deliver what they thought were fatal electric shocks to people just because they were told to do so by a scientist in a lab coat. Zimbardo randomly assigned Stanford University students[6] to serve as guards or prisoners in a mock prison. It may have begun as a mock prison, but a very real prison was what it became when the "guards" started to torture their "prisoners." Lacking support from a supportive community, individuals can behave in disastrous ways. These experiments shed light on the unthinkable atrocities perpetrated by the hitherto regular folks that became monsters when they contributed to the extermination of millions in Nazi concentration camps or took up machetes to hack their neighbors to death in the Rwandan genocide.

Hardin's tragedy of the commons describes how good, rational people can form destructive communities. Finding themselves in an environment with limited resources, people need to form functional communities that can preserve those resources. In this they frequently fail. Instead of protecting their long-term future by conserving resources, they protect their short-term gains by competing, deplete their resources to the point of collapse, and bring about the failure of the community. This occurs again and again, even when everybody in the community recognizes the risk. Forming cohesive communities that can cooperate on the commons is no easy task.

Our values and ideologies often get in the way as well. When it comes to how the world works, we become fixated on ideas. The Inuit of the Canadian Arctic believed that the seals they hunted were replaced by the spirits each season. Their misunderstanding was not important until they acquired guns, but no number of spirits could replace the seals once the shooting began. We used to think the earth was flat and that the sun revolved around it—and it was heresy to think otherwise. We become deeply attached to beliefs that cause us to veer away from a logical understanding of the living world, and it can get us in trouble.

We also become deeply fixated on ideologies, and these can cause trouble too. Communism seemed like a good idea until the first major communist government took over in Russia and swallowed its neighbor states. The Soviet Union attempted to spread its utopian dream around the world, but, as it began to fail, it increasingly repressed the very people it had sought to save. It is very dangerous for a society to become too attached to an ideology because it can be tempted to defend that ideology beyond any point of reason.

ADAM SMITH WAS WRONG

> . . . by directing industry in such a manner as its produce may be of the greatest value he intends only his own gain and he is [. . .] led by an invisible hand to promote an end which was no part of his intention. By pursuing his own interest he frequently promotes that of the society more effectually than when he really intends to promote it. I have never known much good done by those who affected to trade for the public good. It is an affectation, indeed, not very common among merchants, and very few words need to be used in dissuading them from it.
>
> Adam Smith, *An Inquiry into the Nature and the Causes of the Wealth of Nations*[7]

Adam Smith was way ahead of his time, his economic theories were visionary, and his basic premise is true. Markets, left to their own devices, operating under conditions of unconstrained free trade and competition, do appear to be controlled by an invisible hand. Supply and demand set the ideal price for a commodity without intervention. Seeking only their own self-interest by buying and selling the best products at the best possible price, merchants spur innovation and create a level, fair marketplace. But there are problems with free-market capitalism.[8]

The first problem is that free-market economics has been elevated from the status of an economic theory to that of an ideology, sometimes fraught with religious obsession. The Cold War demonstrated the superiority of the capitalist economy of the United States over the centrally controlled economy of the Soviet Union, and we seem to have concluded that capitalism is the only viable economic system. It is considered heresy in some quarters to question this.

The ultimate problem with free-market economics, however, is that while the price of products is controlled by the invisible hand of the markets, the relationship of the economy to the environment is largely ignored. Impacts that occur outside the boundaries of a specific economic transaction are considered irrelevant to it and are brushed aside as *externalities*.

In the short term this may be true, but in the long term it is false. Externalities have a nasty habit of accumulating and then coming back to bite us. The price of resources is also regulated by the invisible hand of nature. Global warming is the simplest measure of this. While it is uncertain that any given economic transaction will generate some measure of "progress," it is quite certain that it will release some carbon dioxide. The carbon dioxide released is completely irrelevant to the transaction at hand, has no short-term impact, and is discounted from the economic calculus. In the long term, however, global warming may become one of the biggest economic factors of all.

The invisible hand of nature is much more powerful than the invisible hand of the market, but since it operates on much longer timescales, we fail to include it in our economic models or even to acknowledge its existence. Nature dictates that externalities will accumulate, that finite resources will eventually be exhausted, and that renewable resources must be harvested no faster than they can renew themselves. Our failure to understand that ecology is the foundation of economics has led us, as it led many civilizations before us, to the brink of disaster.

There are four fundamental laws of ecology that cannot be violated in the long term:

1. *Energy can neither be created nor destroyed.* All energy enters the biosphere from the sun and is transferred to other forms thereafter.[9] This law also applies to fossil fuels that were formed over millions of years underground. When energy is transferred from one form to another, it gradually degrades, releasing wastes and ending up as dissipated heat.

2. *You can never do one thing.* Ecological systems are complex, and one impact is certain to cause others. The secondary impacts may be small, changing the functioning of the system very little, or they may be large with far-reaching consequences. Activities such as the harvesting of resources from the environment and the combustion of fossil fuels should be expected to have multiple unintended consequences. Systems that are tightly interdependent lack resiliency, and the impacts upon them are more likely to spread.

3. *Diverse systems are more stable than simplified systems.* The simplification of ecological systems makes them vulnerable. Agriculture, for example, is a simplified ecosystem in which the dominance of a single species—the crop—is artificially supported. Dramatic population impacts, such as plant disease epidemics, are much more likely in a wheat field than in an unmanaged grassland. This law extends to human cultures, communities, and economies, which are more robust when they are diverse than when they are simplified. One weakness of the global economy is the "one size fits all" ideology of free-trade economics that simply does not work the same way in all countries.

4. *All organisms, including humans and their societies, are subject to the laws of ecology.* Nature is not only those wild places absent of humans but also the primary realm within which humans live. Humans cannot control nature, nor can they escape it.

The laws of ecology have never changed. All civilizations, as they have prospered and grown, have repeatedly violated the laws of ecology and failed. We seem to feel that with our modern world of abundant energy, sophisticated communications, and political freedoms that we have broken the mold: but we have not. We are violating the laws of ecology on the grandest scale ever, and it puts us in great peril.

WHAT SHOULD WE DO? WHAT SHOULD WE SAVE?

> **[. . .] Grant me the serenity to accept things I
> cannot change, the courage to change the things I
> can, and the wisdom to know the difference.**
>
> Alcoholics Anonymous[10]

Are we trying to save the world? There is a huge new green movement afoot (although it sometimes looks more like a big green party). There are lots of books available telling us how to save the world: *How to Save the World*; *365 Ways to Save the Earth*; *How to Save the Planet*; *1,001 Ways to Save the Earth*. We can even *Serve God, Save the World* in an environmentally conscious way.[11] Surely everything will be fine now that we have this new awareness and mobilization of human ingenuity, right?

I think we have passed the tipping point and can no longer prevent a major economic collapse. Our society has grown too large, has depleted too many resources, and has caused too much environmental degradation, and—as our fossil fuel supplies go into decline—we will not be able to maintain this overburdened colossus of a society. The world cannot be saved as it is. The combined impacts of two centuries of fossil fuel–powered civilization building, pollution, and resource depletion will finally overwhelm our support systems. The time has passed for trying to prevent the inevitable; it is time to prioritize the retreat. What should we put on the priority list for saving? What do we have that is irreplaceable? What things will be the most valuable in the generations to come?

PART I
A BRIEF HISTORY OF PROGRESS

CHAPTER 1
SEEDS OF CIVILIZATION

IN THE BEGINNING . . .

**Nature has no mercy at all. Nature says "I am going
to snow. If you have on a bikini and no snow shoes,
that's tough. I am going to snow anyway."**

Maya Angelou[1]

It's quite ironic that we are concerned about changes in the concentration of gases in the atmosphere. The composition of the earth's atmosphere has undergone much bigger upheaval than the meager increases in greenhouse gases that are currently getting us all excited. The planet has been much hotter than it is now. It has also been much colder. The very early earth had no oceans, had an atmosphere devoid of oxygen, was scorching hot, and was frequently bombarded by debris left over from the formation of the solar system. The "first atmosphere," primarily hydrogen and helium, was lost to space; and the "second atmosphere," formed by the release of gases from volcanoes and asteroid impacts, was a toxic brew of ammonia, methane, water vapor, carbon dioxide, and nitrogen. Nonetheless, it was in this seemingly inhospitable environment that life arose.

Molecules that could copy themselves were eventually formed, and these replicators became increasingly common in the primordial soup.[2]

The replicators were organic, digestible, and devoid of structural strength, yet they have turned out to be longer-lived than diamonds or granite. One of these replicators has copied itself through the ages and now finds itself in every living thing as DNA.[3] It has survived for four billion years.

The natural selection of variant forms—evolution—resulted in replicators that could consume their counterparts and protect themselves from being consumed. Replicators interacted as predator and prey, as parasite and host, and formed the bodies and behaviors of the diaspora of life on earth. Humans are just one form in which those ancient replicators live out their primordial game of thermodynamics; but what a game of thermodynamics it has become: humans now seek control over the energy of the biosphere. So it is also ironic that we are nervous about descending into a global energy crisis. We are bathed in, and surrounded by, more energy than we could ever need.

Earth's "third atmosphere" was formed by the first global polluters, a group of microbes that had evolved an ingenious method of harnessing the energy of the sun. These organisms—photosynthesizers—consumed carbon dioxide to build their bodies, and the concentration of this gas gradually declined. Oxygen, which had been virtually absent from the atmosphere until then, was slowly released as their waste.

The atmosphere is now 20 percent oxygen: all of it made by photosynthesizing bacteria, protists, and plants. The first photosynthesizers were horrendous polluters that changed the climate of the planet and caused the extinction of untold numbers of species. We tend to think of them in a kind light because, by releasing copious volumes of oxygen into the atmosphere, the first global polluters paved the way for the evolution that led to us. The atmospheric concentrations of oxygen and carbon dioxide have remained more or less constant for the last few million years; the amount of oxygen released in photosynthesis balanced by the amount consumed in respiration.

Until recently, that is.

At the end of the Jurassic period, sixty-five million years ago, a massive asteroid smashed into the shallow sea between the continents of North and South America, where now sits the town of Chicxulub, Mexico. Two geological findings converge on this date. First, the fossil record of the dinosaurs ceases suddenly and completely. Indeed, fully two-thirds of the species of life on earth became extinct at that time, not just the dinosaurs. Second, rock strata of the same age show a flush of the heavy metal iridium. Iridium is very rare on earth but is found in asteroids and other space debris. The Chicxulub asteroid created a huge pall of dust in the atmosphere that blocked out the sun and threw the planet into a short but deep winter. The poor, old, cold-blooded dinosaurs froze and starved. The dust pall, as it settled, left a layer of iridium to mark the event.

The rest is history. Cute, little, recently evolved, warm-blooded mammals made it through the postimpact winter, evolved into less-cute mammals, and finally evolved into us. It's interesting to imagine what the world would have been like had the Chicxulub asteroid missed. Would cold-blooded reptiles be living in cities, playing sports, writing books, fretting about the future of a planet they were destroying? *Tyrannosaurus* Beck? A scary thought.

The asteroid that ended the dinosaurs was only one of a number that have struck our planet. An even more dramatic event took place two hundred million years earlier when nearly 95 percent of the earth's species were suddenly extinguished in an event known as the Great Permian extinction. NASA scientists estimate that significant asteroid impacts may occur every hundred thousand years or so. In fact, bad news might be coming soon. Astronomers declare it a 250,000:1 chance that the asteroid *Apophis* will strike the earth on April 13, 2036.[4]

No matter how patient you are, it's hard to sense the movement of the continents (unless you are unfortunate enough to witness a tsunami or an earthquake). Billions of years our ancestry may be, but our spheres of influence and experiences are short-term. We now know that the continents drift around the planet like dinner plates floating on a sea of syrup. In its lifetime, the earth has spawned and swallowed entire continents. In only the last hundred and fifty million years (the last thirtieth of the planet's lifetime), the supercontinent of Pangaea split and its shards scattered across the oceans. South America and Africa were riven apart and then separated by the Atlantic Ocean, as Australia drifted lazily (do Aussies move any other way?) northeast across the Indian Ocean. India, meanwhile, was sprinting northward for Asia and the great collision that formed the Tibetan plateau and the Himalayas.[5] The drifting continents have created oceans, land bridges, and inland seas, have baked the planet in prolonged tropical periods and plunged it into ice ages.

Global climate change is one of the great concerns of our time, but it is nowhere near the scale of the dramatic climate changes that have been brought about by natural processes; so if climate change is a bad thing, watch out: there's plenty more where that came from. Over the next fifty million years or so, as the earth's dinner plates continue to meander, California will drift away from the rest of America (geographically as well as politically), Australia will finally make formal ties with Asia, and Africa will smash through the Mediterranean, crushing Europe into another massive range of mountains; a fitting, albeit belated, revenge for centuries of colonial exploitation.

How will life on earth fare as the continents continue their hustle and bustle? As usual, we should expect winners and losers, but it's really no big deal. The planet will be fine. Life will go on.

Relatively humanlike, upright apes have been in existence for only about three million years, but even in that short time, our ancestors have lived on a capricious planet. Although we have known the continents only in their current positions, and an atmosphere only of its current composition, humans have lived through dramatically changing times and survived. Why, then, are we concerned with change in the modern world? Does it really matter that the concentration of carbon dioxide in the atmosphere might increase by a few hundred parts per million, that temperatures might increase by a few degrees, and that sea levels might rise by a few feet? Read on. It matters a lot.

FIRST ATTEMPTS TO HARNESS ENERGY

Stone tools made by our ancestors *Homo habilis* more than two million years ago have been found at various sites in Africa's Great Rift Valley,[6] and the best estimates are that the taming of fire began at least half a million years ago.[7] We have, apparently, been trying to figure out how to harness energy from the environment for a very, very long time.

The use of fire was not a sudden invention but a gradual process of cultural evolution. Ugh Smith did not wake up one morning, fancy some toast for breakfast, and decide to rub two sticks together. The great grasslands of the world are prone to natural fires, and hunters living in fire-prone environments must have figured out not only how to avoid becoming trapped in fires but also that fires might provide opportunities for easy hunting. Observant gatherers presumably noticed that some of their favorite leafy greens sprouted abundantly after fires. Fires must have presented obstacles to early humans, but they also provided opportunities. The first step in the use of fire, then, was probably simply to take advantage of natural fires when they occurred.

The first Australians used fire extensively for the management of grasslands. They lit fires in sequence around their settlements to promote the sprouting of the new shoots of young grasses that would attract kangaroos and wallabies. With areas of new growth under their control, hunting could be focused into a circumscribed area and high-protein food then acquired more efficiently. The Aussie smoker's question *"Got a light, mate?"*[8] might be thousands of years old. Similar activities were probably carried out by the ancient peoples of many grasslands of the world.[9] When humans began to harness fires, maintain them, and then bring them fully under control, the energy-harnessing steamroller began to trundle.

The first technological developments of our ancestors were only small baby steps, and it took millennia to walk them, but they set us on the path that has finally brought us to our twenty-first-century, oil-bathed, energy-rich civilization. Tool technology has gone through a sequence of developments from its primitive beginnings and has incorporated more and more sophisticated materials and techniques. The first tools were made and operated by hand, extending the power of their operator relatively modestly. Tools manufactured using an external power source (e.g., smelted iron knives) or operated with an external power source (e.g., wooden plows, windmills) extended the power of their operator much further. Now, of course, we use a whole host of tools that are both manufactured and operated with an external power source. These tools are truly powerful and can control the world in ways our ancestors never could have imagined. The road of progress has been paved with increasingly sophisticated technologies powered by increasingly efficient means of extracting energy from the environment.

THE MOTHER OF INVENTION

We tend to think of environmental destruction as a recent phenomenon, but the damage wrought by our species is ancient, and it began soon after the adoption of our very first technologies. The archaeological record of North America, for example, reveals a very unusual extinction event that occurred over just a few centuries at the end of the last ice age. North America had been home to a vast array of megafauna—giant ground sloths, mastodons, mammoths, saber-tooth tigers, lions, glyptodonts, horses, camels—an array of supersized mammals that would make the contemporary Serengeti plain look like a second-rate safari park. The archaeological record also shows, at the same time, and often in the very graves of the great mammals themselves, the arrival of the famous Clovis points of the first Americans: efficient stone tips designed to be hafted onto hunting spears. Spilling into the Americas at the brief invitation of Beringia, when sufficient ice retreat had opened the land bridge but melting had not yet flooded it to form the Bering Straits, humans entered a new megafauna paradise and began, quite literally, to eat their way through it.

The destruction of edible animals has been a hallmark of all lands discovered by tool-wielding humans, particularly as seen in islands such as Mauritius, New Zealand, and Hawaii, where it has been sudden and dramatic. Arriving already armed, skilled in hunting, and encountering animals that did not recognize them as predators, humans have repeatedly sent their food into extinction. But the carnage has not been limited to a few special parts of the globe; indeed, it has hardly been limited at all. The consequences of these extinctions have been many and varied. The extirpation of horses from the Americas, for example, would come back to haunt the Inca when they were confronted by Francisco Pizarro's cavalry. Their llamas, alas, were no match.[10] The destruction of game animals has been particularly rapid in newly colonized lands, but it has been a problem wherever human populations have grown.

Growing populations put increasing pressure on supplies of easily hunted animals and easily gathered plants, and people faced their first self-imposed limits to growth thousands of years ago. These limits probably caused significant hardships as formerly abundant sources of food became rare, but these limits also spurred the adoption of a new form of subsistence.

An agrarian lifestyle is generally assumed to be far superior to a hunter-gatherer lifestyle, but why would people dig in the dirt to raise crops if plentiful wild plants could be collected? I don't think they would. They first destroyed the easy life and then necessity became the mother of invention. Only when hunting and gathering could no longer support their needs did they stumble across the next great development in the history of civilization: when people began to farm.

This theme of "destroy first, rebuild later" has been a trademark of our history. We tend to think of progress as a steady stream of innovations, each one building on the last, but nothing could be further from the truth. Progress has more often begun with failure.

PUTTING DOWN ROOTS

> **And he gave it for his opinion that whoever could make two ears of corn, or two blades of grass, to grow upon a spot of ground where only one grew before, would deserve better of mankind, and do more essential service to his country, than the whole race of politicians put together.**
>
> Jonathan Swift[11]

Agriculture was neither invented nor discovered but came about as an exercise in unconscious cultural evolution, and it occurred in a number of different parts of the world independently. In environments with migrating herds, people remained mostly nomadic. Where food could be found year-round, they began to settle, and this simple action of settling down set in motion the first agrarian revolution. Static communities depleted many sources of easily hunted and gathered foods but elevated a select few. Hunter-gatherers traveled large distances to collect roots, tubers, shoots, fruits, and grains to bring back to their families. Returning from gathering trips, people must have inadvertently scattered some seed along the way, where it grew. They eventually realized that they could do this on purpose and began to grow favored plants close to home.

Our modern cereal crops evolved from wild grasses over thousands of years as they adapted to a human-manipulated environment.[12] One key characteristic was a nonshattering seed head on which the seed would mature without falling off its spike and would therefore be collected for planting the next year. The seed that germinated in sync with the rest of the crop would also have a better chance of being selected for growth the next season. Evolution gradually tailored crops to suit the needs of humans. As people began to realize that the plants that produced larger, more nutritious seed one year tended to do the same the next, crop evolution shifted from a process of natural selection to one of artificial selection, and people began to reserve the largest, sweetest seed for planting. Now when we compare a modern crop plant with its progenitor, the two are hardly recognizable as relatives, yet all those differences evolved at the hands of people in the last ten thousand years.[13]

Our transformation of the humble wild grasses has been dramatic, but their transformation of us has been even more profound. Agriculture placed humans much more firmly in charge of their food supply, which not only increased but also was made more reliable. Putting down roots on the same piece of land every year, to raise crops, sowed the seeds of civilization.

Like crop production, animal husbandry first emerged through a sequence of unconscious human activities. Hunting is not a random activity but involves a significant amount of decision making to optimize the efficiency of the hunt. Predators often migrate with herds of their preferred food source. Searching randomly over the plains is useless if you can figure out where the herd is likely to go next and then meet it there. Migrating with your food source delivers the distinct benefit of always being close to your next meal. On the other hand, you have to be always on the move, and you may lose track of the herd. Instead of following the herd, a much better idea is to control where it goes.

Manipulating the movements of animals over grasslands with fire was a first step, but the major step toward the factory farm and feedlot came when animals were consciously domesticated. As with crops, this occurred independently in many parts of the world. Animals were selected and bred to better suit the needs of humans. Those raised for food became larger, fatter, and more muscular; those raised for clothing became woollier; horses became faster; and dogs became more train-able—and then transformed into various ridiculous forms, such as insipid varieties of household pets.[14]

Agriculture made the acquisition of food increasingly efficient and its supply more reliable. The ability to manipulate nature by bringing favored plants close to home, and to control favored animals without hunting, increased our access to calories and led to wholesale changes in the structure of communities. Agriculture generated surpluses of food and enabled societies to support nonfarmers. These nonfarmers would have time on their hands to get into all sorts of mischief.

The first major advances in the harnessing of energy, then, were tools, fire, and agriculture. Tools and fire increased the efficiency of hunting, which was eventually replaced with animal domestication. Gathering was eventually replaced with cultivation. With these efficiencies in place, human societies were primed for rapid cultural change.

THE AGE OF EMPIRES

Until the emergence of agriculture, humans organized themselves primarily into family groups or small bands, and, as long as populations remained small and scattered, there was probably little group organization. As bands grew, social organization increased and the division of labor enabled people to perform increasingly sophisticated tasks as a group. Our small-group mammal tried to figure out ways to cooperate. Leaders emerged, both civil and spiritual, and rules were created to control thieves and freeloaders.

As farming and technology improved and settlements grew, people developed increasingly specialized trades. Farmers continued to farm but could feed more and more people, partly thanks to tradespeople such as millers and blacksmiths who ground their grain and shod their horses. Energy was collected from animals put under the yoke to drag vehicles or to plow the land and with machines that captured the energy of the wind and flowing water. Even people could be captured, enslaved, and used for many tasks, as long as they could be fed and controlled. The energy from burning wood was harnessed to perform myriad tasks, such as smelting metals to construct increasingly efficient tools—and weapons.

The weapons were needed, of course, because as the territories of different communities overlapped, they came into competition for resources. If they generated sufficient surplus energy and food, communities could also invest in soldiers to wield those weapons.

With increased access to energy in the form of animals, wind, water, slaves, and with surplus agricultural production, populations grew and filled the landscape and the human experiment was under way in earnest. The great empires—the Sumerians, the Harappans, the Qin, the Han and the Ming Chinese, the ancient Egyptians, the Greeks, the Persians and the Romans, the Maya, the Inca, and the Aztec—were all built on the same basic premise. Energy from agriculture (for human calories) and from human labor, animal labor, wind, water, or burning wood (for industry and motive force) was drawn from their immediate environment.

Control of the immediate environment, however, is not the hallmark of an empire. An empire is a dominant civilization that grows beyond the limits of its environment and subjugates or conquers its neighbors to commandeer theirs. The result has always been the same. A vast, complex civilization is created. It flourishes at the expense of its environment, then at the expense of its neighbors, and then at the expense of its neighbors' environments. Stratified societies are formed; wealth is created; government bureaucracies are put in place; there is a burgeoning of the arts; and great monuments are erected. And then it is all swept away.

CHAPTER 2

THE GHOSTS OF EMPIRES PASSED

THE IMPOSSIBLE MOAI

Easter Island[1] is just about the most isolated scrap of habitable land on earth. More than two thousand miles west of South America, it was colonized around 900 CE by Polynesians canoeing from islands more than a thousand miles to the west:[2] a fifty-thousand-acre green space adrift in the heart of the world's biggest ocean. When the Dutch explorer Jacob Roggeveen came across the island on Easter day, 1722, it presented a confusing paradox. He found a barren, unproductive landscape and described its few thousand inhabitants in disparaging terms as impoverished, malnourished, primitive, and uncivilized. Their agriculture was unproductive and their canoes were small and leaky.

But poverty and windswept hills were not all that Roggeveen found.

He also found carved statues of solid stone, the fabled Moai, up to twelve feet in height perched atop massive stone platforms. Most of the Moai weighed in at around ten tons, but some were much larger, and hundreds of these things were to be found around the island. The largest was a seventy-foot monster of 270 tons. The apparent impossibility of the Moai left Roggeveen completely confused. How could this small population of primitive, destitute people possibly have constructed and erected such magnificent statues in this barren place? The same paradox would lead the great Norwegian explorer Thor Heyerdahl to conclude that the Easter Islanders must have been in contact with traders from South America. It would convince Swiss author Erich von Däniken that the island must have been visited by aliens.[3] But the truth is much more compelling, and the secrets of Easter Island have now been uncovered from oral histories and detailed paleoarchaelogical studies.

Easter Island has always been significantly less resource-rich than other Polynesian islands, being too far south of the equator for coral reefs, for example, and therefore poor in nearshore fishing. The small island has also been rather lacking in wildlife and, even more important, short of freshwater. But despite the assumptions of the early European visitors, Easter Island had all the resources necessary to support a thriving society, and when it was first discovered, Easter Island was covered in something quite surprising: trees.

The analysis of pollen grains taken from soil cores shows that at the time of its discovery Easter Island had been largely forested and supported a number of species of large trees, including a giant palm tree with a broad trunk and other species from which fibers could have been stripped to make strong ropes.

Large oceangoing canoes were built for deep-sea fishing. Large, sturdy buildings were erected. The giant palm trees also provided the answer to the paradox of the Moai. Given large tree trunks and an abundant source of fiber, only a relatively simple combination of manpower and mechanics would have been required to move and erect large stone slabs.[4]

Fueled by their island's forests, the Easter Islanders developed a complex society. They fished in the shallows and the deeps, harvested land birds and sea bird eggs, and cultivated crops. They grew sugarcane to provide juice for drinking to alleviate the limitations of freshwater.[5] Their population grew rapidly, to at least fifteen thousand, and became increasingly complex and stratified, with different parts of the island managed by different groups.[6] The Easter Islanders erected hundreds of Moai as symbols of power around the shores of their island. The Moai were carved out of the rock of a large volcano, Rano Raraku, transported around the island on rolling logs along more than twenty miles of roads[7] and lifted vertically onto platforms with ropes, levers, frames, and pulleys.[8]

The Moai became larger and larger through time as bigger and bigger statements of power were made. In the latest period of Moai construction, the practice of adding an additional large stone slab, called a *pukao*, to the Moai's head must have further strengthened the statement of power. As Jared Diamond, author of *Collapse: How Societies Choose to Fail or Succeed*, puts it: "All right, so you can erect a statue 30 feet high, but look at me; I can put this 12-ton pukao on top of my statue; you try to top that, you wimp!"[9]

At its height, life on Easter Island was probably decidedly pleasant, with adequate food, security, and social interaction. The Easter Islanders had devised ingenious means of harvesting their diminutive island environment to produce food and harness energy for a burgeoning society. But all that would change. Isolated from the rest of the world by hundreds of miles of water, the Easter Islanders needed to conserve their resource base. They failed.

The first resource to be overexploited on Easter Island was the bird life. The island had originally supported at least six species of land birds and around twenty-five species of nesting sea birds, but these species rapidly disappeared as they were exploited for food. The land birds were completely extirpated, and the surviving sea birds moved their breeding grounds to the rocky islets offshore. Birds and their eggs, initially an important and easily obtained source of protein, became unavailable.[10] The fisheries of Easter Island also suffered from the growing human population, with many species of fish and shellfish depleted from the shores.

Agriculture went through a set of transitions, intensifying as the population climbed. The perpetual shortage of water for irrigation led the Easter Islanders to attempt more and more elaborate methods for its conservation.[11] But as wild sources of food were becoming gradually depleted, and the population was becoming increasingly reliant on agriculture, the island's soils were gradually eroding, and agriculture was failing, too.

The biggest problem on Easter Island was unsustainable logging. The rich and diverse forests of the island were the islanders' most valuable assets, and so, as the landscape became gradually deforested, the very underpinnings of Easter Island society were threatened.

The big trees were important for many things. They were harvested for fuel and construction. One of the most important parts of the local diet was dolphin, which could be caught only in deep water, by harpoon, from large, seaworthy canoes. As the big forest trees were depleted, the canoes shrank, and an important part of the people's diet was lost. Building construction also declined, and, eventually, so did the quality of firewood: by 1600 the Easter Islanders were burning grass for warmth and cooking. Deforestation also dealt a crushing blow to agriculture, as the soil, no longer held in place by tree roots, was increasingly washed into the ocean.

One of the most visible problems with the loss of trees was the inability to transport and erect Moai. The leaders of the various competing groups continued to commission more and more, larger and larger Moai, and the sculptors continued their diligent work. Eventually, however, the wheels of industry ground to a halt, and, judging from the large numbers of part-sculpted Moai abandoned at various stages of completion in the Rano Raraku quarry, the end came rather suddenly. Moai were still being commissioned even as the last of the trees needed to transport them was being felled.

Eventually, the Easter Islanders fell into conflict: some reports claim that, at their nadir, the desperate islanders suffered serious famine and may even have resorted to cannibalism.[12] In the end, they formed into two groups and fought a final battle on the slopes of the volcano, Poike. The battle, dated 1680,[13] occurred just forty-two years before the island was "discovered" by Roggeveen; and when he arrived in 1722, the population of the island was a mere three thousand.

The Easter Islanders had discovered a new land replete with resources, developed a thriving society, destroyed their land base, and fell into decline and collapse. Incredibly, they had done all of this in the space of only seven hundred years. The overall history of the rise and fall of Easter Island seems relatively clear, but two troubling questions are raised: First, *Did the Easter Islanders realize that they were destroying their forests?* Because the forests were so central to their way of life, it is difficult to imagine that the Easter Islanders could have been unaware of the deforestation they were causing, but it is possible. The process of deforestation occurred over a period of seven hundred years, which represents approximately fifty generations of people, and it may have been imperceptible to any single generation. That the island had been replete with forests may have been just as much a mystery to the fortieth generation of Easter Islanders, who lived at the apparent height of its civilization, as it was to the fiftieth generation encountered by Roggeveen, and to Roggeveen himself. The hand of nature, clear as day in the soil cores examined by today's paleoarchaeologists, may have been invisible at the time.

Creeping environmental degradation such as this is occurring around the world today. Deserts are expanding, forests are retreating, freshwater aquifers are declining, and the atmosphere is filling with greenhouse gases. This has been happening for some time now, but we have only recently understood its extent and potential consequences.

The second question is even more troubling: *If the Easter Islanders did recognize the importance and vulnerability of their resources, why were they unwilling or unable to preserve them?* Surely a society that recognized a serious impending danger would be able to find a way to protect itself, right? Well, given the current state of our planet, we'd like to hope so. We are acutely aware of a suite of dangerous environmental problems and would like to think we can muster some sort of effective response. We'd hate to see our world become a global Easter Island.

Archaeological evidence and oral traditions indicate that Easter Island was divided into about twelve different territories, each operating somewhat autonomously. Tongariki territory contained the Rano Raraku crater. Anakena territory had the best beaches for launching canoes. The best agricultural land was in the four or five regions of the south, and the nesting sites of seabirds were mostly in Vinapu territory. It is likely that the territoriality of Easter Island society became a significant weakness, as none of the individual territories was able to take a lead in the conservation of vital resources. The need to continue trading with neighbors may have applied a disastrous pressure to harvest and distribute resources. Each territory might rather have risked possible long-term environmental damage than forego short-term economic needs.

The comparison of Easter Island's interacting territories with the world's interacting economies is inescapable. The resources of many countries are suffering rapid depletion in the name of global trade. The consumption of meat in European restaurants demands the production of soybeans on the Brazilian cerrado, which encourages logging of the pristine Amazon rain forest. Cheap Christmas presents from a midwestern Wal-Mart come at the expense of the shrinking resources of China and consume huge volumes of fuel for shipping. The need for construction materials in China comes at the cost of knocking down forests in Southeast Asia.

The specialization of regions in the production of globally traded commodities and services accelerates resource depletion. To abandon a particular specialty, no matter how obviously damaging and unsustainable it may be, is to risk an immediate loss of competitive advantage in the global marketplace. The hand of nature, even if it is visible, cannot always be stayed.

The idea that the Easter Islanders were aware that their actions might be disastrous but continued them nonetheless is not inconceivable at all. Buildings and oceangoing canoes were needed *now*. Demonstrations of power—the impossible Moai—were needed *now*. Leaving resources unused could result in a rapid and obvious loss of competitive advantage against other territories that might use them instead. And, in any case, environmental degradation, the consequences of which may have been highly speculative anyway, would be shared out among all.

And shared out among all, they were.

Easter Island is a cautionary tale of civilization collapse. Here, in the middle of the Pacific Ocean, a society grew in size and complexity—made progress—by harvesting the resources of its environment for food and energy. But its growing population became too demanding of its resource base, and its supply of resources went into decline. The over-exploitation resulted in land degradation, further steepening the collapse.

The Easter Islanders, at least some of them, at some time, must have feared the worst. I wonder if anyone called for restraint, recognizing the peril caused by their reckless exploitation of resources and degradation of the environment. Perhaps a few Easter Island Al Gores voiced the need to figure out a way to cooperate, to conserve their essential resources, and to curtail the disastrous degradation of their land base. But, if these objections were raised, they were not heeded, and the Easter Islanders competed and consumed themselves into oblivion.

WHERE DID ALL THE PEOPLE GO?

The American Southwest has always been a difficult, unproductive, and arid landscape.[14] One need only stand on one of the ruin sites at Wupatki National Monument in northern Arizona and look out across the vast, inhospitable expanse of the Painted Desert and wonder: How on earth did people manage to build a civilization here? Of course, the second question is: Why did it fail?

When the Diné (more commonly known as the Navajo, a name given by the Spanish) moved into the American Southwest sometime before 1400, they could tell from the ruins of dams, earthworks, and buildings around them that the land had been occupied before. They named these former people *Anasazi*, which can be translated as "ancient people" or sometimes as "enemy ancestors." The Hopi name *Hisatsinom* has less of a negative connotation and simply means "people of long ago."[15]

Wupatki National Monument. A Hisatsinom building still stands vigil over the vast expanse of Arizona's Painted Desert, centuries after its inhabitants moved away. Photograph courtesy of Steve Hallett.

In more recent times, the rise and fall of the Hisatsinom has been calculated with great accuracy and precision from two principal pieces of evidence. First, the timbers used in the construction of Hisatsinom buildings have been well preserved in the arid environment and can be accurately dated from their ring patterns.[16] Second, a cute little rodent has left us a remarkable archaeological legacy.[17]

The southwestern packrat has the habit of gathering bits and pieces from around its burrows, creating large trash piles, and then urinating on them. The urine of the packrat crystallizes on the trash pile and preserves it, so packrat middens contain exquisitely preserved records of the flora of the region for thousands of years. By dating the timbers found in ruins and delving into layered piles of ancient rat garbage, paleoarchaeologists have been able to reconstruct the natural history of the Amer-

Canyon de Chelly. The "White House" overlooks the Canyon de Chelly in northern Arizona, a river valley that once supported a large population of Hisatsinom farmers. Photograph courtesy of Steve Hallett.

ican Southwest over the entire history of the Hisatsinom, and a compelling story of the rise and fall of a civilization can now be told.

Agriculture came to the American Southwest around 2000 BCE from Mexico; as the Hisatsinom incorporated it into their hunter-gatherer lifestyle, they began to settle into small villages. They had to contend with shallow, weathered soils, scant, widely spaced rains, and periodic droughts. Cropping was restricted to moist canyon bottoms, and long rotations and fallow periods were used to allow the soil to recover after each cropping cycle.

As the population of the region began to climb, the Hisatsinom began the construction of various water-management basins, channels, and levees. The renowned pottery skills of the peoples of the region were probably also born out of the need for large water-storage vessels. Water conservation was effective as long as population pressure remained low, but the Hisatsinom were developing an increasingly large, complex, and stratified society. They were setting themselves a trap.

As the resources close to major settlements became depleted, the Hisatsinom began to import increasing volumes of goods from the surrounding countryside, and their settlements became large sinks into which resources increasingly disappeared. The depletion of gathered foods, the depletion of easily hunted game, and their growing population also forced the Hisatsinom to attempt the cultivation of increasingly marginal land. The water-management programs became more elaborate, but their cropping systems became increasingly vulnerable to damaging soil erosion, serious washouts during storms, and the gradual depletion of soil fertility. Agriculture, stretched to its limits, was robbing the Hisatsinom of the precious soil upon which their civilization depended.

The Hisatsinom could ill afford to put stress on any other resources, but they also locked themselves onto a path of unsustainable logging. Trees are very slow growing in this harsh environment, and it would have been easy to remove stands of timber faster than they could recover. The removal of local trees forced the Hisatsinom to search farther afield for timber, and, as the local pinyon pine and juniper trees became increasingly scarce, teams of loggers traveled deep into the surrounding mountains to recover the wood they needed. This must have taken enormous effort, and feeding all the laborers required for the work must have exacted a significant toll on the meager resources of the region.

The Hisatsinom became committed to the lifestyle of a complex, interconnected civilization, but they were exceeding the capacity of their rugged and fragile corner of the world. After a period of burgeoning culture lasting approximately six hundred years, the Hisatsinom civilization went into rapid decline. The archaeological record shows increasing numbers of human remains scarred by malnutrition and a dramatic increase in fortifications suggesting conflict in the final years. The Hisatsinom had attempted to control and exploit their environment, and, in fairness, they had managed for a remarkably long time, given its fragility. But, as their population grew, and even as their civilization appeared to flourish, their demands on the environment became unsustainable.

In the end, it was probably the environment that dealt them the final blow. A prolonged drought hit the area beginning in 1130 CE. Hisatsinom agriculture could no longer support its population, and the end had come. The areas around their settlements were now so depleted of wild food that they were unsuitable even for a hunter-gatherer society, and so the Hisatsinom abandoned their towns and villages and moved away, leaving nothing but ghosts to haunt the next civilization that would follow.

The Palace, Mesa Verde National Park, Colorado. The cluster of kivas—round sunken rooms—indicates that the Palace was probably an administrative and ceremonial site. Photograph courtesy of Steve Hallett.

The Hisatsinom teach a simple lesson. You may be able to impose your will upon the environment for a while, but if you lose your power over nature, you will be reminded just how unforgiving nature can be.

THE LEGACY OF EIGHTEEN RABBIT

The great Mayan civilization ruled over a large part of Mesoamerica for two thousand years. It built great cities and supported a population in the millions. But by the time the Spanish conquistadors passed through the area in the early sixteenth century, there was virtually no trace of the Maya. The Spanish had no idea that one of the great civilizations of the world had flourished there. The ruins of the Maya had been reclaimed by the forest, and few had any knowledge of the great civilization that had gone before. The breathtaking hieroglyphic staircase at Copán, the immense pyramids at Tikal, the intricate carvings at Uxmal, and the limestone palisades of Palenque had been lost so thoroughly that they had disappeared even from memory. It was not until 1839 that explorers John Stephens and Frederick Catherwood went to investigate rumors of ruins in the Central American jungle that, to their astonishment, pyramids, monuments, ceremonial arenas for ritual human sacrifice, carved stelae and tablets, observatories, and ball courts[18] were revealed.

To walk around the ruins of a Mayan city is to take a journey into the imagination. The complexity and size of these places is overwhelming, and the thought that a civilization of such magnitude and splendor could simply vanish, and its great cities could be swallowed by the jungle, lost and forgotten for generations, is astonishing. In Mesoamerica, around 900 CE, a civilization died. This was not an assembly of hunter-gatherers but a flourishing region of cities, towns, and villages. The Maya had advanced agricultural systems, elaborate religious ceremonies, a calendar based on planetary cycles,[19] and a system of writing. The pyramids of the Maya would remain the tallest buildings in the

Americas until the twentieth century. To this day, you can stand atop the Great Pyramid at Ek Balaam[20] in northern Yucatán, and the only humanmade structures big enough to see are the Sun Pyramid at Chichen Itza and the Great Pyramid at Coba.

The Mayan civilization was built in a relatively productive environment. Explanations of its collapse based solely on the careless overexploitation of highly limited resources will not be sufficient here. The southern lowland forest of the Mayan world in Central America is not the most productive part of the world, but it is far from fragile. The city of Copán, for example, was founded in a river valley with fertile soil. The disappearance of the ancient Maya clearly requires some explaining.

Mayan villages have been dated back to 2000 BCE, and settlements at that time may have contained as many as two hundred or three hundred people.[21] Over the next two millennia, a gradually rising population was supported by the intensification of agriculture. Large reservoirs and canals were built in the area of modern-day Belize by 50 BCE.[22] Raised fields and canals enabled effective irrigation and drainage and supported high-yielding agriculture in fertile valleys. Check dams and walled field complexes were used in most areas. Some canals were big enough to serve for transportation as well. As the human population climbed, leading into the preclassic era,[23] competition for resources began to emerge. By 1 CE, the conversion from swidden (slash-and-burn) agriculture to permanent cultivation was also well under way on less productive lands beyond the valley bottoms.

The sophistication of Mayan agriculture is testament to effective management and a complex society. The construction of terraces, canals, drainage ditches, and raised fields was not haphazard. Some canal systems were huge undertakings comparable to the construction of the pyramids, and their maintenance would also have required effective government. The Mayan civilization was strongly stratified into ruling classes: an extensive midlevel hierarchy of bureaucrats and artisans, peasants, and subclasses.

The first fortifications of Mayan settlements began to appear around various population centers, notably a remarkable complex of earthworks around Becan, as the Mayan civilization entered its classic period. Fortifications were primitive at first, but they attest to the emergence of competition and conflict. Raids by one city on another became common, and various Mayan writings brag about the prowess of their leaders, their conquests of other cities, and the torture and execution of enemies. Perhaps even more important than the raids and occasional large battles was the threat of them. Such threats probably promoted a continual need to maintain and project power, causing the Mayan exploitation of its resources to continue relentlessly.

Not long after the birth of Jesus of Nazareth, but a continent away, the Maya had built a complex, stratified, organized society with productive agriculture, and the erection of their great public buildings began. Population densities across the southern lowlands may have been the highest in the world at that time. More than five hundred people per square mile lived in the immediate vicinity of Tikal, which had a population in the tens of thousands.[24] By 600 CE, truly monumental buildings were being erected, fortifications became increasingly robust, and displays of power became larger and more elaborate. The glory days of the Maya came in the seventh century CE. In Copán, the reign of the ruler known as Eighteen Rabbit saw the initiation of the marvelous hieroglyphic stairway, an architectural wonder constructed from thousands of intricately carved steps that climb an immense pyramid and record the history of a dynasty of rulers of Copán.

But Eighteen Rabbit also marked the beginning of the end. He was captured and executed during a battle with the nearby city of Quirigiá.[25] The hieroglyphic stairway was completed just a few decades later, but then the hammers and chisels of the stone masons of Copán fell silent forever. By 750 CE, populations appear to have maxed out across much of the Mayan region, and the rot began to set in. The cities of Quirigiá and Piedras Negras show no inscriptions beyond 810 CE. There was no construction at Tikal after 830 CE. Copán collapsed around 800 CE. The cities fell, one by one, across the entire Mayan civilization, and, as the people left, the forest quietly returned. The Maya had finally outgrown their ability to produce food.

In Copán, agriculture had gradually crept out of the safe valley bottom onto the forested slopes. The land became increasingly liable to erosion, and the eroded slopes became uncultivable. What's more, the soil that eroded from the slopes clogged irrigation and drainage systems, wrecking crops in the fertile valley below.

Giant trees are now anchored in Copán's hundred-foot-tall Temple 16, abandoned approximately twelve hundred years ago and reclaimed by the jungle. Photograph courtesy of Steve Hallett.

Agriculture in Copán seems to have succumbed to a fairly sudden decline consistent with the last recorded dates of Mayan inscriptions. The valley had been an ideal place for the establishment of a small settlement, a reliable river beside fertile land, and a forest rich with plants and animals for hunting and gathering. But the Copán River valley became a trap for the big, cumbersome city. The lords of Copán gradually destroyed their environment—and then it, much more suddenly, destroyed them.

Similar problems were occurring everywhere. The analysis of sedimentation patterns has shown that soil erosion became a problem across the region. Particularly detailed analyses come from the stratigraphy of Peten Lake sediments near Tikal, where large influxes of soil into the lake bottom correlate with the loss of trees from the paleoarchaeological record and the cessation of building in the archaeological record.[26] Eventually, the Mayan population could not be supported on its land base. Resource competition broke out, and fighting became widespread.

As if they were not already having enough problems, it seems likely that climate change also afflicted the Maya. The rainfall of the region is not entirely reliable, as any Guatemalan farmer will tell you, but the period of 800–1000 CE seems to have been unusually dry.[27] Thus a particularly dry period may have challenged the Maya at the time of their greatest vulnerability, and climate change may have contributed to the Mayan collapse.

That a civilization could damage its land base and suffer as a result is not hard to understand. It is relatively easy to imagine that environmental damage could send a civilization into an economic depression or protracted period of hardship. But that is not what happened to the Maya. There was no gradual contraction and then recovery, no transient Mayan Great Depression. Rather, the Mayan civilization, thousands of years in the making, suddenly imploded and was gone. It passed from being dominant and powerful to being utterly destroyed within a few generations. By 1000 CE, the population of the Mayan lands had fallen from more than three million at its height to only tens of thousands.

Some of the Maya's most incredible structures were built in their last century. The massive pyramids at Tikal towered over everything that had been erected over the preceding one and a half thousand years, but barely a century after the erection of the great 230-foot Temple 4, dedicated to Yik'in Chan Kawil in 810 CE,[28] all memory of its construction and the ceremonies and executions carried out there were erased. These displays of power just before collapse are reminiscent of the Easter Islanders, whose Moai were produced on a grander and grander scale right up to the end; some of the biggest of all still lie, unfinished, in the Rano Raraku quarry.

It seems that the desperate lords of Tikal were erecting colossal pyramids as displays of strength in times of trouble. Even as their prospects for a sustainable future were crumbling around them, they were desperate to prevent anyone from detecting any whiff of weakness. A similar sudden display of power occurred at Copán, where the writings on stelae in the last century before its collapse were the most stridently patriotic of all, and the work on the hieroglyphic stairway remained a priority.

The struggling Maya turned their attention in the wrong direction. Where conservation, sustainable agriculture, and land management might have paid dividends, they instead became more competitive with their neighbors. The competition was expensive and put greater and greater burdens on their strained resource base. Resource wars and displays of power were not the solution and became an increasingly important part of the problem. The Maya were fighting the wrong enemy. They were fighting their neighbors for resources; however, the enemy was not outside but within: the enemy was their own exploitation of the environment.

FORESTS TO PRECEDE CIVILIZATIONS, DESERTS TO FOLLOW[29]

Although much of the Middle East is now an arid desert, the region was [once] rich with trees and ani-

mals when Moses led the children of Israel through the Sinai wilderness. The mountains of the Promised Land were then cloaked with dense forests; Asiatic lions stalked abundant wildlife . . . today one can go for days and never see a living thing.[30]

René Dubos, *The Wooing of Earth*[31]

Soils are created naturally by the weathering of rocks and the decay of organisms and their wastes. Soil building is a slow process, but a steady one, and soils are reasonably resilient when left to their own devices. Take a sand dune, for example. A few tough grasses such as marram grass eke out a living on the blowing, shifting sands. They are repeatedly buried but grow back to the surface, their woody rhizomes[32] building and stabilizing a dune. Once the dune has reached a certain size, other plants can establish behind it, sheltered from the wind. After this weedy zone has been established for a few years—dying, regrowing, and releasing nutrients—a soil begins to build, and other plants can then establish. By now the shifting dunes have crept away. It is perhaps two hundred years since the first brave marram grass rhizome snuck out onto the beach, but something very cool has happened. Dig out eighteen holes and fill a couple of the hollows with sand, grab a mashie and a niblick, and off you go: you're on a golf course. Where once was sand, now soil is supporting a healthy sward of grass. Make sure you mow it, or the succession will continue, and in another hundred years or so your golf course will be a forest.

If we leave nature alone, it can turn a beach into a pasture or a forest. This process can be extremely slow, particularly in harsh climates, but the principle is more or less the same in any environment.

Of course, the opposite is also true: we can, and much more quickly, turn a forest into a beach.

On the banks of the Euphrates, tangled dunes, long-disused canal levees and rubble-strewn

mounds contribute only low, featureless relief. Yet at one time here lay the core, the heartland, the oldest urban, literate civilization in the world.
Robert M. Adams, *Heartland of Cities*[33]

The name Fertile Crescent sounds like some kind of sick joke in reference to one of the most arid, unproductive, degraded regions of the world, yet for millennia the Fertile Crescent was just what its name denoted. It was the land of plenty and the most valuable real estate on the planet. It was not simply random chance that dictated that the world's first great civilizations would emerge across central Eurasia, along the Tigris, Euphrates, Nile, and Indus Rivers: it was the availability of resources. Central Eurasia provided the rich bounty that would propel the cultural evolution of small bands of hunter-gatherers to become the first complex societies.

But these large, complex societies set in motion a long sequence of global slash and burn. Over the centuries that civilizations have risen and fallen in central Asia, they have scarred and depleted the landscape. It should be no surprise that the seat of power crept out into more fertile, less exploited regions, beginning in central Asia and inching its way west. Each civilization trashed its environment, and a new one set up shop next door.

The Greek Empire grew in population from less than one million to nearly fifteen million between 800 and 400 BCE, as they took up the mantle of civilization in the eastern Mediterranean.[34] Although there is no treatise on ecology in the classical literature, many of the greats have painted a vivid picture of ancient impacts on the environment.[35] Herodotus, the "father of history," gives a number of descriptions of environmental damage, frequently commenting on the vulnerability of Lower Egypt and its reliance on the flooding river Nile. In his magnificent *Histories*, written between 431 and 425 BCE, Herodotus describes mines on the island of Thasos: "A whole mountain there has been turned upside down for gold," and at Laurium: "A great scar upon the Attic landscape [and] by the time of Strabo the wooded surface of the region had been completely bared to provide timber for the mines and charcoal for the smelting of the ore."[36] Plato (428–348 BCE), in *Critias*, makes it clear that the logging of forests over large areas of the Mediterranean continued to be widespread during his time, and that it was evident that this was contributing to extensive soil erosion.[37]

Greece had been a productive, forested land, but, as had occurred with the Sumerians and the Egyptians before them, the long occupation of the Greek Empire degraded its landscape. Greece fell vulnerable in its turn, and the next civilization rose, yet one more peninsula to the West, when Greece was consumed by the Roman Republic in 146 BCE.[38]

THE SCOURGE OF GOD

> **In the second century of the Christian Era, the Empire of Rome comprehended the fairest part of the earth and the most civilized portion of mankind.**
> Edward Gibbon, *The History of the Decline and Fall of the Roman Empire*[39]

Rome's origins are attributed to Romulus,[40] the founder of a small settlement on the banks of the Tiber in 753 BCE. The settlement flourished and developed into the Roman Republic and then the Roman Empire; it controlled the Italian peninsula by 300 BCE and most of the Mediterranean by 100 BCE. The expansion of the empire continued with the additions of Britain, parts of central Europe, Palestine, and southern areas of Egypt as late as 180 CE. At its peak, the Roman Empire extended from the Atlantic Ocean to the Euphrates River and the deserts of Africa. It controlled a population of more than one hundred million people over an area twice the size of the modern United States.

The achievements of the Romans were, well, legion. Its army was large, organized, and well equipped. Roads were cut through the landscape, great sporting (and not-so-sporting) events were staged at colosseums, and a high standard of living was maintained with baths, heated buildings, and exotic foods transported from around the empire. Take a trip to the English city of York, or any of a thousand other sites around Europe and west Asia, and you can't help but be impressed by the reach and power of this empire. Even an outlying site like York, two thousand miles from Rome—and probably viewed as a rather crappy place to get posted—is astonishing. But within two hundred years of its peak, the Roman Empire had collapsed catastrophically.[41]

The downfall of the Easter Islanders, the Hisatsinom, and the Maya can be clearly linked to overpopulation, overexploitation of resources, and environmental degradation, with their descent into collapse steepened by infighting and climate change. These were all impressive civilizations, but they were geographically limited and are therefore relatively easily understood. The Roman Empire was something quite different altogether. Rome was not defeated by a better-organized civilization possessing more advanced technology or superior firepower. It was not superseded by a more sophisticated or even a more populous society. Rather, the Roman Empire was swept away by relatively disorganized "barbarians," and its fall was followed by the Dark Ages: a period of artistic, scientific, and political vacuum that lasted a thousand years.[42] That this could happen to Rome should give all would-be empire builders some pause. So why did the Roman Empire fall?

In order to get a feel for this subject, I began by calling a few historians. Their explanations were almost identical. The Roman Empire fell, it is said, because it developed a pathology of decadence and decay. Its government became inward looking and too concerned with the affairs of the elites. The corruption of the government resulted in the squandering of economic opportunities and poor distribution of funds. This eventually weakened the military, which was eventually defeated by the

Huns. Historians, it seems, still walk in lockstep with Edward Gibbon, who described this process in excruciating detail centuries ago.[43] But perhaps there is more to the story than meets the eye.

The study of the decline and fall of the Roman Empire has almost exclusively been the realm of historians, who tend to be people with an economic and political bent. Only recently have people from other specializations brought different skill sets to bear. Ecologists seem like an unlikely group to be providing explanations to conundrums such as the collapse of empires, but perhaps they are attuned to explanations that classically trained historians may have overlooked.

At the height of its powers, the Roman Empire was a colossal machine dominating the resources of a huge region. Massive amounts of construction were undertaken, and the Romans enjoyed great luxuries. They produced tons of charcoal for metal extraction and manufacturing, built kilns for the firing of bricks, and created extensive fleets of trading and fighting ships. The Roman Empire was built on a key, seemingly inexhaustible, resource. It was the material of choice for all construction,[44] and it was the sole source of fuel for every aspect of its industry: the Roman Empire was powered by wood. That wood was the key resource on which the Roman Empire was founded is clear. Is it possible, then, that a lack of wood was the key to its fall?

It is very difficult to imagine how a civilization emerging in Europe in the first millennium BCE could possibly have suffered from a shortage of wood. Much of Europe was forested at that time, and the growth rate of its forests is not especially slow. Europe is no fragile ecosystem and enjoys plentiful rainfall and good soils. It is hard to imagine that forests of such high productivity, growing on such a huge scale, could be depleted. But the demands that the Romans made of the European forests were prodigious and lasted for many years.

Deforestation may seem (to historians, at least, maybe not to ecologists) to be a banal explanation for the fall of an immense and all-powerful empire. There is, however, good evidence that the Roman

Empire depleted its land base of its most essential commodity. Picture thousands of public baths supplying heated water year-round—all of them heated by wood fires. Bear in mind that all Roman industry, from the firing of bricks and glass to the smelting of iron and silver, was fueled by wood and charcoal prepared from wood. The Roman fleets and nearly all Roman buildings were made from wood. Even the colosseums and other great public structures were initially made of wood until it became cheaper to use stone. The lack of charcoal for smelting eventually resulted in the downgrading of the imperial coins, which, by 300 CE, contained hardly any silver and were effectively valueless. It has been estimated that a single iron smelter could consume a million acres of Mediterranean forest per year; a rate of harvesting that could not have been sustainable, even in Europe.[45]

The biggest impact on forests probably came from the clearing of land for agriculture. Virgil describes how a Roman farmer should "subdue his woodland with flames and plow."[46] The great Roman agriculturalist Columella describes techniques for the removal of forestland for farming in his amazing twelve-volume *De Re Rustica*, published in 60 CE.[47] The process of killing trees by girdling and then burning the next year was already thousands of years old, having been first performed with flint axes in the Stone Age.[48] Forests were decimated with each burst of civilization, as it slashed its way westward though ancient Greece and reached its climax in the western Mediterranean at the hands of the Romans.[49]

The lack of wood on the Italian peninsula required its transportation from increasing distances and the relocation of industries based on wood to different parts of the empire. By the end of the Roman Empire, the Mediterranean had been virtually stripped of trees.[50] Seneca,[51] circa 20 CE, commented "In a moment the ashes are made, but the forest is a long time growing."

But much of the Roman Empire clearly remained forested, and there was certainly still enough wood available for all the needs of the

Romans. Why could they not simply bring wood from central Europe or conquer more lands to extract the wood they needed?

Resources that exist in finite amounts tend to be extracted following a rather predictable pattern: slowly at first, accelerating, then peaking, and finally declining. This pattern is the same for nearly all resources, and this fact will become very important again, later in the book, when we discuss oil. It is an iteration of the economist's law of diminishing marginal returns, and it can be visualized using the "woodlot scenario":

Imagine you buy a new house on a wooded lot and you decide to set up a small timber business. You buy a chainsaw and head for the trees. You pick a couple of nice big ones just behind the house and fell them (what fun!). You buy a truck to drag the logs and build a saw shed to prepare them into planks. It takes you a week or so to get organized, but that's OK; you're having fun, building a business. It turns out that the timber is pretty good and you soon get a few customers. You hire someone to work the shed so that you can focus on your Paul Bunyan thing with the chainsaw. After a few months, you have generated some good business, and a local hardware store places a big order. You abandon the chainsaw to work in the office, and you hand over the tree chopping to some more hires. Soon enough, you're a successful timber merchant.

But here's the woodlot problem:

You start to notice that things are going wrong with your cash flow. You're selling more wood than ever, but you're making less money. You look out toward the back paddock and still see trees, and your chainsaw guys are still heading out looking for wood, but they are spending more time finding the best trees and traveling farther to fell them. You're using more fuel than before and paying more wages. Your business starts to struggle long before you run out of trees because you are beginning to experience the law of diminishing marginal returns. You had better figure out what's going on soon or you'll be in big trouble. You have equipment and hired hands. You took out a loan to finance the construction of the saw shed and that new office—you're wishing you hadn't bought that fancy new Wii system for the kids.

The quality of your wood continues to decline, and your production costs are still increasing. It's time to get out because the longer you wait, the worse it will get. Hang on too long, and you will be stuck with useless gear and will end up defaulting on your loans. Your banker (let's call him Attila[52]) may realize before you do just how bad your situation really is and will move in to repossess your home. The bailiff (let's call him Alaric[53]) will come to evict you. And here's the really important point: this will all happen long before the woodlot runs out of wood. You might have been better off simply conserving the woodlot and hanging out in the summertime collecting berries, but that's not how it is. Now the berries are gone, too.

The Romans depleted their local forests and then more distant forests as the empire grew. A complex society formed that was predicated on the supply of huge amounts of wood. Then, around 200 CE, as demand continued to grow, supply flattened, went into irreversible decline, and the cost of wood began to climb. Even with large forests still standing on the periphery of the empire, the Roman economy began to fail. Short of affordable wood, the Romans became short of everything.

Various other forms of environmental degradation and depletion were found across the empire, particularly in the Mediterranean, as the Roman machine attempted to extract the massive amounts of resources it needed.[54] Agriculture suffered as topsoil was washed away from deforested hillsides. The cleared land, vulnerable to erosion and fertility declines, worsened through time. Advice to farmers for avoiding soil erosion is to be found in Columella's *De Re Rustica*. There are some very enlightening passages citing common complaints by Roman farmers that their soil had become "all used up and unfruitful" and lamenting that "Romans live on imported grain, and farming is regarded as employment for which no training is necessary."[55] His writings frequently comment on the oft-cited Roman decadence when he laments:

"The Old Romans, such as Cincinnatus, tilled the land allotted to them after their victories with an energy that matched their bravery in war, but nowadays men care only for luxury and pleasure."[56]

The acquisition of new food supplies was a major driving force for the expansion of the empire through the conquest of new lands, and the Roman experiment was degrading the farm as well as the forest. The extent of soil erosion is illustrated by the silting-up of Mediterranean Sea ports from soil lost from the denuded slopes. The North African port of Leptis Magna was completely swamped by silt and then abandoned. The huge volumes of soil washing down into the sea attest to the scale of the problems that must have been occurring on the farm. The massive Pont du Gard aqueduct that once watered the provincial city of Nemausus (Nîmes) of Gaul (France) records increasingly dirty and friable layers of limestone deposit along its walls: the legacy of a water supply coming from an increasingly eroded landscape.[57] And the amount of farmland needed to support the food requirements of the builders, slaves, and draft animals involved in Roman construction projects was prodigious. Authors Karen Frecker and Thomas Homer-Dixon calculated that the construction of the Roman Colosseum commanded the food production of fourteen thousand acres of land every year for five years—an area the size of the Manhattan Island for one building alone (albeit a big one . . .).[58]

The Romans reacted to their emerging economic hardships in a similar way to the Maya: they beefed up their efforts to protect the empire and maintain control over its resources. But once their principal commodity was too expensive to recover, they could not last for long. They consumed more and more resources in a vain effort to maintain their lifestyles until they were left stranded in a huge, complex, expensive, wood-dependent society. The environment around them was stripped of trees and agriculture was failing. The Roman experiment grew more and more massive even as resources that had once existed in colossal quantities were declining.

The Roman Colosseum. It might seem as though a civilization powerful enough to build a structure as indestructible as this must be indestructible itself. But perhaps the opposite is true: any civilization that is willing to plunder its environment for such follies can never last. Photograph courtesy of John Hallett.

Although its resource base was crumbling, the empire probably felt secure. It had displays of strength in abundance, great buildings, a decadent society, and an army flung to the far reaches of Europe, North Africa, and the Middle East. But Rome was becoming an empty shell. Even the mighty Roman army became vulnerable. Centurions found themselves wearing inferior chain mail rather than the solid armor breastplates their fathers had worn, and holding shoddy, flat shields rather than the tall, curve-strengthened ones that had protected the armies of the glory years. Once the pride of the empire, the Roman legions—as soon as rations began to decline and paychecks became interrupted—lost their edge. By 400 CE, the Romans were no more powerful than the barbarians; they just wore fancier clothes. They had all the pretense of wealth and power but had overdrawn their account in the ecological savings bank. They eventually became easy pickings for the Huns, led by Attila—the Scourge of God—and the Roman experiment in empire building was over. But the real scourge was not Attila at all: it was the Romans' own scourge on nature.

The barbarians did not take over a great empire, and there was no chance to rebuild what had been cast down. Attila the Hun did not emerge as the leader of a great, new empire in the region, because this region was done. The Huns simply showed up after the Roman Empire had deforested itself to collapse and gave it the final push into oblivion. The Roman Empire had grown into a massive, unresponsive colossus that seemed to believe it could make even nature submit. But when nature raised its invisible hand, the fall of Rome was so dramatic and so complete that Europe would languish in the Dark Ages[59] for the better part of a millennium.

RECURRING THEMES

> **Collapse is recurrent in human history . . . fundamentally a sudden, pronounced loss of an established level of sociopolitical stability. A complex society that has collapsed is suddenly smaller, simpler, less stratified, and less socially differentiated. Economic activity drops to a commensurate level, while the arts and literature experience such a quantitative decline that a dark age often ensues. Population levels tend to drop, and for those who are left, the known world shrinks.**
> Joseph A. Tainter, *The Collapse of Complex Societies*[60]

The human cultural experiment has grown exponentially. We hung out in bands roaming the savannahs of Africa for a few million years before we learned how to manipulate the land with fire and how to hunt with primitive tools. We spread across the landscape and developed agriculture over the next ten thousand years or so. It took a few thousand years for our experiment in civilization to spawn nations and empires. The fossil fuel era is only two centuries old, the petroleum interval only a century, and the computer age began just a few decades ago.

The world seems incredibly complex, but the path of progress has always been the same. Civilizations have emerged thanks to the ability of an intelligent, upright ape to figure out how to get its dexterous hands on food and fuel from the environment with ever-increasing efficiency.

But the pathway traveled by civilization has been decidedly bumpy, and neither progress nor survival has ever been guaranteed. In order to sustain our civilizations we have needed to maintain the integrity of our resource bases in the face of escalating demands. In this, we have nearly always failed. Progress has not been gradual: it has been a sequence of booms and busts. Collapse is no freak occurrence that befell the odd ancient civilization here and there following some unusual stroke of bad luck or unexpected act of folly. Collapse is the norm and is consistently linked with the depletion of resources and ecological damage.[61]

All civilizations that have begun to fill a geographic region with people have become endangered. The Easter Islanders, isolated on a small island by thousands of miles of open water, developed a complex society and then trashed their resource base in only a few hundred years. The Maya filled Mesoamerica over a period of a few thousand years, finally causing overpopulation-driven resource depletion only a few short years before the arrival of the Spanish conquistadors. The Romans packed the Mediterranean full of people and then scraped it clean of resources, like hyenas over a wildebeest carcass. Their empire eventually fell when it could no longer afford to ship in all its excessive luxuries from an extended region.

The obvious question, then, might be: Is the world now full?

There are certainly signs that it might be. Many of the problems that brought about the demise of past societies, including overexploitation of our principal source of energy, environmental damage, and declines in agricultural productivity, are clearly visible in the modern world. We are also experiencing substantial climate change, another factor frequently implicated in civilization collapse.

Perhaps the strangest aspect of civilization collapse is the human angle. How could complex societies allow such collapses to occur? Is it possible that they have been unable to recognize the calamities that were about to visit them? Is the hand of nature truly invisible? At first pass, it is hard to imagine that a complex society could fail to perceive an encroaching environmental disaster that might threaten its survival. But if this is the case—if societies were able to recognize impending calamities—we must conclude that societies failed to react to problems that they understood threatened them. Joseph A. Tainter was particularly troubled by the suggestion that complex societies were not responsive to their environment:

> The resource depletion argument, at base, ascribes collapse to economic weakness, often suddenly induced. One supposition of this view must be that these societies sit back and watch the encroaching weakness without taking corrective actions. Here is a major difficulty. Much of [the structure of complex societies] seems to have the capability—if not the designed purpose—of countering deficiencies in productivity. Dealing with adverse environmental conditions may be one of the things that complex societies do best. It is curious that they would collapse when faced with precisely those conditions they are equipped to circumvent.[62]

Tainter concluded that societal decay was the root cause of collapse and that those other factors, such as environmental degradation and climate change, were only of secondary importance. But, although he has been one of the most important analysts of civilization collapse, and incredulous though he may have been, Tainter was quite wrong on this point. Societies are exquisitely capable of failing to respond to a danger even if they understand it quite thoroughly. Alas, we demonstrate this fact in the modern world every day.[63]

The study of past civilizations leaves us with some surprising and chilling conclusions. First of all, civilization collapse is not some unusual, rare occurrence: it has happened again and again. Even more sobering is the realization that the succession of civilizations has not been a gradual procession of more efficient challenger civilizations conquering established ones. Rather, it has been the result of the failure of the established civilization to protect its resource base. Factors of both the environment and the socioeconomics of the civilization are important, with a common feature of collapse being the simultaneous growth in size and complexity of the society and the expansion of its resource demands beyond the capabilities of its environment. The environment is generally degraded in the process, making matters worse.

The size and political and economic dominance of a civilization does nothing to protect it from collapse, nor does its social complexity. Civilizations both large and small have fallen, and although social complexity supports rapid growth, it stagnates into selfish interdependence. It provides no resilience against failure when the established elites increasingly defy the laws of ecology to preserve their entrenched position.

The most ominous aspect of the demise of civilizations, however, is that they have been so sudden and dramatic, as if nobody could see what was coming. The empires that passed have left behind their ghosts. The pensive Moai still stand guard over Easter Island. The desert winds still blow sand through the empty buildings of the Hisatsinom. The Parthenon still glares down upon Athens from the Acropolis. The immense Roman Colosseum, where one all-powerful civilization put half a million people to death for entertainment, still stares back, unimpressed, as yet another civilization bustles around its travertine façade. These ghosts were the last follies of doomed civilizations. They were intended as enduring symbols of power and security, but, though they endure, the societies that created them do not.

A gradual contraction into more sustainable patterns of resource use is not the norm for a society that is overexploiting its environment. The norm is a last-ditch effort to maintain outward displays of power, and then a sudden, and dramatic, collapse.

CHAPTER 3

THE FOSSIL FUELS SAVINGS BANK

An official-looking letter arrives in the mail, and when you open it you discover that some distant relative just died and left you a billion dollars in her will. Shame that what's-her-face is dead 'n' all, but you are suddenly a billionaire: sweet. You spend a few hundred bucks to throw a party, of course, and then dump the rest into a savings account and think about what to do with it. How to invest it—how to spend it? Only if you are an idiot do you just leave the money in the savings account and continue to party. Only if you are a fool do you allow the money to alienate all your friends and family and turn you into a miserable wretch. Only if you are a complete loser do you use the first half billion to make gambles that the second half billion can't pay down.

So you have to ask yourself why humankind has squandered its natural inheritance so badly. A prime example is the use of fossil fuels.

Coal is a rock formed from the remains of plants that died in anaerobic swamps during the carboniferous period 280 million to 345 million years ago and were compacted, dehydrated, and gradually degraded into simpler hydrocarbons. Four broad categories of coal are found in a number of places on the planet. The lowest-quality coals are known as lignite and today are used only in power plants. Lignite is not a whole lot more than rather dry, solid peat. Intermediate grades are the subbituminous and bituminous coals; the bituminous are used for multiple applications, including the production of coke. The highest-quality coal, reserved for residential and commercial heating, is anthracite. (Super-compressed coal is a semiprecious stone called jet).

Oil is found in fewer locations than coal because the conditions for its formation were more specific. Most of our oil was formed during two relatively short periods in prehistory, one around ninety million and one hundred million years ago, and another about five million years ago, when organic-rich[1] sediments became buried under rock. If they were buried at depths greater than seventy-five hundred feet, large organic molecules were degraded into chains of between five and twenty-five carbon atoms: crude oil. If they were buried at depths greater than fifteen thousand feet, they broke further to form a small molecule with a single carbon atom: natural gas. The "oil window," then, is a layer of rocks that have been buried at a depth of seventy-five hundred to fifteen thousand feet for much of their geological history. Oil and gas can only be extracted from porous source rocks, through which they can move, and those source rocks must be located beneath an impermeable cap rock through which they cannot leak away.

If any of these geologic requirements has not been fulfilled, there is no oil. It is not surprising, then, that oil is found in relatively few places on the planet. Source rocks from oil-window depths beneath deformed impermeable cap rocks are particularly common in the Middle East and in the Caspian Sea region. Most of the planet lacks one or more of the geological requirements and is not blessed (or cursed) with oil.

Coal, oil, and natural gas are finite resources. A finite amount of organic material was trapped below ground, at the appropriate depth, in the appropriate types of rocks. Once we have extracted all the coal, oil, and natural gas that we can, the age of fossil fuels will be finished.

We received a huge inheritance from generous ancestors who died millions of years ago. It took a long time for the attorney's letter to arrive in the mail, but we finally set up our savings account about two hundred years ago. We spent tentatively at first, but we soon got used to being rich. We've done so well off this inheritance that we pat ourselves on the back for being such great innovators and investors, as if we made all this happen. But it's been so long since we first opened that savings account that we seem to have forgotten where it came from.

BLACK GOLD AND THE BRITISH CENTURY

> **The carpenters' tools were of wood but for the last cutting edge: the rake, the oxyoke, the cart, the wagon, were of wood; so was the wash tub in the bathhouse; so was the bucket and so was the broom; so in certain parts of Europe were the poor man's shoes . . . the loom . . . the pipes that carried water into the cities . . . the ships, of course. . . .**
> Lewis Mumford, *Technics and Civilization*[2]

Europe is a continent of cities, towns, and agriculture. Its wild places are few and far between, and the only pristine areas of any size are hidden in the mountains or in the far north. But Europe used to be a continent of forests. Hansel and Gretel, Little Red Riding Hood, William Tell, and Robin Hood all lived in the great European forests.

The Romans took their toll on the forests of the Mediterranean region, and many of these forests never recovered, but the northern forests were less affected, and most of Europe recovered ecologically after the fall of the Roman Empire. Medieval Europe was densely forested with scattered villages and towns and few significant cities.

Energy use in medieval Europe was dominated by the burning of wood, with wind and water power used for special purposes such as grinding grain, and animal power used for transportation and farmwork. Medieval construction was also almost entirely from wood[3] and, as the population of Europe began to climb, forests fell increasingly to the axe. A big increase in the demands for wood came from increasing demands for iron, smelted using charcoal.[4] Iron needed lots of charcoal, charcoal needed lots of wood, and, before too long, the forests were being cut faster than they could regenerate. Europe was heading toward and beyond its "peak wood."[5]

Europe had developed in relatively benign baby steps in the centuries following the fall of Rome, and it took a long time to degrade its huge, productive forests, but, in the second millennium CE, Europe's wood resources slowly but surely began to decline.[6] By the thirteenth century, wood was becoming expensive, and by the sixteenth century, the forests of Europe had shrunk to a quarter of their former size. The most productive land had been cleared for agriculture, and a struggling Europe was primed for the next stage in the history of civilization. Necessity would, once again, become the mother of invention. This time, the exemplars would be the British.

The dominance of the British Empire began with its mastery of wind power, through which mighty Britannia's warships ruled the waves. This naval dominance enabled the expansion of trade and conquest overseas. Colonialism included the advent of a new, cynical model of slavery, which became one of the first large-scale, multinational capitalist enterprises. The capitalist machine demanded vast amounts of energy and burned through huge volumes of wood. As its forests disappeared, the British Empire turned to coal, the Industrial Revolution was launched, and the modern era had arrived.

Once they had taken to the seas, the Europeans soon figured out that there was a whole world of resources—and people—to be exploited. William Catton refers to the European colonies as "ghost acreages"; a means of extending a nation's effective production acreage by the capture of resources from overseas.[7] At its height, the British Empire controlled the resources of nearly half of Africa, parts of Central and South America, parts of the Middle East, South Asia, and Australia, and held sway over many other regions, including China.

This first era of globalization set into motion two interrelated trends: a huge expansion of the global economy and the divergence of rich countries from poor countries. As the Europeans extracted resources from around the world, wealth flowed from poor, who became poorer, to rich, who became richer. The relative wealth of nations today is still linked to the degree to which resources were gained or lost during the colonial era. Those enjoying a net gain in resources gained wealth and power; those that suffered a net loss of resources were left behind.

The advent of "institutional slavery" by the colonial British was a special case in the progress of civilization, not least for the scale of the horror that it perpetrated. Slavery was by no means a new phenomenon. It had been employed by nearly all the civilizations that had gone before, but it was institutionalized by the British on a far grander scale. Slavers stole people from Africa, sailed west on the trade winds to trade for sugar, tobacco, and other products in the Americas, and then sailed back to Britain on the westerlies to cash in. The so-called triangular trade was openly funded from both private and public coffers and operated under the protection of British law.

Institutional slavery also represents a special case in the history of energy. It was an efficient means for generating products to supply the new consumers in the emerging capitalist markets of Europe. Slavery declined only when the capitalist economy it had bolstered spawned the Industrial Revolution and made coal more efficient than slaves. We thank the brave and noble actions of great figures such as William Wilberforce and Abraham Lincoln for defeating slavery—and their moral stance, in their time, was nothing short of heroic—but it is doubtful that their efforts could have prevailed until the economic climate had changed. In the same way that colonialism had created the preconditions for institutional slavery, so industrialization sounded its end.[8]

At the height of its colonial expansion, the British Empire was putting immense pressure on its forests. A lack of wood might have brought an end to the British experiment in empire building before the eighteenth century but for Britain's eventual, albeit reluctant, embrace of coal. Waiting beneath the rural landscapes of England and Wales lay an immense energy inheritance, and Britain was about to begin withdrawing from the fossil fuels savings bank.

The dusty black rock that could be burned to give heat—and an icky sulfurous mess—had been used for some time by peasants unable to afford wood.[9] Coal was known as a nasty polluter used only by the poor, but, as wood became scarce, people from all segments of society were forced to use it. The switch from wood to coal was not easy, and people resisted, but coal was about to change the world. Like the Stone Age hunters whose careless overhunting had made them reluctant farmers, the colonial British logged their way, reluctantly, into the Industrial Revolution.

The British had stumbled on a truly civilization-transforming opportunity, and they became the first to access stored geological energy. No longer would it be necessary to harness energy as it was delivered by the sun, flowed on the wind and water, or needed to be grown before it could be collected. Now it was possible to delve into a source of energy that had been prepared millions of years before and stored underground, awaiting the civilization that could tap it. Nobody at the time could have had any inkling, but a new era in the history of civilization had begun.

The advantages of coal became apparent only when coal was adopted on a large scale. One key development was the use of coal for the production of coke, which burned extremely hot and allowed the production of large volumes of high-quality steel, the likes of which had been impossible with charcoal-fueled smelters. Coal gradually became the mainstay for a wide array of burgeoning industries, such as glass-making and brick making, and the nasty black rock became essential to the economy of Britain and the other nations of western Europe.

The Industrial Revolution was poised for takeoff, but the coal industry was dogged by inefficient mining, especially seepage and mine flooding, which required massive amounts of pumping with teams of horses. So, ironically, the major breakthrough that catalyzed the Industrial Revolution was an application of coal for the mining of coal itself.

The steam engine, first used to pump water out of coal mines, represents a genuine "moment in history" because the world now had its first machine powered by fossil fuels.

By the middle of the nineteenth century, the steam engine had found numerous other applications, on steamships that could bring materials from overseas colonies more efficiently and on trains that could transport coal and other commodities rapidly over land. Trains had never been possible before because the first locomotives could never have carried enough wood to fire their boilers. Other applications for coal included a wide range of new chemicals that could be synthesized from coal, such as new dyes for the textiles industry. The British Empire, rather than fading into wood-deficient obscurity, went from strength to strength. But as surely as coal had catapulted the British Empire to world dominance, so would the lack of coal seal its fate. By relying so heavily on a finite resource, the British Empire had ensured its eventual demise.

The Deep Duffryn mine in the town of Mountain Ash, in South Wales' Cynon[10] Valley, was sunk to a depth of two hundred and eighty-three yards in 1850 and began producing coal at a rate of approximately a hundred and fifty tons per day. At its height, over two thousand men worked down the mine, and when the coal became harder to mine by hand, machinery was brought in and the mine was sunk deeper, to the Gellideg seam, over four hundred yards underground.

In order to reduce the horrendous pollution caused by millions of homes around Britain that were burning coal for heating, a Phurnacite[11] plant was built in the Cynon Valley, where coal was treated to remove sulfur. The coal shipped out of the valley was cleaner, but the pollution in the valley became extreme. The Phurnacite plant, once named the dirtiest plant in Europe, polluted the surrounding areas with a toxic cocktail of sulfurous emissions, heavy metals, and a pall of fine coal dust. Vegetation and wildlife was destroyed for miles around. The horrible irony of the town's name after the once-common mountain ash tree[12] is self-evident.

Mountain Ash, 1934. Coal miners open up land on the hill above Mountain Ash to grow vegetables during the Great Depression. The father and son in the center of the photo are David and Thomas George Hallett, the author's father and grandfather. Photograph courtesy of Steve Hallett.

The Deep Duffryn mine was still producing nearly four hundred and fifty tons of coal a day into the 1970s until it closed, suddenly, in 1979. Its entire workforce was laid off, and hard times fell on Mountain Ash. And here lies one of the great ironies of my family history, mirrored in the family history of many and a microcosm of the Industrial Revolution.

My great-grandfather migrated from rural Somerset to mine coal in the Welsh valleys when workers were needed in the newly opened collieries. He was part of the transformation of the sleepy pastoral town of Aberpennar into the (then-renamed) mining town of Mountain Ash. My grandfather, Thomas George Hallett, spent much of his working life in the Deep Duffryn mine and died prematurely of black lung (I knew him for a short time but remember him fondly as "Bubbles"; he did cool magic tricks). My father, David Hallett, suffered significant peer and parental pressure to stay in the valleys to become a miner, but he developed a passion for nature from wandering the green slopes of the valley as a child. He left for university to pursue a career in botany. By the time he returned, the green hills were black and dead.

Thus, the Industrial Revolution drew my great-grandfather to the coal that would take the life of his son and the passion of his grandson. Those three generations saw the birth, peak, and death of an industrial town; the peak and decline of the British Empire; and the promise, power, and horror of the fossil fuel era.

Such is progress.

BLACK GOLD AND THE AMERICAN CENTURY

> **Oil has literally made foreign and security policy for decades. Just since the turn of this century, it has provoked the division of the Middle East after World War I; aroused Germany and Japan to extend their tentacles beyond their borders; the Arab Oil Embargo; Iran vs. Iraq; the Gulf War. This is all clear.**
> Bill Richardson, US secretary of energy, 1999[13]

John Maynard Keynes, the father of macroeconomics,[14] commented that the period from the dawn of man clear through to the middle of the eighteenth century could be viewed as a single, more or less monolithic "period of scarcity." This period, he suggested, eventually culminated in the Industrial Revolution and a new "period of abundance." This view overlooks some glorious achievements of, say, the Romans or the Inca, but his point is well met. Even the burgeoning wealth of Europe in the sixteenth century was merely a function of its ability to control territory. The European colonies solved the problem of resource depletion by expanding their sphere of influence overseas, and their colonies provided the raw materials that were needed at home. Once the resource hot spots of the world had been claimed, however, this avenue of development was closed, and it would fall to the Industrial Revolution—Keynes's period of abundance—to reinvigorate the restless engine of progress, powered by coal.

But it was not the Industrial Revolution that brought us to the pinnacle of human achievement upon which we stand today. Even as the coal-fired Industrial Revolution was booming, a new era began, almost without us noticing.

The last century has seen an incredible explosion in population, industry, technology, and consumption far beyond the promise of the Industrial Revolution. In just a hundred years the world's population has tripled; millions of miles of roads have been built for a billion cars (in 1900 there were approximately twenty-five hundred worldwide), electricity has illuminated homes and businesses; planes were invented, used, and perfected—as were synthetic fertilizers, computers, iPods, Barbie dolls . . . and the list goes on. Why did all this happen in the twentieth century? Why did the modern world arrive so suddenly—and why at this time? Did Western civilization simply reach a certain critical mass, a certain stage on its inevitable pathway of progress? Or was there something special about the twentieth century that propelled the development of this glittering modern world?

I submit that the explanation is oil. At the end of the nineteenth century, the Industrial Revolution morphed into the petroleum interval.

At the turn of the twentieth century, the United States of America was emerging as an economic power but was far from being the dominant nation it would, so suddenly, become. Oil was about to change everything, and America was about to assume the center of the world stage. Oil had been found in Pennsylvania and Ohio, making millions for a young entrepreneur named John Davidson Rockefeller. Within a generation, an immense fleet of American cars would drive on tens of thousands of miles of new American roads. Britain entered the First World War as the world's biggest empire, but American troops and American oil were needed to secure victory. By the end of the Second

World War, the United States was undoubtedly the most powerful country, and all this had happened in the span of a single generation. We often refer to this as the Greatest Generation. In truth, it was the Petroleum Generation.

Rockefeller was not born rich; he dropped out of school early and held a few mediocre jobs for the first years of his working life. By age thirty-eight, however, he controlled 90 percent of the oil refined in the United States. He had taken a small, speculative company in an emerging commodity, recognized its potential, and skillfully—sometimes ruthlessly—transformed it into the most efficient oil company in the world. Standard Oil[15] was eventually singled out by President Theodore Roosevelt as unfairly monopolistic, and, at the judgment of the Supreme Court in 1911, Standard Oil was split up (the pieces would become Exxon, Mobil, Chevron, Amoco, Arco, and Conoco). And then, on New Year's Day, 1901, the age of the gushers was heralded just outside Beaumont, Texas. Oil exploded from the ground at the Spindletop well in a deafening blast that shot a black plume hundreds of feet into the air. The first Texas well was suddenly producing thousands of barrels per day—at least twenty times more than any well before. Thousands of wells rapidly sprang up around it, and the first century of the petroleum interval had begun.

In Europe, meanwhile, oil was coming from the area around Baku, Russia (modern-day Azerbaijan), with the Rothschild and Nobel families vying for control. The Russians resisted, thanks to a local agitator called Joseph Dugashvili, whose understanding of the importance of Caspian Sea oil would be essential in the defeat of Nazi Germany a few decades later (after he had changed his surname to Stalin). The Europeans were sending their exploration teams out into the world. They first explored their colonies. The Dutch discovered oil in Indonesia, and Royal Dutch (eventually Shell) was formed. The British discovered oil in Persia, and Anglo-Persian (eventually BP) was formed. The French discovered oil in North Africa, and Elf was formed. The most obvious sites around the world were quickly explored, and most of today's major oil-producing regions were established. By the middle of the twentieth century, seven oil companies owned nearly all the oil reserves in the world; they produced nearly all the oil and distributed it with tankers they owned or through pipelines they owned. These seven companies became known as the seven sisters: Exxon, Mobil, Chevron, Gulf, Texaco, BP, and Shell.[16]

One of the lovely ironies of cars is that when they were first being promoted, it was claimed that they would reduce urban pollution by freeing the streets of stinky horse manure. Cars looked to remain a novelty item until the construction of enough roads made it worthwhile for the average person to own one. Heavy lobbying by the automobile and oil industries pushed a massive government investment in roads. The automobile industry blossomed rapidly, but often unfairly. General Motors teamed up with Chevron to buy the electric light rail system around Los Angeles, only to remove it. Angelinos have many hours to ponder the wisdom of this transformation as they sit in gridlock every day. Streetcar and light rail systems suffered across the country as the United States was redesigned and built for cars.

Air travel remained largely a luxury until new efficiencies enabled it to expand through the 1950s and 1960s. Today, air travel is a common activity for many people, especially in large countries such as America and Australia, where it has eclipsed bus and rail systems.[17] Cars, in the last century, and planes, in the last half century, have been responsible for a major overhaul of our societies. The whole concept of suburbia is a construct of the oil era, predicated on the availability of efficient private cars. People from the wealthier nations now globe trot and globe trade with ease.

Oil has transformed our world rapidly and completely. It can be refined into a range of energy-dense fuels, and so some of the most obvious transformations have been seen in transportation—but oil has transformed the world in a thousand other ways. Oil is the chemical feedstock for countless materials. Nylon[18] was the first true plastic, invented in the 1930s. It was first used for parachute material, replacing silk during the Second World War, and then it hit the big time on American legs during and after the war. Nylon was a major winner, and the battle of the synthetic chemists hit high gear. It is now hard to find many things that don't contain petroleum products. To demonstrate this point, go find something in your house that does not have a plastic part. Good job. I'll bet it's something very simple—what did you choose? A knife? Check the handle. A table? Check the stain and varnish. A mug? Sorry, the paint. A glass? Sure, but it was fired using . . .

Petroleum products have completely pervaded our civilization, and there are no substitutes for many of them. Plastics are essential for computers, and computers are essential for many other applications. Petroleum products are essential for weapons, drugs, Xbox consoles, smartphones, hospital machines that go "bleep," breast implants, golf balls, cars, dog bowls. You name it—oh, and fertilizer. Did you know that roughly half the protein you eat comes from natural gas? We'll get to that later.

THE GLOBAL ECONOMY

The world has been getting effectively smaller since the Europeans first shrank it under sail power in the eighteenth century. Globalization gathered steam[19] with the Industrial Revolution in the middle of the nineteenth century and accelerated with the adoption of oil as the fuel of choice in the twentieth century. The silicon age, especially during the period of rapid adoption of computers in the 1980s, heralded a new era of globalization in which information could be transmitted around the world instantly just as goods were moving in huge volumes on a sea of oil. New efficiencies permitted tasks to be shared across borders. The intertwining of the affairs of the world over the last two decades or so has weaved the world's economies together in a closer and closer mutualism. But while a mutualism can be beneficial by delivering mutual benefits, it can also spell danger as mutual dependency.

The first event of the new millennium was a collective sigh of relief as we survived Y2K.[20] Many people had predicted a huge disaster with the world's computers going berserk as their clocks attempted to record the date 01.01.00. The Y2K problem was largely avoided, thanks to the stalwart efforts of devoted computer geeks, but it was a bizarre example of how technological progress can put civilization in a pickle. We had become so reliant on computers that a major computer glitch, no matter how comical the cause, would have been very damaging. We organized well for Y2K and avoided the disaster with relative ease, but it was a teachable moment.

Thomas L. Friedman, in his book *The World Is Flat: A Brief History of the Twenty-First Century*,[21] argues that globalization has been a process of flattening the earth, and I think this is a good image. He talks about a range of "global flatteners" that have been rapidly seized upon in the last decade. Developments in telecommunications, computers, the Internet, and software have enabled outsourcing, off-shoring, and the development of complex supply chains. Global access to information has made the linkage among different regions of the world more rapid and has broken down national boundaries in many ways.

Globalization is essentially the combination of rapid communications and cheap, long-distance transport. India has been a huge beneficiary of advanced communications and computer technology. Its economy has blossomed as a result of its ability to supply quality services and high-tech goods from a remote location. China, meanwhile, has become the world's newest manufacturing hub. Its economy is booming in the era of globalization on the back of its natural resources and huge labor pool. Cheap oil enables it to deliver manufactured goods cost-effectively anywhere in the world.

It is not surprising that few people understand how the economic world is linked to the natural world. Consider the products available at your local big-box store. Stuff appears, miraculously, on the shelves, but where did it come from and how was it made? Was some hardship endured by someone, somewhere, in order to make it? Was a forest felled or a hillside eroded?

You would think that understanding the fruit and vegetable section would be relatively easy, but it may be the most confusing section of all. Consider the large volumes of organic food with which the big stores are now well stocked. This would appear to be the heartening result of the tireless efforts of environmental activists, but it has been perverted too. I picked up some organic asparagus at my local Wal-Mart the other day: "product of Chile." OK, so it may be pesticide free, but since it was raised by underpaid workers it hardly fits the bill as the model of social development; and since it was flown in from half a world away, it hardly represents the environmentalists' dream of sustainability. The asparagus is cheap, tastes vaguely like asparagus, and sells well. It has become an economic irrelevance that asparagus grows perfectly well in Indiana.

One of the major products of the global economy has been the proliferation of corporations, large companies owned by shareholders that enjoy legal rights as entities. In the United States, for example, corporations enjoy First Amendment and Fourth Amendment rights, as if they were individuals. Since corporations are owned by shareholders rather than by their directors, the directors enjoy rights of limited liability. The role of corporation directors mandates shareholder primacy, which dictates that they should increase the wealth of the corporation's shareholders above all other concerns. These three principles: special constitutional rights, limited liability, and shareholder primacy, have transformed corporations into massive, dominant capitalist machines that now generate the vast majority of the global economy. They deliver high levels of productivity by ensuring the greatest possible competition between economic rivals. But corporations are unresponsive to long-term dangers because they must report to shareholders who demand short-term rewards, and environmental problems are ignored if they do not affect the bottom line.

A series of energy transitions has brought us from our nomadic pasts to this twenty-first-century world. First stone tools, then agriculture, fire, wood, and coal enabled the emergence of a sequence of advanced societies across the globe, and, through the last century, oil has brought us all together. This single resource has enabled the construction of a monumental global civilization in which we have become dependent on the increased productivity and efficiencies of scale it can provide. The energy density of oil has enabled us to produce more goods than previous generations would have thought possible. It has, however, also enabled us to overwhelm many of our other resources and support systems and generated pollution on a global scale. Oil has helped to push our global population close to seven billion, not all of whom can be fed. The blessing of oil has been a double-edged sword.

But the biggest news about oil is neither the wonders it can create nor the scale with which it can destroy. The biggest news is that its supply is flattening. We suddenly find ourselves at the very middle of an amazing, two-hundred-year glitch in history. As surely as the last century saw the emergence and dominance of oil, the next century will see its decline, demise, and disappearance. This is the peak of the petroleum interval, and we are about to embark on the next great energy transition. It will bring the greatest upheavals in the history of civilization.

CHAPTER 4

DIVORCED FROM NATURE

To sit back hoping that someday, some way, someone will make things right is to go on feeding the crocodile, hoping he will eat you last—but eat you he will.

Ronald Reagan[1]

Human societies have been repeatedly caught out by failing to see slow but pervasively dangerous changes. The gradual deforestation of Easter Island may not have been noticed by its inhabitants, the gradual erosion and degradation of the fragile lands of the American Southwest may have been overlooked by the Hisatsinom, and the dangers of increasing population pressure were probably not recognized by the Maya. For modern societies with extensive historical records, however, there is no excuse for letting this happen again. We should be able to understand the true nature of these slow changes that put us in jeopardy.

Global warming is a classic example of slow change. We now know that humans have been enriching the atmosphere with greenhouse gases for thousands of years,[2] but global warming was understood only in the last few decades. We finally have some agreement on the issues, and some action is being mustered, but the response is minuscule compared to the size of the problem, and we have, again, been blindsided.

Creeping problems are hard to see at the best of times, but we make them even harder to see in a number of different ways. Religion can obscure problems when it seeks to insert simplistic phenomenological explanations or advises us not to worry because some supernatural being has it all under control. Poor government can also easily overlook creeping problems whose impacts are separated from the center of political power. Government can also get horribly in the way of solving environmental problems when unyielding economic growth is its first priority. Most important, however, is the way we have become divorced from nature. How can we expect to see nature's invisible hand if we don't even consider ourselves a part of it?

If only carbon dioxide was a rich puke-green color, it would spew out of the back of your car and leave an icky trail. Over the last century, the air we breathe would have gradually changed color and we'd now be living under a vomit-colored sky. Humans react best to things they can see. Invisible carbon dioxide is no less damaging, but we need science sightedness to understand why.

The first important step, then, in facing some of our pervasive environmental challenges, is to find ways to see the invisible hand of nature. What you see is, most demonstrably, not always what you get. What you can't see but can figure out with an open, inquiring mind might be much more important. You might think that if people understand the nature of a problem, then they will figure out a way to solve it. It's an important first step, but if only it were that simple. . . .

CAN THE LEOPARD CHANGE HIS SPOTS?

Scorpion wants to cross the river but he can't swim, so he asks Frog to carry him across.

"If I give you a ride on my back, how do I know you won't sting me?" asks Frog.

Scorpion replies: "It would not serve me to sting you for I cannot swim."

Frog agrees, and braves the surging waters with Scorpion on his back. Halfway across the river, Frog feels the burning spear of Scorpion's sting in his back.

"Mr. Scorpion! Why did you sting me? Now we will both die!"

Scorpion replies, sadly, "I can't help it; it's in my nature."

Aesop

About seven million years ago separate populations of African apes began to evolve into the distinct groups that would lead to the modern gorillas, chimpanzees, and humans. The one destined for humanity evolved an upright posture, improved vision, and dexterous hands. Agile tongues and big brains followed, leading to complex language. Communication must have assisted the coordination of hunting and promoted social cohesion, and it eventually enabled the storage of information within communities and its transmission from generation to generation: *"Where was the wild honey last year, honey?"*

With fine motor skills, powerful intellect, and sophisticated communications, humans then evolved in a very unusual way—we evolved culturally. While our biological evolution is slow and clunky, as in the rest of the living world, our cultural evolution has exploded like a Bill Gates experiment gone mad. We update our cultural software rapidly but still run it on outmoded hardware. We are hardwired with a set of biological capabilities that are more or less unchanged since our caveman days, yet we are attempting to manage a decidedly unnatural and complicated world. It should be no surprise that a small-group mammal adapted to hunting and gathering on the African savanna can feel out of place in this modern world, and that it can be stunningly unaware of problems beyond the scale of its local environment and personal life experience.

If you draw a line with our ancestors of about three million years ago,[3] we have spent roughly two hundred thousand generations as hunter-gatherers, and a few hundred generations as farmers, but only seven generations since the Industrial Revolution. The first two hundred thousand generations figured out fire and stone tools. The last seven generations gave us trains, planes, and automobiles, electricity, computers, and liposuction.

Our cultural evolution began to outstrip our biological evolution at least fifty thousand years ago when the archaeological record shows a rapid burgeoning in the arts, dramatic developments in tool technology, and signs indicative of religious rituals. Skulls and skeletons from this era, the so-called great leap forward, are virtually indistinguishable from our own. I have a mental image of a group of regular modern humans sitting around a campfire debating the meaning of life fifty thousand years ago. They were probably every bit as intelligent as you or me. Oh, to be a fly on the cave wall.

You may, or may not, wear a suit and tie, but you probably consider yourself more advanced than a caveman—more sophisticated, more thoughtful. You probably consider yourself more sophisticated than some loincloth-clad dude chipping flint knives in the African Rift Valley, hunting wooly mammoths across Siberia, or gathering grass seeds on the banks of the Mediterranean Sea. But you are not inherently smarter at all. You feel sophisticated because you have been the beneficiary of thousands of years of cultural evolution.

This rapid cultural evolution has had enormous advantages. In communications, for example, we are no longer limited to passing campfire stories down through the generations; we can store terabytes of information in libraries and cyberspace. We do not have to reinvent the proverbial wheel each time we slay a boar and need to transport it to camp. We now have books on wheel making. But our rapid cultural adaptation has also sent us down some unfortunate dead ends. Let's call these dead ends maladaptations. There are plenty of parallels in biological evolution: flightless birds are well adapted to predator-free islands because they don't waste energy with unnecessary aerial sightseeing. But throw some foxes, cats, or humans into the mix, and the evolution of un-flight suddenly seems like an oversight—a maladaptation—making the moa, dodo, and dozens of other flightless birds, well, sitting ducks. Similarly, the appendix was presumably valuable to our herbivorous ancestors, aiding the digestion of large volumes of cellulose, but it's a bursting maladaptation now that we are omnivores.

But, like our bodies, our cultures have also adapted in some very unfortunate ways. Sugar-rich treats are rather rare in nature and greatly prized by hunter-gatherers, but are a dime a dozen at your local 7-Eleven. Gorging on sugar is a great thing if you are hungry and active—let's say you raided a nest of wild bees to get it—but if the closest you get to the wild is the Discovery Channel, that box of Twinkies on the coffee table is a health hazard. We know this, and yet we gorge nonetheless. It's in our nature to crave sugar because sugar is packed with energy that can be stored away as body fat for later use. We evolved to love the taste of sugar when getting as much of it as possible was good for us. Now if you live near that 7-Eleven, it's a maladaptation.

Another cultural maladaptation was the Chinese custom of foot binding. Small feet were considered a highly desirable trait in Chinese women. Judging that they could become more desirable by making their feet as small as possible, women bound their feet, and even broke them, to inhibit growth. An imperative for generations of Chinese women was to limp down the aisle to a suitable marriage in agony on disfigured feet.[4] Generations of Papua New Guineans ritually consumed the brains of deceased family members in the belief that they could retain some of their admirable traits. In the process many consumed an infectious prion disease (similar to mad cow disease) called kuru, which reached epidemic proportions until a group of Australian researchers figured out its epidemiology and the practice ceased.

Culture is acclaimed as our finest characteristic. A procession of philosophers has pronounced culture to be that special quality that separates "us" from "the animals." My heart is with them. I love my cultural trappings and occasional indulgent pretensions. But culture is much more than fine art, music, or poetry. Culture is a complex but hastily erected scaffold of human life that has evolved above our biology as a small-group mammal, and it divorces us in pervasive and dangerous ways from our environment. That culture makes us feel separate from the rest of the living world is a maladaptation in itself. We are naked apes in suits and ties, and that's fine and part of the fun. Like the leopard, we can't change our spots, and nor should we try, but understanding how we got those spots and what they actually do is part of the key to protecting our future.

ARE HUMANS INNATELY RACIST AND VIOLENT?

I grew up in Oldham, a town on the edge of Manchester, in Northwest England. It's a very interesting place to have grown up, although I didn't recognize it at the time. Oldham is an unusually segregated town, and when I went back home to visit for a few months in the late 1990s, having been away for years, it was obvious that trouble was brewing. In May 2001, race riots broke out across the town. Petrol bombs were thrown, scuffles developed into little pitched battles, many people were injured, police arrived by the busload, and significant property damage occurred over a period of three semianarchistic days.

Why does this kind of thing happen? Are humans innately racist and violent? We certainly have a significant capacity for racism, but then we also have the ability to resist it. In Oldham, for example, things can go either way. When times are good, people of different races can live together rather peacefully, but when times get rough, things can fall apart.

Oldham was once prosperous and the center of the cotton milling industry; at its height, nearly a fifth of the world's cotton was woven in

Oldham. Much of the work in the cotton mills was drudgery, so when immigrants were shipped in from Commonwealth countries[5] to work the mills, Oldhamers were grateful. Since the new immigrants were poor, they settled in the cheapest areas of town. So, when the cotton industry went into irreversible decline in the middle of the twentieth century, and the economy of Oldham was decimated, the town was left with a poor, segregated community. The Oldham of my childhood never had any truly ghettoized areas, but it was obvious, even to a kid, that there were areas where white folks lived and areas where the Asian folks lived. I remember no mixed-race relationships, and schools were either all white or all Asian. Asians ran the corner shops, the chippies, and drove the taxis. The entire staff of the large stores was white, and you'd be pretty sure that the cashier at the bank would be white.

It seems to me that a number of things predispose people to racism and violence. There is certainly some measure of innate tribalism in humans, as there is in many animals, including all the other apes. An individual chimpanzee's defense of territory, for example, will favor his immediate family first and then his troupe. An individual that wanders into the wrong territory had better beware. Humans display this characteristic to a considerable degree.

As discussed in the prologue, Stanley Milgram showed us quite categorically that regular folk can be led to support evil-doing relatively easily.[6] He did not study prison guards at Auschwitz or Abu Ghraib, but he showed that your average Yale University student could behave rather like them. With relatively little overt coercion, the erstwhile Yalies delivered what they thought were painful and even fatal electric shocks to subjects in a psych experiment simply because they were told to do so by an authority figure in a lab coat. Most were willing to inflict serious pain, and nearly two-thirds were willing to deliver a shock they believed would be fatal. Milgram's experiment has been repeated a number of times and across cultures, with similar outcomes.[7]

In another landmark experiment in social psychology, Phil Zimbardo created a mock prison in a hallway beneath the psychology department at Stanford University.[8] He selected eighteen Stanford students and young Palo Alto residents and assigned them randomly to the role of prison guard or prisoner for the two-week experiment. To his great surprise, the participants rapidly adopted their new roles in the "Stanford Prison," and, when the "guards" began to torture the "prisoners," the experiment had to be terminated early. Many among us, it seems, are capable of being Adolf Eichmann, William Calley, or Lynddie England[9] when pushed. Perhaps we need to worry less about the few "bad apples" out there and focus more on the bad barrels that rot them. Our innate tribalism—racism—(and there will always be unashamed Nazis out there)—cannot be expunged, nor can our tendencies for violence and cruelty. On the other hand, while these tendencies can be ramped up, they can also be tuned down.

First, experience and education are priceless. As Mark Twain said: "Travel is fatal to prejudice, bigotry and narrow-mindedness." It is difficult to recognize the prejudices around you until you have a deep understanding of other cultures and can appreciate your home as if through the eyes of an outsider.

Second, segregated communities and unequal educational and economic opportunities can lead to conflict and can unearth latent racism. The danger grows if the social or economic divide between communities is allowed to widen. The danger abates if the divide is narrowed. Thus, by promoting laws that prohibit discrimination in education and employment, and by promoting mixed-income, multipurpose communities, we inhibit the development of racial tensions.

Third, the general economic health of communities has a huge bearing on their ability to get along. When there are enough territories and resources for everyone, communities tend to appreciate the enrichment they gain from diversity, and they tend to thrive. But when times are tough and the competition for resources is strenuous, enrichment through diversity can morph, disastrously, back into tribalism. Witness the hundreds of thousands of Tutsi hacked to death in 1994 at the hands of their hitherto cordial Hutu neighbors in the chronically overpopulated Rwanda. When times are tough and a region is dominated by one ethnic group, there is a tendency for tribalism to be expressed as the victimization of out-groups. Witness the millions of Jews, Roma, and ethnic Poles murdered by the German Nazis who fomented violent fascism from latent tribalism following the economic ruin of the 1930s. Economic sustainability, then, is not just needed for the accumulation of individual wealth but to stave off some of the social calamities that can be confounded by economic hardship.

THE TRAGEDY OF THE COMMONS

Ruin is the destination to which all men rush, each pursuing his own best interest, in a society that believes in the freedom of the commons.
Garrett Hardin[10]

Garrett Hardin's famous paper "The Tragedy of the Commons" describes in a clear and compelling way a counterintuitive phenomenon that has implications for the biological and social sciences, politics, and economics. The tragedy of the commons highlights the danger of overexploitation of common-pool resources by rational groups of people. "We may call it the Tragedy of the Commons," explains Hardin, "using the word 'tragedy' as the philosopher Whitehead used it; 'the essence of tragedy is not unhappiness. It resides in the solemnity of the remorseless working of things. . . .'"[11]

Hardin conjures the image of a farmer with access to a shared pasture who has the opportunity of adding sheep to his flock. The farmer recognizes that the extra animals may place additional stress on the pasture but calculates that he has more to gain than to lose by doing so. It is clear that he will make additional income from these added animals. The damage they might cause is speculative and seems rather minor. He adds the sheep. It is the only rational thing to do.

All the other farmers, however, have reached the same conclusion, act in the same way, and the number of sheep on the pasture increases considerably. The pasture becomes degraded and all the farmers suffer as a result.

And then the situation worsens.

The pasture is now degraded, but the farmer still has the same choice. Indeed, given his reduced income from sheep grazing on poorer land he may be even more compelled to increase his flock. Again, all the farmers reach the same conclusion and act in the same way. The pasture is degraded further and all the farmers suffer more. The situation may persist until the pasture is degraded to the point of complete failure.

The tragedy could have been averted by the reduction of animals on the pasture, but, for each individual farmer, that was never the rational thing to do. Each farmer's ability to improve the pasture by reducing his flock would never have been clear while his loss of income would have been obvious. Furthermore, his act of altruism would have resulted in larger benefits to his neighbors (competitors?) than to himself since the pasture would have served their expanded flocks more than his reduced flock.

The importance of Hardin's tragedy of the commons is that it explains how disastrous choices, such as those made by these farmers, can be entirely rational. People can act disastrously and rationally at the same time, and even in full recognition of the likely consequences. Their chance to gain is clear, whereas the damage they may cause is speculative and shared out among all. The tragedy of the commons has been played out on thousands of commons for thousands of years, and it is being played out in a thousand more right now. Hardin shows us that it is not only idiots who destroy the environment but clear-thinking individuals making rational choices. Rational, that is, only in the strict sense of the term, and in a community that cannot find ways to cooperate.

The threat posed by allowing free access to common-pool resources has prompted much discussion, and the prevailing wisdom is that there are really only two ways that such resources can be sustained. Both aim to prevent a commons scenario from existing.

The first way is to place the resource under government control and to limit, by force of law, the extraction of resources by each user. This can be extremely successful, but government control can cause problems, especially if management is poor or distant.

The second way to manage the commons has been to divide and sell them into private ownership. This ensures that the costs of any damage will be borne by the owners themselves rather than passed onto others, thereby increasing the incentive for stewardship. This approach has also been successful in many cases. The problem here, however, is that the ownership of the resource tends to gradually accumulate in the hands of fewer and fewer owners, and local communities are removed from their land base.

Both these approaches have yielded considerable successes in the remediation and protection of common-pool resources, but there is a third way. When communities understand how to protect and conserve their resources, they can exist sustainably on their land base. Where this can be achieved, it is by far the best possible outcome. We will examine the management of the commons in the last part of the book.

HOLDING ONTO DISASTROUS VALUES

> **Doctrines may be a frightful burden, for, with the prestige of antiquity and tradition, they deprive the living generation of an open-minded capacity to face facts.**
>
> William G. Sumner, "The Banquet of Life"[12]

A population of Norse settlers established a colony in Greenland in the 900s that lasted for five centuries, eventually disappearing, with everybody dead.[13] Things went reasonably well for a while, and the settlers developed a pastoral farming society in two fjords with about two hundred and fifty farms gathered in fourteen separate parishes. Their demise was by no means inevitable; their Inuit neighbors, after all, continued to thrive after they were gone. The Inuit harvested abundant resources such as whales and seals by harpoon from kayaks, but the Norse settlers considered themselves superior to the Inuit and did not learn from these scallies[14] they called the Skraelings.[15]

The Norse made the mistake of holding onto disastrous values. First, they had tried to carry on living as "Christian farmers" in their new land and maintained as much contact as possible with Norway, sending tributes back "home," as well as receiving religious leaders that were really of little value in this desperately harsh landscape. Second, they not only failed to learn by observation of their Inuit neighbors but also probably made enemies of them. In short, the Norse attempted to lead a Norwegian way of life thousands of miles from Norway in an environment that was significantly different and considerably harsher than Norway's. What might have saved them was the adoption of culture from the Inuit; but the Inuit were the despised Skraelings, so the Norse held onto their disastrous values to the end.

One deep-rooted part of our cultures has been the habit of conjuring up the supernatural. This appears to have extremely ancient origins[16] and to be more or less universal. Events such as earthquakes, storms, and the movements of celestial bodies inspire fear and awe and warrant explanation. Remarkable monuments such as Stonehenge, erected by Neolithic Brits, and the Caracol observatory at Chichen Itza, erected by the Maya, are testaments to our stubborn desire to connect ourselves to the cosmos—and the millennia over which we have striven. We are an innovative and inquisitive species, and we will go to great lengths to figure out how things work. When we lack sufficient knowl-

Stonehenge. These slabs of rock were transported to the Salisbury Plain in southwest England from the Marlborough quarry twenty-five miles to the north, around 2500 BCE. The site had been used for burials and had already been developed using wooden structures at least five centuries earlier. The immense standing sarsen stones are each thirteen feet tall and weigh in at an astonishing twenty-five tons. They were shaped with chisels to create mortise joints before the lintel stones, themselves weighing nearly eight tons each, were lifted on top. Why? Well that's the great "Mystery of Stonehenge." The Neolithic culture that went to such great pains to build it left no user's manual. Most believe it served as some sort of astronomical and religious site. Stand inside Stonehenge at dawn on the summer solstice and look back through the entrance. The sun will rise directly over the fabled "heelstone" visible through the entrance, 250 feet to the northeast. Photograph courtesy of John Hallett.

edge of the natural world, however, we have a tendency to invoke the supernatural.

Religion is our principal mechanism of invoking the supernatural. The gods—whether they be the panoply of gods worshipped by polytheists such as Hindus or the various iterations of the One God worshipped by Jews, Christians, and Muslims—are the quintessential

EAGLE VALLEY LIBRARY DISTRICT
P.O. BOX 240 600 BROADWAY
EAGLE, CO 81631 / 328-8800

supernatural beings. They are conceived as larger than nature and beyond it: supernatural, in the literal sense.

The principal questions tackled by religion have generally been the big ones that could not be answered any other way. What is the meaning of life? Why are we here? What happens after we die? How do the celestial bodies move around the earth? Where did we come from? Religion can serve a role in centering people by giving them a sense of place amid the workings of the cosmos, but it provides no substantive answer to any of these questions. It is intellectually lazy.

The last two seemingly unanswerable questions, of course, were eventually answered by careful observation of the natural world, and it turned out that the supernatural answers were plain wrong. Copernicus showed that the earth actually orbits the sun, and Darwin provided the first detailed exposition of where we come from. It took the Catholic Church more than a century to finally accept the correction provided by Copernicus, and millions of people still continue to resist Darwin's theory of evolution. This has prompted Richard Dawkins to quip: "We no longer have to resort to superstition when faced with deep problems [such as] 'What is Man?' All attempts to answer these questions prior to 1859[17] are worthless and we are better off if we ignore them completely."

Dawkins may be right, but more Americans believe the creation story than the theory of evolution. I have a hard time getting my head around that, but there it is. In this regard, religion presents a societal danger. Evolution is the scientific bedrock upon which an understanding of ecology and the environment is based. It also gives us the understanding needed to manage problems, such as antibiotic resistance, which are direct and recent consequences of evolution in action. When religion inhibits people's ability to understand the environment, it can prevent them from taking the right action.

The Mormons believe that Jesus Christ visited North America and that the American Indians are the descendants of the so-called Lamanites who traveled out from the Middle East around 600 BCE. It gives me a headache trying to figure out why anyone would believe this, but plenty do. I have a colleague who is both Native American and Mormon, and, frankly, I have difficulty reconciling that. It seems to me that imperiled Native American cultures are not well served by the belief that they sailed out from the Middle East. Other theories are better supported by the evidence.

When religion steps out of bounds and reduces people's ability to think clearly about real problems, it poses a problem. Science, imperfect as it is, has a much better track record for explaining life's mysteries. When it comes to times of crisis and an accurate worldview is needed, religion can present significant obstacles.

There are some expressions of religion that do much more than simply inhibit curiosity. Some religious movements cross far more boundaries, and they do this in two ways. First, they act in a coercive and controlling way and attempt to influence public policy. Fundamentalist Christian sects in the United States are particularly guilty of this. They link Christianity with so-called moral values, particularly abortion rights, and with the Republican Party. Their primary agenda is not spiritual but political, and they wield their religion like a gun; their congregations are their ammunition. Second, of course, are the fundamentalist Muslim sects that use terrorism as their weapon of choice. We should probably not even consider these groups as primarily religious. This is organized crime of Sicilian Mafia proportions. Their principal method is brainwashing, and their objective, again, is power.

Mainstream, nonfundamentalist religious groups need to take more of the responsibility for their coercive and violent cousins. Their religious sources and many of the core messages that moderates and fundamentalists share are the same. Moderate groups need to do much more to rein in fundamentalism.

But despite these objections, I can't bring myself to evangelize against religion. It's not for me, that much is clear, but it is undeniably important for many people—probably the majority. In any case, any attempt to silence religion would be futile. The Soviet Union's attempt to do that merely drove the church temporarily underground from where it eventually reemerged, undiminished. And while it concerns me that religious teaching can blur people's understanding of how the world works, it clearly provides substantial comfort for many people and helps them cope in an admittedly confusing world. Furthermore, religious groups often form cohesive communities that provide effective social support to their members, and some serve as something of a model. Many religious groups are very active in aid and social justice causes. These actions may piggyback on the cause of "converting the natives," which is a little unnerving, and they may also be vulnerable to bad logic if they overstress the role of the supernatural, but they are valuable. Those interested in building communities have a vast array of religious-based models from which to learn.

Resolving the risks and benefits of religion in society is no cakewalk. For my part, I conclude that religion is, at base, a set of cultures that inhibits free thinking and has the potential to generate coercive and violent offshoots. I also conclude, however, that the solution lies not in combating religion but in strengthening the human sense of inquisitiveness that religion tends to weaken. I think there is a desperate need for societies to understand their true natures and their relationship with the environment. The problem is not that people cling to a supposed supernatural world but that they are divorced from the natural one.

HOLDING ONTO DISASTROUS IDEOLOGIES

> **Capitalism is the legitimate racket of the ruling class.**
>
> Al Capone

Innovative ideas are a dime a dozen; most of them do not pass detailed scrutiny and are abandoned. Others face scrutiny and survive, or are even enhanced by further study, such as Darwin's theory of evolution. The immense attention that has been trained on that theory has only strengthened it. Still other innovative ideas fail under scrutiny but are retained nonetheless.

Karl Marx's *Communist Manifesto* is a brilliant work by almost any measure. Despite the protestations of anticommunists, it was written out of a will to improve the lot of working-class people, and it contains some wonderful social analyses. When the Soviet Union and Mao's China tried to put Marx's theories into action in large countries, however, communism did not pass muster. It turns out that people will not conform to a strict communist ideal on a large scale and that a command-and-control economy cannot be successfully maintained by a central government, no matter how coercive and desperate it becomes. And yet many people still maintain a communist ideology. Revolutionary communist leaders have repeatedly risen to power leading popular movements to overthrow repressive regimes, but they have then struggled to maintain a functioning economy and wound up resorting to the repression of the very people they emerged to save. Ideology can be a significant burden if one is unable to relinquish it when it no longer serves.

Like all the social thinkers who have gone before them, modern capitalists proposed systems that they believed would promote the welfare of all people, and, like their predecessors, they began sincerely. Capitalism does not aim to steal from the poor and give to the rich, as some claim, nor does it aim to damage the planet. It does both these things, however, because (like communism) the ideology of capitalism is too simplistic and does not account for all contingencies. Now that it has been tested over the decades, we can see that capitalism has significant flaws.

The first major flaw is that it is difficult to keep free markets truly free. There is always a tendency for those in power to tilt the game in their favor. The second major flaw is that capitalism has a tendency to discount the environment. The invisible hand of the market seeks the lowest price but does not value the externalities that it accumulates in the land, water, and air.

John Perkins's *Confessions of an Economic Hit Man*[18] provides an illuminating description of his life working for the National Security Agency (NSA) through private corporations with interests overseas. Perkins describes how he was trained to promote the interests of American companies overseas by fair means or foul. The overall goal, he argues, was to manipulate foreign government agencies and companies to facilitate the acquisition of resources and the export of products by American companies.

One important strategy, he claims, was to trap foreign countries in debts that would force them into unfavorable trade deals. Loans made by the World Bank and the International Monetary Fund (IMF) were instrumental. Once trapped, countries would be compelled to service their debts by trading away their resources to the United States. Principal among those resources was oil, which would be siphoned off by the West as payment for the debts they had artificially created. Perkins's assertions are eerily reminiscent of those made by Smedley Butler, general in the US Marine Corps in 1935: "I helped make Mexico safe for American oil interests ... [make] Haiti and Cuba a decent place for the National City Bank ... purify Nicaragua for the international banking house of Brown brothers ... [prepare the] Dominican Republic for American sugar interests ... [and make] Honduras 'right' for American fruit companies. . . . Looking back on it, I might have given Al Capone a few hints."[19]

It has become increasingly difficult to separate the desires of corporations from the policies of their governments: to which nation does a multinational corporation owe its allegiance? President Bill Clinton's secretary of labor, Robert Reich, commented that "the very idea of an American economy is becoming meaningless, as are the notions of an American corporation, American capital, American products and American technology."[20] The ability of large corporations to influence government policy through lobbying gives them enormous power—bolstered by the Supreme Court's reaffirmation, in March 2010, that corporations are, indeed, people.[21]

The actions of powerful Western corporations affect the welfare of people in many nations. Small nations with desired resources are particularly vulnerable. It is not surprising, then, to discover that the pathway to free trade has been littered with the corpses of the policies, regimes, and people who have stood in the way of this new form of progress.

A CIA-orchestrated coup solidified the position of United Fruit in Central America by encouraging the removal of the elected government of Guatemala. Senator Hubert Humphrey once commented, "[The food dependence of foreign nations] is actually good news, because before people can do anything, they have to eat, and if you're looking for a good way to get people to lean on you, and to be dependent on you, it seems that food dependence would be terrific."[22] Gulf Oil lobbied against US intervention to assist UNITA rebels in Angola because it perceived the status quo as preferable to its business, thus supporting a Marxist government against the avowed US policy in the 1970s. Union Carbide moved into India with explosive results. The CIA's involvement in the assassination of Patrice Lumumba of Zaire and his replacement with the despot Mobutu Sese Seko could hardly be viewed as a job well done for the forces of good in the world. America supported Saddam Hussein when he looked like a reasonable oil supplier and then fought two wars against him when he went bad. America funded, armed, and fought alongside Osama bin Laden before he became public enemy number one.[23]

How can all this happen? The Western world is the bastion of democracy and observant of international laws and agreements—we're the good guys, right?

The opposition to free-market economics has begun to swell. The World Trade Organization meetings of 1999 in Seattle were unexpectedly interrupted by a massive antiglobalization demonstration that turned into the three-day riot now known as the Battle of Seattle. It was a sign of things to come. The voices of dissent have become louder, more numerous, more diverse, and, since they are also becoming increasingly articulate, they can no longer be disparaged as hippies and loons. Two voices at the forefront of the antiglobalization debate are Naomi Klein,[24] who rails against the warlike tactics of Western governments, agencies, and corporations, and Vandana Shiva,[25] who counters the arguments that the mechanisms of capitalism benefit the poor: "Globalization was promised to spread democracy under the assumption that free trade equals open markets, which equals open societies. This equation does not hold. The markets of corporate globalization are not open—the trade rules give control to the giant corporations. The resulting societies are not open."[26]

Perhaps the most telling voice is that of a longtime insider, former senior vice president and chief economist at the World Bank, Joseph Stiglitz. His seminal work *Globalization and Its Discontents*[27] describes his increasing alienation from the World Bank, which, in his view, became increasingly ineffective and gradually more damaging, serving to shore up Western corporate interests rather than providing genuine opportunities in poor countries.

The World Bank and the International Monetary Fund (IMF) have operated three main pillars of economic development: fiscal austerity, the promotion of privatization, and the liberalization of markets. This has repeatedly opened countries to international trade, but it has also caught them in debt traps.

These organizations have not helped poor countries. They were supposed to promote the development of poor nations, but they have been corrupted into the promotion of Western agendas. The most fundamental problem is that the World Bank and the IMF embrace the concept of globalization and free-market economies without question. They are holding onto a disastrous ideology whose failings have now been revealed.

Humans, like all living things, have been shaped by the environment in which they have evolved, but we have evolved some peculiar attributes that have enabled us to plan and organize. We have created special environments and processes and can control nature in profound ways. We have become the masters of this planet, using and shaping it to suit our needs. Indeed, we have become so efficient that we increasingly forget that our artificial systems all draw, ultimately, upon the natural systems that we are damaging and depleting. The walls we have erected shield our eyes from the carnage and the danger. Few seem to be able to see beyond these walls, and fewer still seem concerned that the walls may not hold.

Perhaps this is not surprising. We live, after all, in a world that is now predominantly urban: we even call our cities "man-made environments." But the problem runs much deeper than simply a lack of education. Those who understand the threat posed by environmental degradation and depletion are more likely to reduce their impacts and to find ways to mitigate the damage, but they still find themselves swept along by the tide, impotent to bring about the sweeping changes that are needed because human societies appear to be repeatedly prone to divorcing themselves from nature.

The development of societies and civilizations is fundamentally a process of separation from the natural world and a means of controlling and subduing the hardships normally enforced by nature. We control plants and animals through agriculture and harness the materials around us for energy and construction. A hunter knows where her food comes from, and the inhabitant of a mud hut knows that his home comes from the earth. But as our societies develop we become more and more sophisticated, and we increasingly forget. And so it is, ironically, as we reach the pinnacle of our powers to control the natural world, when our grip on the planet seems to be the strongest, when our fear of nature is the least, and our divorce from nature is complete, that we fail.

PART II

THE PETROLEUM INTERVAL

History was first, and for the longest time, recorded as a succession of "Great Men." Much as I love history, I have always found this focus unsatisfactory, and it's not just the glaring lack of "Great Women." There seems to be a tacit assumption that the great men of history possessed some sort of exceptional characteristics that enabled them to guide us on our pathway of progress. The world was shaped by them and, without them, things would have been very different—or at least that is what we seem to have been told.[1]

First of all, many of these supposed great men were not as great as our history books might have us believe. There are myriad examples, from Augustus to Zedong, of people of questionable talent and dubious morals serving as heroes, and none is a better example than Christopher Columbus, who has been served up to generations of Americans as the brave, brilliant mariner who discovered the New World. The treatment of Columbus has been a near deification—states, provinces, cities, and towns across the nation are named for the man—but he was actually little more than a brutal conqueror. America would have been—and was—discovered by any number of Europeans even if Columbus had stayed in Italy to become a gnocchi sous chef. His relevance to the great sweep of history is minimal to nil, except as a name for a place marker.

The same argument can be made for many other historical figures. Brilliant they may have been, but how much longer would it have taken the world to invent electricity without Marconi and Edison? Would we still be draining water from coal mines with horse-powered water pumps were it not for Newcomen and Watt? Would we still be flummoxed by the mystery of the origin of species had Darwin not voyaged on the *Beagle*? Without the unique brilliance of Albert Einstein, the general theory of relativity may have had to wait a few decades, but it's hard to imagine that progress in physics would have been delayed significantly. These were clearly brilliant people, but I doubt they were irreplaceable.

A second account of history has considered the natural world: natural history. This field has run on a parallel course to the rest of history, operating on much larger timescales. Natural history has provided a detailed time line of the geological and living history of the earth, beginning four and a half billion years ago with the formation of the solar system, and less than a billion years thereafter with the origins of life, and it has grown into many branches of science. We now have a comprehensive understanding of how organisms interact within communities, ecosystems, and biomes.

What is surprisingly new is the recognition of humans as a powerful force in nature, but the far-reaching impacts we can have on the land, the seas, and now the atmosphere are becoming only too clear. Our renewed awareness of the degree to which civilization has been shaped by the environment is probably the most important development in the discipline of history. Many of the key developments in human history have their origins not in the brave or brilliant (or foolhardy) actions of great men but in the opportunities or limitations presented by the dynamic environments in which they lived. Human history and natural history are now indelibly linked.

Innovation and leadership have certainly played consequential roles. The emergence of a militaristic Germany seeking territorial expansion at the end of the colonial era may well have been inevitable, but it might not have mushroomed into one of the worst genocides and international conflagrations in history were it not for the megalomania of Adolf

Hitler, who amply demonstrated that bad government, especially in a time of crisis, can make matters decisively worse. On the other hand, cool heads and thoughtful minds sometimes do prevail, and people of strength and conviction can help societies transition through difficult times by the best path, rather than the worst.

While history's finer details have certainly been shaped by individuals, the larger picture of history has been painted by our use and misuse of resources on the canvas of the environment. This relationship with the environment has brought us through a series of enormous transitions since we became an intelligent, upright ape on the African savanna a few million years ago. Our cultures and societies developed achingly slowly at first, as we mastered fire and primitive tools through a protracted Stone Age and then gathered momentum over a few millennia of agriculture. Our ability to draw power from the environment was initially modest, and our impacts upon it were mostly gradual. Eventually, however, we found ways to commandeer larger acreages of land for agriculture, to channel rivers to drive watermills, to gather the wind in the sails of oceangoing vessels, and to put forests, efficiently, to the axe. Great empires emerged as they gathered the plentiful offerings of the planet but repeatedly fell into decline or collapse as they overdrew from the ecological savings bank.

The pace of progress accelerated rapidly about two centuries ago when fossil resources were harnessed for the first time. Coal powered the world into the Industrial Revolution, which was thrown into high gear with the advent of the steam engine. Monumental changes have come thick and fast in the seven generations that have followed. Oil has propelled us into the modern era in barely the blink of a historian's eye. This most recent transition began barely a century ago, with oil, but it will end just as quickly a century hence. The planet has only two centuries of oil to offer, and the first is complete. A period as short as two centuries can hardly be called an "age," or an "era," so I call it the "petroleum interval." As short as it may be, however, the petroleum interval is a historical period of enormous consequence.

Oil is a multitrillion-dollar-per-year business that has been the centerpiece of trade battles, embargoes, assassinations, regime topplings, and major wars. The economic success of nations has been linked to many factors, such as good government, an effective health system, and technological innovation, but nothing has been more predictive of economic dominance in the last century than a country's access to oil.[2] The equation is clear: get your hands on lots of oil and burn it to make your economy turn. It's hard to overstate the importance of oil, and yet we take it so much for granted.

But rumors are emerging that the oil is running out. Many geologists and other energy experts are predicting production declines in the next decade or so. But we've heard that kind of scaremongering before, haven't we? And even if it's true, surely we can switch to one of the much-discussed alternatives, right?

People underestimate the degree to which our economies rely on oil; they underestimate the rate of depletion of our oil reserves; and they expect too much of the so-called alternatives. The fact that the world's supply of oil is running out is a daunting proposition. The fact that oil will be extremely difficult to replace is just plain scary.

Or is it?

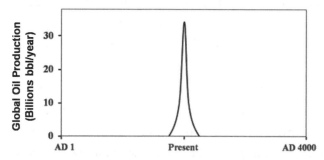

When will oil begin to run out? Well, taking the long view, that's fairly irrelevant. We find ourselves at the peak of this two-hundred-year glitch we call the petroleum interval. Image courtesy of Steve Hallett.

It seems imperative that we should do whatever is necessary to keep the wheels of industry turning because it is industry that has provided us with this wonderful world in which we live. The demise of oil and the passing of the petroleum interval may bring an end to this era of glittering progress that has been so wonderful. But there is another way to look at the petroleum interval.

This same interval has tripled our population, destroyed forests, turned farmland into wasteland or urban sprawl, filled our oceans with plastic and vacuumed them for fish, emptied freshwater aquifers, shaved mountains, sent untold species into extinction (and cultures too), developed nukes—and tested them on each other, drained lakes and rivers, and stuffed the atmosphere with climate-altering gases.

The petroleum interval is a historical era like no other, and it is an interval of only two hundred years: the twentieth century and the twenty-first. By its end, we will look back on the petroleum interval as the most incredible two-hundred-year glitch in the history of civilization.

CHAPTER 5

THE GREAT ENERGY TRANSITION

My grandfather rode a camel. I drive a Mercedes.
My son flies a jet plane. His son will ride a camel.

Sheikh Rashid al-Maktoum, emir of Dubai

We opened our account in the fossil fuel savings bank with the coal inheritance we first uncovered in western Europe at the start of the nineteenth century. Coal-powered machines led us to another part of our inheritance beneath the farmland of rural Pennsylvania, and then to troves of riches in odd places like Texas, the Persian Gulf, the North Sea, and Siberia. We have been spending our inheritance like drunken sailors—has anyone checked the balance of that savings account?

AMERICAN PROPHET

We are facing an unprecedented problem. World oil production has stopped growing; declines in production are about to begin. For the first time since the Industrial Revolution, the geological supply of an essential resource will not meet the demand.

Kenneth S. Deffeyes, *Beyond Oil: The View from Hubbert's Peak*[1]

How much oil may lie in reservoirs underground was the big question that troubled geoscientist Marion King Hubbert in the 1950s. Hubbert made a number of contributions to the field of geophysics during his career with the University of Chicago, Amerada, Shell, and the US Geological Survey. His science was thorough, and he was well recognized and respected in his field. In 1956, however, Hubbert presented a paper at the spring meeting of the southern district of the American Petroleum Institute predicting that oil production in the United States was about to go into decline.[2]

The pundits of the time were predicting a very rosy future for US oil production. Production had climbed every year since its discovery, almost without a hiccup, and the scale of recent production increases had been staggering. The overwhelming consensus was that production would continue to increase and that the rate of increase would probably even accelerate. Hubbert's reputation was damaged by his contrarian views.

But Hubbert quietly stood by his numbers. He had recognized that oil fields tend to go through a predictable production cycle. Production would be slow at first, as the field was discovered and confirmed; would then increase rapidly as multiple wells were drilled; and would then decline as the oil became increasingly difficult to extract. Production would eventually fall to zero—even while there was still oil in the reservoir—because the oil would become uneconomical to extract. Most reservoirs yield less than half their oil before production ceases. Hubbert noticed that he could quite reliably fit a logistic curve to the production data of oil fields to describe the production cycle mathematically. The peak of his logistic curve has become known as "Hubbert's Peak."

Hubbert concluded that if each oil field went through roughly the same cycle of discovery, production, and decline, then it should be possible to combine the predicted output of individual oil fields to describe the production cycle of the United States. When he did this, he discovered—to his great dismay—that American oil production was rapidly approaching its peak. Hubbert reported that US oil production would peak around 1970 and then go into irreversible decline. The respected geologist became something of a laughingstock in the oil industry because his predictions flew in the face of conventional wisdom.

But Hubbert only needed to put up with the laughter for a while. By the mid-1970s, it was clear that he had been right. US oil production peaked in 1971 and began its inexorable decline. Today, the United States produces little more than half the oil it produced in its heyday and imports more than two-thirds of its oil needs: more than twelve million barrels per day.

So, if the oil production of the United States can go through a cycle of growth, peak, and decline, what about the rest of the world?

There's an extremely important debate going on about Hubbert's Peak that the media largely ignore:

On the one hand there are the pessimists (I hope they won't mind me calling them that). The core of the pessimist camp is a group of petroleum geologists, many of them ex–oil industry geologists following in Hubbert's path. They are raising awareness of the prospect of global peak oil, and they claim that oil production is about to go into decline worldwide. The pessimists believe that the world economy will be decimated as a result.

On the other hand there are the optimists. Principal among this group are the oil-producing countries, the oil companies, and government agencies such as the US Geological Survey[3] and US Energy Information Administration.[4] This second group contends that the world's oil production is not in imminent danger of decline and, in any case, that the world will have time to switch to alternate energy sources before any such decline begins. Most of the optimists expect peak oil will not come until 2020–2030. This group is also supported by most economists who believe that the production of oil is driven primarily by demand rather than supply.

But here is the really important point: The difference between the optimists' and pessimists' outlook for world oil production is almost negligible. Oil production may be declining right now, in a few years or—in the absolute best-case scenario—in a decade or so. But decline it will. In the worst-case scenario, you will watch the world begin to run out of oil this decade. In the best-case scenario, your kids will watch. These are the facts, and they are undisputed.[5]

> **There is no such thing as scarcity and no such thing as surplus. There is only price.**
> Henry Groppe, "Peak Oil: Myth vs. Reality"[6]

The issue of oil supply and demand often comes down to questions such as, how much oil is left? or when will the oil run out? These, however, are the wrong questions. Whether or not oil is running out is irrelevant. Oil is a finite resource, so it has been running out since the first barrel was produced. How much oil is left? Well, this is not the most important question, either. There is quite a bit of oil left in the ground, but by the time we are scraping the bottom of the barrel for the last drops, it will have become practically useless.

In the times of plenty that we have enjoyed for the last century, the supply of oil has been driven by demand. The oil-producing nations and oil companies have responded to the world's seemingly insatiable appetite for oil with an astonishing amount of investment, exploration, and infrastructure. Thousands of oil fields have been discovered by tens of thousands of geologists drilling hundreds of thousands of wells. Tankers and pipelines crisscross the globe from oil fields to refineries. Apart from a few temporary glitches,[7] we have seen consistently increasing global supplies of oil matching the consistently increasing global demand.

Economists remind us of the basic rules of supply and demand: "Did we not get this in ECON 101?" they wearily groan. A supply shortfall, they claim, would spur increased demand, which would increase exploration... discovery... production... and the market will correct itself naturally. But since oil reserves are finite, no amount of demand can increase supply when the oil truly starts to run out. An alternative must be found, or the scarcity will continue to inflate prices.

What is important, then, is the availability of oil, on demand, at an acceptable price, and so the question that really matters is this: When will oil production (supply) go into irreversible decline no matter how great the demand? When this happens, prices will climb even as the supply declines, and there will be nothing we can do about it.

PREDICTING GLOBAL PEAK OIL

Hubbert predicted the peaking of oil production in the contiguous forty-eight states of the United States from an extension of the analysis of the peaking pattern of individual fields. A number of people, including Hubbert himself, have taken this approach to the obvious next step and extended the analysis to the rest of the world. The advantage of this approach is that it does not depend on estimates of reserves supplied by oil producers. It simply requires an analysis of cumulative production, which is a much more reliable set of data.

Amazingly, oil production has already peaked in the majority of countries, including the United States, Venezuela, all the countries of North Africa, Kuwait, Iran, Iraq, Russia, Norway, and the United Kingdom. There are significant concerns that production may also have peaked in the world's biggest oil-producing country, Saudia Arabia. Analysts who have studied Hubbert's curve for world oil production using this method have concluded that the world's oil peak may have already occurred and will come before 2012 at the latest.[8]

Kenneth Deffeyes has used an alternate model that simply calculates the point at which the proportion of annual production will equal zero at current production trends.[9] Put another way, it calculates the total volume of oil that is expected to be removed from the ground before production ceases. By his estimates, the world will ultimately produce a little over two trillion barrels of oil. There is more oil than that in the ground, but it will stay there. We have already produced half this amount, so Deffeyes also predicts that the global oil peak is upon us. He put the date of peak oil on Thanksgiving Day (November 24), 2005, and nominated it "World Oil Peak Day." Not only does that day fit his mathematics, but Deffeyes argues that it's a fitting day to give thanks for a century of abundant oil. It has been a day for nonindigenous Americans to thank the American Indians whom they then went on to murder, cheat, and dispossess of their land. What better day to thank the oil with which we have caused environmental pollution and global warming, over which we destroyed economies, fought wars, and perpetrated genocides?

As we have seen, individual oil fields tend to go through a reasonably predictable production cycle. Following discovery, there is a lag period while the extent of the field is confirmed and infrastructure is developed at the site. Production thus begins slowly, then accelerates, and, as the field becomes depleted, declines.

As a rule of thumb, peak production from existing oil fields has been reached roughly forty years after discovery. In the United States, the peak of discovery did indeed precede the peak of production by almost exactly that period. Production in Iraq, by contrast, did not peak until sixty years after the peak of discoveries, a delay probably due to the Iran-Iraq war. Production in the North Sea passed from peak discovery to peak production in only thirty years, probably because the fields were discovered relatively recently (1970s) and were rapidly put under the yoke of the most advanced exploration and production techniques. The actual interval for any given oil field, or producing region, is affected by many different factors, but forty years turns out to be a reasonable average over thousands of fields.

We can use this knowledge, then, as a third method of predicting the date of global peak oil. This analysis is admittedly crude, but it is simple and robust. We know for a fact that global oil discoveries peaked in

1963. If the forty-year rule is reliable, then global oil production would have occurred in 2003. Again, this third analysis predicts that peak oil is upon us.

The world's biggest oil fields are aging, and precious few large discoveries have been made in the last two decades. The supergiant oil fields (those containing more than ten billion barrels) are now reaching old age. The second-biggest oil field in the world is Kuwait's eighty-billion-barrel Burgan field, and it was discovered in 1938. The biggest field ever found is Saudi Arabia's ninety-billion-barrel Ghawar field, uncovered just a decade later in 1948. The most recent supergiant finds are not recent at all: the Daqing field in China (1961), the Samotlor field in Russia (1963), the Prudhoe Bay field in Alaska (1967), and the Cantarell field in Mexico (1975) are the newest. The only exception is Kazakhstan's Kashagan field (2000).[10] In total, there are approximately fifty supergiant oil fields, and all but one of them were discovered before 1975.[11] Only two of the world's giant fields (those containing five hun-

Oil terminal, Valdez, Alaska. Photograph courtesy of John Wright.

The Trans-Alaska oil pipeline runs 880 miles from Alaska's North Slope to the oil terminal at Valdez. Photograph courtesy of John Wright.

dred million to ten billion barrels) were found in the last ten years. We are still finding new oil fields, but they are increasingly small. It seems like the feast is over, and we are now relegated to scratching together the scraps from under the table.

Now consider that the global consumption of oil is around thirty billion barrels per year. This means that the discovery of a new billion-barrel field (of the type that we don't seem to be able to find very often) would provide the world with a pathetic ten days of additional supply. The peak of world oil discoveries occurred in 1963, and we started consuming more oil than we discovered in the early 1980s. Worldwide, oil is being consumed four times more rapidly than it is being discovered.

This cannot go on much longer.

WHY IS NOBODY WARNING US?

> **For demand to exceed supply is supposed to be good for capitalism, leading to increased production and often to lower costs. Oil, however, is not really produced, but extracted . . . [from a finite pool].**
> James W. Loewen, *Lies My Teacher Told Me: Everything Your American History Textbook Got Wrong*[12]

If only we could trust the reserves estimates supplied by the oil-producing nations and the oil companies, life would be so much simpler. Alas, the words *trust* and *oil company* seldom fit comfortably in the same sentence, unless that sentence also contains the word *not*. A detailed understanding of oil reserves would enable us to calculate the rate at which we need to develop replacement technologies. If detailed data were collected and reported honestly, it would be much easier to predict the state of oil reserves, and we wouldn't need to do all this second-guessing. But the oil producers have been deliberately vague about the reserves in their possession.[13]

The members of the Organization of Petroleum Exporting Countries (OPEC) have been tempted to overestimate their reserves since the countries with larger reserves are allocated a larger share of exports. Nearly all the OPEC countries suddenly "discovered" a whole bunch of oil in the 1980s without any increased exploration.[14] We can only conclude that they simply fudged the numbers. Oil companies have been tempted to overestimate the reserves in their possession to encourage investors. In January 2004, Shell reduced its reserves estimate by a fifth. Now that's like coming home from work one day and telling your significant other: "Oh, and by the way, love, I thought my salary was $50,000, but it's only $40,000. Sorry about that. I hadn't noticed. What's for supper?" Your sweetie figures you're either stupid for not noticing or else you've been lying about the other $10,000 all along and spending it in that seedy part of town. Your argument that everyone else is in the same boat (the claim made by Shell's CEO Jeroen van der Veer[15]) convinces your partner that either all men are bad or that you're *really* full of it! You might end up shelling out a large settlement to those hurt by your, er, inaccuracy. The announcement by Shell was followed by a similar one by BP (British Petroleum).[16] All the folks in a position to know how much oil there actually is in the ground have every reason to lie about it. And lie they have.

So where do the oil companies get their reserves information from anyway? The gold standard is BP's Global Oil Reserves Estimates, which are compiled from, in their own words: "a variety of different sources, data from the OPEC secretariat and a few other places [outside] BP."[17] BP also provides the small-print disclaimer that "the data do not necessarily meet the US Securities and Exchange Commission definitions and guidelines for determining proved reserves, nor necessarily represent BP's view of proved reserves by country."[18] In other words, BP puts out reserve estimates that are compiled from various estimates that BP does not trust, and then everyone else takes these estimates as the gospel truth. Any wonder why there's so much doubt about existing reserves?

Are oil companies unaware of the state of their business? No, we can be reasonably confident that the oil companies know what's going on. Perhaps we can judge the mood of the oil companies by their actions rather than by their words.

There has been an active market for takeovers and mergers in the oil business in recent years: BP with Amoco, Exxon with Mobil, Total with Elf and Fina, Conoco with Philips, Statoil with Saga, and Repsol with YPF. This oil company feeding frenzy looks like trends we have seen in other industries. Nobody wants to admit it, but the rash of mergers looks like an early symptom of a doomed industry. Also very revealing is the fact that the big companies have been investing less and less in exploration despite high prices and a lack of supply. Even though they are running close to capacity, old refineries are being decommissioned faster than new refineries are being built. Ditto oil tankers, which are being retired even while shipyards stand idle.

Why are the big oil companies reducing their investment in future oil discoveries and production? There is certainly no shortage of demand, and oil will continue to extract a higher price for a number of years. There is a windfall to be made. The oil companies clearly know that most of the oil has been found, half of it has been produced, and there is no place for the oil business to go but down. It's time the rest of us wise up. What would your endgame strategy be? I would pretend that all is well, but I would shed infrastructure, consolidate, keep prices high, and prepare for a future *beyond petroleum*.

The calculations of the pessimists are truly compelling and the actions of the oil companies are revealing. I am extremely concerned that the world is pumping at peak capacity already. Declining oil production over the next few years seems likely, and it will cause economies to stagnate. Rising oil prices will have an inflationary impact. We have already seen some economic stagnation and oil price volatility, and this is only the beginning.

Despite my general distrust of "economic wisdom," I do expect the demand for oil to drive additional discoveries that will stretch the oil peak into a plateau for a few years and delay the initial decline. But a few years are about all we can hope for. Around 2015, oil production will show a clear and convincing decline, and the world will be at the beginning of the end of the petroleum interval. The changes it will bring will be staggering. We're fussing about being in a recession now, but in the words of Ronald Reagan: "You ain't seen nothin' yet!"

THE RED QUEEN AND THE LAST DROP OF OIL

> **Alice looked around her in great surprise. "Why I do believe we've been under this tree the whole time! Everything is just as it was!"**
>
> **"Of course it is," said the Queen, "what would you have it?"**
>
> **"Well in our country," said Alice, panting a little, "you'd generally get to somewhere else—if you run fast enough for a long time, as we've been doing."**
>
> **"A slow sort of country!" said the Queen. "Now here, you see, it takes all the running you can do just to keep in the same place. If you want to get somewhere else, you will need to run twice as fast as that!"**
>
> Lewis Carroll, *Through the Looking Glass, and What Alice Found There*[19]

If the world has spent half its savings of conventional oil, its ability to supply increasing volumes of oil to the global economy is at an end. This is extremely scary and must spell economic disaster, yet a significant sense of hope remains that this decline in oil production will not actually happen for some time, thanks to three much-discussed avenues of escape.

The first escape hatch is advanced oil recovery technology that would increase the amount of oil extracted from existing wells, producing more oil without the need to discover new fields. But these "new technologies" are not actually all that new: most have been used since the 1980s. The most valuable contribution has come from horizontal drilling,[20] which, incidentally, was one of the reasons claimed by Saddam Hussein for his invasion of Kuwait in 1990, as he accused Kuwait of drilling into oil fields under Iraqi soil.[21]

My August 2007 copy of *National Geographic* contained a DVD produced by Shell. Cringing, I popped it in the player and sat back for nine satisfying minutes of happy time with Jaap van Ballegoolien, a real-life Shell engineer, and his teenage son, Max. Poor old Jaap was in a bind. A reporter had come to ask how things were going with Shell's explorations in Brunei. Lots of worried faces. Not good. Lots of tiny oil fields ... environmentally sensitive area ... how to extract the oil without screwing up Brunei more than necessary? What to tell the reporter?

Good old Jaap takes the reporter on a helicopter tour of the area, explaining the problem. Phone rings—it's Max. Uh-oh. Max is wrestling with a decline in core values as a result of Daddy's absence from home finding fuel for the world. Jaap, the good father, scoots back to Amsterdam to hang out with his impressionable young lad. And then it happens: Max drinks a milkshake and the world is saved. In a moment of Einsteinian brilliance, Jaap recognizes that his son's upside-down bendy-straw technique for the extraction of a thick shake can be applied to the extraction of oil from the picky little fields off Brunei. The snake drill is born. All is well. Shell has access to untold volumes of new oil. Worried faces become happy faces.

So what of this Jaap and Max story? Well, first of all, congratulations to Jaap for a really cool discovery (no irony) and to Max, for proceeding smoothly into adulthood (no irony). Really, though, the enduring image from the Shell ad should be the worried faces. The snake drill changes the big picture not one iota. It is a cool but minor modification of existing horizontal drilling technologies. Despite improvements like this, the underlying, and much more important, truth is that there is no more oil to be found, except in much smaller fields. The enduring line from the ad should be this one, from Jaap: "We all know easily accessible oil is a thing of the past. The challenge now is to get at those reserves we know about, but haven't yet been able to reach—reserves that would otherwise go to waste."

We should thank Shell for its moment of candor.

Another technique that has increased extraction rates is water injection, the pumping of seawater into oil fields to maintain their pressure, raise and concentrate the oil layer, and prevent the oil from dissipating into the surrounding source rock.[22] This technique was used in old, declining fields in the United States and Saudi Arabia, and recovery rates were increased significantly. The technique is certainly valuable, but it is hardly new and is already used in most of the fields where it is suitable.

The second escape hatch is to make new oil discoveries, but with the world now picked over by petroleum geologists like a maggot-ridden antelope carcass on the Serengeti, major discoveries seem rather unlikely. There are, however, three notable exceptions.

Significant reserves probably exist in Antarctica, but, thankfully, there is a global moratorium on drilling and exploration there at present. The Antarctic climate is harsh, and oil production would be difficult, but if reserves were large enough, production might be feasible.

At the other end of the planet, reserves also exist beneath the Arctic Ocean, and there is an emerging kerfuffle about drilling rights at the top of the world. Each of the nations neighboring the Arctic Ocean—Canada, the United States, Russia, Finland, Norway, and Denmark (Greenland is Danish territory)—has obvious claims to the region. The fact that we may soon be able to drill for oil in the high Arctic is perverse when you consider that it is only feasible thanks to oil-induced global warming. Perverse or not, drilling will presumably begin as soon as it is feasible. There will be a long lag time since superstrong rigs will be required, and transportation will remain extremely challenging for some time, but, as prices climb, the incentives will increase and oil will flow from new fields in the far north. The volumes of oil extracted are unlikely to make any significant difference to the overall global oil production picture, and the predominant hydrocarbon under the Arctic Ocean will probably be natural gas, rather than oil, as in Alaska and Siberia.

Another "safe bet" for new oil supplies is the North American continental shelf. New drilling close to the US shore was banned in the

1970s to protect the environment—especially the environment visible to tourists—from unsightly offshore rigs, onshore refineries, oil spills, and tar balls gumming up the beaches. President Barack Obama lifted the ban in early 2010 and was soon reminded that fortunes change quickly in politics by the explosion and sinking of the "Deepwater Horizon" drilling rig operated by BP in the Gulf of Mexico. Eleven workers lost their lives, and the oil spill continued for months, becoming the worst in American history. The disaster provided ammunition for antidrilling activists to press their case against offshore drilling and Arctic drilling, as well as fodder for myriad lawsuits.

And why not? Americans had been told by the oil companies and the government that oil could be produced more safely and cleanly, yet it appeared that regulations were lax, enforcement was inept, and the response was reminiscent of the Keystone Kops. As the supplies of "easy" oil are exhausted, producing oil in the new frontiers will carry increasing risks for disaster as demand soars, desperation grows, and companies are tempted to cut corners. The technical difficulties will be greater and tougher for regulators to oversee.

The overall potential for recoverable US offshore oil is rather modest anyway, in the order of twenty billion barrels, or roughly nine months' global supply, which is not to be sniffed at but also is not a game-changer to significantly extend the petroleum interval.

Is there any hope that improved technologies will lead to increased rates of discoveries? Again, the outlook is not promising, and the so-called new technologies are not particularly new.[23] The largest of the more recent oil discoveries have been in deep water, and their production is much more difficult. Discoveries in the Gulf of Mexico, Nigeria, Angola, and Brazil appeared to bring renewed growth to the oil industry. BP, in particular, began hitting sizeable oil reserves in the Gulf of Mexico, but the hope was short-lived. Deepwater oil discovery is already past peak, and deepwater oil production is projected to peak around 2014.[24] A measure of the disconnect between hope and reality was revealed by the Jack 2 field in the Gulf of Mexico in 2006. This discovery hit the news as a major breakthrough, but, with wells passing through seven thousand feet of water and then four miles of rock, the costs of production from Jack 2 are five times higher than land-based rigs. Big as it is, this oil field can supply only two years of US consumption. It seems that even the oil companies are jaded by this, and their excitement over deepwater exploration has declined significantly.

The third escape hatch for the oil era is through so-called unconventional oils. There are huge reserves of poor-quality, hard-to-extract oil around the world, especially in Alberta, Venezuela, and the American Rockies. It is tempting to hope that, as we become more desperate for oil and as oil prices rise, these sources of oil will become more available, but this is, literally, a case of trying to squeeze oil from a stone.

Alberta, Venezuela, and the American Rockies hold in the order of six trillion barrels of oil. That's three times the total endowment of conventional oils, and it's enough to feed our addiction for another century. But the devil is in the details: these oils can only be extracted very slowly, and most of this untapped resource will remain exactly that: untapped. Unconventional oils are either very viscous and flow very slowly, or else they need to be mined as solids. If producing conventional oil is like sucking back a soda, then producing heavy bitumens is like a triple-thick milkshake, tar sands are a slushy (best use a spoon), and oil shales will make you reach for a knife and fork.

Venezuela's Orinoco Belt may contain more than a trillion barrels of "triple-thick" extra-heavy crude oil, but only a fifth of it is likely to be recovered. There may be as many as two and a half billion barrels of "slushy" tar sands beneath Alberta, but less than a tenth of this will ever be extracted. From their massive oil reserves, Venezuela and Canada combine to produce a not-so-whopping two million barrels per day, about 1 percent of global production.

The extraction of unconventional oils is very damaging to the environment. Alberta is a land of glorious sweeping prairies, some of the most spectacular mountains in the world, and Wayne Gretzky's Edmonton Oilers.[25] There's a lot of oil in the ground here, but not all is well with Albertans and their oil blessing. The extraction of oil from tar sands is horribly polluting. For every barrel of oil produced, two barrels of a nasty, oily, waste-slime yuck is pumped into giant sludge ponds. Picture a pond fourteen miles in circumference with icky water floating on a forty-meter-thick layer of oil/sand/dirt slurry, and you won't be surprised that some Albertans want to see the tar sands plants closed down. So will tar sands replace conventional oil? Picture the seven hundred plants that would be required, along with a waste pond the size of Massachusetts. Many have legitimate reasons to hope that the tar sands will not "save us."

The oil shales are the nastiest reserves of all, making up the balance of the unconventional oils portfolio, and it may take a decade or more to start up the oil shale production business in earnest. Recovery percentages are likely to be very low, cost/profit ratios high, and when we begin to seriously contemplate turning over the American Rockies for oil, it will be a very sad day. Oil is not pumped from oil shales but mined and extracted; it is a very energy-intensive proposition, and the environmental damage will be horrendous. Huge volumes of water would need to be used for extraction and processing, and the American West is already short of water. Diverting precious water resources to oil shale production would be an environmental catastrophe.

These energy-hungry extractions present additional problems during an energy crisis. A case in point is the extraction technology known as steam-assisted gravity drainage, which uses large volumes of natural gas to generate steam to improve the flowability of the oil, used extensively in Alberta tar sands. As natural gas becomes more expensive and scarcer, the extraction efficiency of unconventional oils will decrease even more.

Despite the disappointment that they will not prevent the decline in world oil production, the slow rate at which unconventional oils can be produced does present one interesting opportunity for Venezuela and Canada, which in the last decades of the twenty-first century are destined to be the world's dominant oil producers . . . in a world that produces and consumes less than a tenth of the oil that it produces and consumes today.

THE MANY LIVES OF METHANE

Methane (CH_4) is a particularly interesting molecule and a major source of energy. It is one of the principal greenhouse gases when it is released into the atmosphere from rice paddies and belching, flatulent cows; it is the infamous "firedamp" when it explodes in a coal mine; and when it is produced by microbes in stinky bogs, it is "swamp gas."[26] Methane is found in great abundance in solid form under the Arctic tundra and deep in the oceans, as methane hydrate (also known as clathrates). There is more methane on the planet in this form than in any other—perhaps by one or two orders of magnitude. Alas, nobody has yet figured out a way of getting their hands on methane hydrate, so, if you want to be rich and famous and save the fossil fuel world, here's your big chance. Be careful, though. Given that methane is more than twenty times more potent a greenhouse gas than carbon dioxide, the last thing we need is folks stirring up methane hydrates and sending them off into the atmosphere. If this were done on a big scale, global warming would quickly become a global cookout.[27] In energy circles, however, it's not cool to call methane *methane*, so we'll switch back to calling it natural gas, or gas.

Natural gas is produced (extracted) in more or less the same way as oil, by puncturing wells into gas-rich porous source rocks that sit beneath an impervious cap rock. Gas is extracted much more easily than oil because, being a gas, it simply escapes through wells under its own pressure and does not need to be pumped. Once the gas is no longer coming out of the ground under its own pressure, however, there is little that can be done to remove it, and production ceases rather suddenly. Gas can be coaxed from shales by creating cracks, through which the gas can move. Large deposits in West Texas (Barnett shale); Louisiana (Haynesville shale); Arkansas (Fayettcville shale); the Appalachians, centered on Pennsylvania (Marcellus shale); and Southern Quebec (Utica shale) are attracting significant investments at the moment as high prices and improved technology make larger volumes from these reserves economically recoverable.

For many years, natural gas was considered a wasteful byproduct of oil production and was burned off. This seemed reasonable at a time when few considered either oil or gas to be particularly limited resources and when gas was only a fraction of its current price. Gas-only fields were also avoided by oil companies for many years, but gas is now in high demand. Natural gas is widely recognized as one of the cleanest sources of energy. It releases roughly half the carbon dioxide per unit of energy than coal and much smaller amounts of other forms of pollution, especially particulates. Natural gas consumption has increased dramatically in the last decade or so with an increasing number of new power plants using this cleaner fuel.[28]

The gas industry is largely an extension of the oil industry and is controlled by many of the same players. Small gas reserves are held in a large number of countries, but the biggest reserves, by far, are found in Russia and the Middle East. In the world of gas, Russia is dominant, with nearly a third of the world's known reserves. Europe and North America are in relatively bad shape with very small reserves.

THE PROBLEM WITH NATURAL GAS: IT'S A GAS

Natural gas is produced in some of the world's remotest places. A case in point is the twin island nation of Trinidad and Tobago, a tropical paradise that sits at the southern tip of the Caribbean chain only a few miles from Venezuela. The rain forest of the Northern Range is replete with colorful tanagers, motmots, hummingbirds, and the remarkable oilbirds. The Nariva swamp has red howler and capuchin monkeys. The coral reefs ringing Tobago attract divers from all over the world. You can take a boat out onto the Caroni swamp and watch the fabled scarlet ibis flock home to roost after a day's feeding in the Orinoco delta. Drive to the north coast for some of the best beaches in the world, kick back on the veranda of the Mount Plaisir Hotel in the late evening with a rum punch, and watch the sea turtles nest. Trinidad is the land of calypso, sagga boys, bobbol and commess, dingolay and macotious neighbors, steel bands and a colorful, buoyant carnival celebration. Everyone is happy, liming, acting up like "dey's no tomorrow and like dey is yuh friend or yuh tantie." But take the Solomon Hochoy Highway south toward San Fernando, and you'll see another side of Trinidad altogether.

The Point Lisas industrial estate is a sprawling tangle of towers, stacks, tanks, and scaffolds that would not look out of place in Merseyside, Rotterdam, or New Jersey. You see, Trinidad has gas, and quite a lot of it.

Trinidad was "blessed" with oil for a short time. The oil was found in the early days because its presence was betrayed by bitumen, which seeps out of the ground in the south of the island (the tar pits at La Brea are an interesting tourist attraction if you ever feel like visiting a big natural parking lot), but the oil was pretty much played out by the end of the 1970s. Many of those gas guzzlers that jammed you up on the highway have been maintained by Trinidadian mechanics ever since. Trinidad has an oil refinery—a legacy of the earlier oil era—but it no longer operates anywhere near the nation's previous refining levels because its own crude output has slackened. Natural gas has taken the place of oil in Trinidad and Tobago and has become a much bigger "blessing" than the oil ever was.

The problem with having natural gas fields in Trinidad is that Trinidad is pretty much in the middle of nowhere. Check out a map. The island is just off Venezuela, but it is the uninhabited, deepest, darkest jungle part of Venezuela. It's a long trip down to Brazil and a long way up to the United States. How on earth are you going to go about wasting all that natural gas as quickly as possible if there's nobody nearby to buy it? You see, the problem with natural gas is that it's a gas, and this makes it extremely difficult to transport.

Enter the Point Lisas industrial estate. Thankfully, Trinidad is a well-behaved, civilized (former British colony, you understand, old chap), English-speaking country, so it has lots and lots of nice friends (companies from the United Kingdom, Australia, the United States, and Canada, among others). Its friends have figured out some really great ways of moving natural gas, and they have set up chemical plants that convert the natural gas into something that can be carted away more easily. The former canelands of the old colonial sugar plantations, suddenly, are home to ten ammonia plants, an immense iron and steel complex, various miscellaneous petrochemical plants, and seven methanol plants, one of which is the biggest in the world, producing eight hun-

Pointe-à-Pierre. The tropical Caribbean paradise of Trinidad is home to more than just rain forests, hummingbirds, and sea turtles. Its economy is dominated by oil and natural gas. For now. Photograph courtesy of Steve Hallett.

dred fifty tons of methanol per year. Alcoa is in the process of building an aluminum plant. Bauxite from South America will be shipped to Trinidad and smelted using Trinidadian natural gas. The aluminum—along with most of the ammonia fertilizer and methanol—will be shipped off to America. Presumably, the tons of waste and pollution will be taken as well, right? Trinidad has become the Western Hemisphere's leading supplier of liquid natural gas (LNG), supplying more than three-quarters of the shipments to the States. Huge tankers packed with supercooled LNG ply the waters from Port of Spain to New Orleans.

Trinidad's dilemma is typical of the problems posed by natural gas, but Trinidad produces only approximately one two-hundredth of the world's supply. Russia, meanwhile, produces a third of it and faces some of the same transportation issues. The Russian gas fields are in remote Siberia, but Russia's massive reserves, and the fact that wealthy Europe is desperate for natural gas, have enabled it to invest in transcontinental pipelines that now crisscross western Eurasia like a spider web.

Gas markets have always been more or less restricted to the producer continent because of the problems of transportation, and this presents a major problem for North America. Alaska wants to build pipelines to bring natural gas from the North Slope to the rest of America, but these are unlikely to flow for at least a decade. Even then, Alaska will supply barely five percent of America's demand. Development moves frantically ahead in the shale deposits, but these are expensive to develop, and it is still uncertain that they will ever be fully exploited.

There is a dire need for investment in LNG terminals for gas imports, but LNG is expensive too and presents the ever-present risk of explosions. The fear of an explosion of an LNG tanker in a major American harbor is perhaps the reason that one of the biggest LNG terminals in North America is just south of the US border in Baja California, Mexico.

The infrastructure for the transportation and storage of natural gas into North America is not even close to being sufficient, and North

America will run short on gas while Russia and the Middle East are still producing, and Europe and east Asia are still consuming.

HUBBERT'S PEAK FOR NATURAL GAS

We know that reserves of gas are significantly larger than reserves of oil, but just how much bigger has been hard to determine. The production curves for gas fields are not the same as those nice, reliable, logistic Hubbert curves that we see for oil, and we do not know how much gas has been removed from many fields by flaring.[29] Natural gas is also often used directly at the plant, or locally, without being metered (oil has to be refined, and it is metered at the refinery), so we don't even know how much gas has actually been produced.

Despite these difficulties, the general consensus seems to be that the global natural gas peak will likely occur approximately two decades after the global oil peak.[30] Most people tend to be equally optimistic or pessimistic about oil and gas, so the optimists tend to expect peak gas around 2040 to 2070, and the pessimists expect peak gas around 2020 to 2040.[31]

A very serious concern with gas production is that the decline side of the production curve tends to be steeper for gas than for oil. Once the gas quits coming out of the pipe, there's not much you can do to pump it, and natural gas wells often go out of production rather suddenly. Whereas global oil production will suffer a long, drawn-out decline, global natural gas production will end rather suddenly, within a few decades of peak. So, while the beginning of the end will be later for gas than for oil, the end itself may be sooner.

Although the global picture is unclear, and supplies in Russia and the Middle East are impossible to estimate accurately, there is little dispute that natural gas production is in strong decline in the Western Hemisphere. Natural gas production in America has remained constant for the last decade, but only as a result of the drilling of an increasing number of wells. The gas wells rapidly added to production in recent years have been added without providing additional overall output, which is extremely worrying. The US gas industry is drilling frantically just to stop output from falling. The natural gas crunch could come very soon and very suddenly in North America, long before global peak.

DESCENDING FROM HUBBERT'S PEAK

In the waning years of the petroleum interval, we'd like to believe that our economies will switch seamlessly to renewable, nonpolluting forms of energy. We'd also like to believe that our civilization will continue to find increasingly powerful and efficient forms of energy beyond oil. It is much more likely that we will first reach for whatever alternative energy source is the easiest. For many nations, this will be coal. Coal is already heavily used in most industrial nations, and the necessary infrastructure and knowledge are already in place. Increasing the output of the coal industry should be relatively straightforward.

But coal is a monster. It is a horribly polluting fuel that causes heavy-metal contamination, land degradation, and untold human suffering. Coal is also horribly inefficient compared to oil, especially for transportation. Taking your next transatlantic flight on a coal-powered steam plane might not be the image of the new energy economy that you had in mind. Is coal really going to be the future energy source of the world? There must be something else.

What about nuclear power? Nuclear offers enormous opportunities but is also rife with problems. There is undoubted potential in nuclear energy, but, given its track record, it may not offer a rapid resolution to an energy crisis. Like coal, nuclear is an old technology, not a new one, and our enthusiasm for it is mixed.

The bright, shining future envisioned by most people would bring us into a new era of renewable fuels in which energy can be generated without detriment to the environment. There is a wide range of energy options available, including solar, hydro, wind, geothermal, and biofuels. But the hopes and dreams are simply not matched by reality. These are not new sources of energy but old ones. These too are not more efficient sources of energy; in fact, they are far less efficient.

As we approach the end of the petroleum interval, we'd like to think that a better and brighter world awaits us. It may, eventually, but the transition will be extremely slow and painful, like all those that have gone before. We have not planned well, and we are desperately short of solutions, but a growing energy crisis is calling out, like an impatient child: "Ready or not; here I come!"

ALL ABOARD THE CARBON EXPRESS!

As oil supplies dwindle, most people seem to have high hopes for a bright, shining new future of clean, green, renewable fuels *beyond petroleum*. We may get there eventually, but it seems much more likely that the next century will see most countries reach for more coal. What we have to look forward to in the near future is not clean, green fuels, and a cleaner, greener planet, but coal and a planet that is likely to get dirtier, dustier, and more sulfurous.

A number of the world's biggest and expanding economies retain significant reserves of coal, and it seems inevitable that they will exploit it as an initial response to oil and natural gas shortfalls. The United States has huge reserves, in the order of two hundred and fifty billion short tons: more than twice as much as any other nation except Russia (160). China (110) and India (85) each have large reserves, as do Australia (80) and South Africa (50). The largest holders in Europe are Germany (66), Ukraine (34), and Poland (22).[32]

The rush to coal is likely to happen in many countries. China and India, in particular, have economic growth as their number one priority.

Purdue University Power Station. This is where the electricity is produced for one of the world's great land grant institutions at which cutting-edge environmental research is performed. It's a little disappointing. Photograph courtesy of Steve Hallett.

They realize that energy drives economies, and they are working hard to get their hands on as much energy as they can. They have the attitude that their economies should develop first and then clean up later. China consumes more coal than America; a whopping 70 percent of China's energy comes from coal. This is why China is now the world's biggest emitter of greenhouse gases and why the sun can hide behind a blanket of smog over Chinese cities for weeks on end.

Being a solid, coal presents the opposite problem to natural gas. It can be shipped and shunted around by trains, but it is bulky and cumbersome and cannot be sent through pipelines. Most important, coal is significantly less energy-dense than oil or gas, and a return to coal would represent a return to a much less efficient source of energy.

Trucks pound mountain roads hauling coal from hundreds of small mines to dumps and chutes that fill the thousands of barges that ply the Yangtze River. Photograph courtesy of Steve Hallett.

One of the biggest problems at the end of the oil era will be the production of transportation fuels. Here again, coal has some dubious potential. Coal can be broken down at high pressure to produce liquid fuels. Coal-rich but oil-desperate Nazi Germany and apartheid-ruled South Africa both carried out significant amounts of coal liquefaction when it became a costly necessity, but the process uses huge amounts of coal and is horribly inefficient. Lots of energy is used, and carbon dioxide released, in both the manufacture and combustion of these fuels. The widespread conversion from petroleum products to liquid fuels from coal would result in a disastrous increase in carbon dioxide emissions, and the possibility of this happening is real. What else can we do but turn to coal if we have no other alternative?

The 2005 Sago mine disaster in West Virginia trapped thirteen miners underground following a gas explosion; only one was rescued. The 2007 Crandall Canyon mine collapse in Utah killed six miners and three rescue workers. When coal-mining disasters occur in technologically advanced countries, people are shocked and horrified, and I suspect part of the reason for this is that they think of coal-mining disasters as a thing of the past, from the gloomy, sooty days of the Industrial Revolution. Yet more than five thousand miners die every year in mining disasters in China.

In the United States, much of the coal is mined in the west but burned in the east, so mile-long trains chug out of Wyoming's Powder River basin, hauling half a billion tons of coal per year across the continent. The American railroads have a love affair with coal, which serves as their core business. Ironically, the trains don't use coal. Diesel fuel, of course, is a much more cost-effective, efficient, and compact form of energy.

There are significant opportunities to prevent excessive carbon dioxide emissions from coal-fired power plants. The carbon dioxide can be sequestered underground or pumped deep into the oceans from where, scientists assure us, it would not surface. Governor Brian Schweitzer of Montana is a big believer in carbon sequestration from coal-fired power plants. Coming from coal country, and governor of a state with more than 5 percent of the world's coal reserves, this is heartening: "For the last hundred years we have built coal plants like this one [at Colstrip, Montana]. It takes crushed coal, ignites it to heat water that produces steam, and that turns a turbine and produces electricity. [. . .] You build that smoke stack real high so that nasty stuff goes to someone else's backyard. Well," says Governor Schweitzer, "we've run out of backyards."[33] The best way to capture carbon from coal-fired power plants is to build a type of power plant known as an Integrated Gasification Combined Cycle (IGCC) plant. This type of plant employs a two-step process that first converts the coal into syngas (a crude mixture of carbon monoxide, carbon dioxide, and hydrogen) and then uses the syngas to drive the turbines. While it might seem a no-brainer to build IGCC plants, they cost about a fifth more than standard pulverized-coal power plants, and few are planned.

These approaches do offer some potential for mitigating the effects of diminished oil supplies, but a rush to coal would result in drastically increased carbon dioxide emissions. The legacy of burning fossil fuels is already certain to affect the planet for centuries to come; the last thing we need is a last-ditch, half-century, coal-burning spree. The combustion of coal releases twice as much carbon dioxide per unit of energy gained than does oil. A desperate rush to coal threatens to send the industrial era out with a global warming bang.

Just as peak oil guru Marion King Hubbert would predict for oil, a century later William Stanley Jevons forecast "peak coal" in Britain.[34] Like Hubbert, Jevons caused great hilarity among his colleagues, and, like Hubbert, he was right. Britain's coal production peaked in 1913 and went into a long, gradual decline. So is there a global peak date for coal? But that's a silly question, because everybody knows that there is enough coal to last for a very, very long time, right?

Shockingly, no.

There has yet to be a convincing Hubbert-style global coal reserves analysis to guide us, but there is significant doubt that coal production will be viable for as long as many of the throwaway statistics suggest. There is certainly lots of coal in the ground, but the best and most easily accessible coal reserves have already been taken. The first phase of the Industrial Revolution gobbled up most of the anthracite. Britain's anthracite was removed decades ago. In the United States, the best anthracite was found in northern Pennsylvania, and that is mostly gone too. What's left is now deep down and more expensive to remove. The big active mines in America are out west, and they contain mostly lower-grade, subbituminous coals. The same pattern has been repeated in most countries. Peak coal might come sooner than people think, as the mines go deeper and the quality of the coal gets worse.

The other largely ignored aspect of coal mining is that it is a very oil-intensive business. Those massive yellow dump trucks with the twenty-foot wheels that pound through open-cut mines don't run on coal. The pumps, winches, drills, and all the rest of the paraphernalia that goes into mining is powered by petroleum products. Mountaintop mining involves the removal of mountaintops. And what about those mile-long trains that thunder across the prairies bringing coal to the east? The coal industry cannot run on coal, and getting our hands on the black rock may be surprisingly difficult as we start to run out of the black gold.

There is the shocking possibility that coal might have a significantly shorter effective lifetime than most people think. China, in particular, has only half the coal reserves of America, yet the country consumes it twice as fast. China probably has reserves of a little over a hundred billion short tons but consumes nearly three billion tons per year. It is, of course, taking the best and easiest coal first.[35]

As with oil, coal will become increasingly concentrated in a relatively small number of nations, and the hundreds of years of coal supplies often promised may be a gross overestimate. If your major concern is the economy, this should be very worrying. If your major concern is the environment, this might be some cause for comfort. Pick your poison.

THE GIFTS THAT KEEP ON GIVING

> **Nuclear fission and fossil fuel burning amount to global pyromania. Renewable energy is the fire extinguisher.**
> Hermann Scheer, German member of parliament
> and founder of Eurosolar

Planet earth is not a closed system. It receives a steady stream of energy from the sun that ultimately makes everything go. It's only in the last two hundred years that we stumbled on a way to unlock some of the sunlight energy that had been stored underground, millions of years ago, in the form of fossil fuels. The reason we created our modern world so quickly, and at this time, is that we figured out how to release this stored energy on a large scale. By the same token, the reason we have been able to change the global climate so dramatically is that we have been releasing the stored carbon of more than one geological era at the same time. Our civilization has become highly dependent on these geological energy stores, but, as they gradually run out, we will need to revert to harnessing the sunlight as it arrives. This is the renewable energy conundrum.

Energy from the sun can be trapped on the earth in a wide variety of different ways. Direct entrapment includes the use of solar, or photovoltaic (PV), cells and can be harnessed judiciously in well-designed houses. The greatest solar trappers of all are plants that store sunlight as organic chemicals simply by grabbing a little carbon dioxide and water. As the sun shines, it warms different parts of our spinning planet in different ways, resulting in "weather," including winds that can also be harnessed. The heat of the sun lifts water out of the oceans and dumps it on the land from where it flows downhill along rivers and can be diverted through turbines. Lastly, the moon orbits the earth free of charge, pulling the oceans from side to side and packing them, too, with gazillions of watts of kinetic energy.

Some countries are also lucky enough to have heat popping out of the ground. OK, so some of them explode in a big ball of ash and lava every now and then, which might be a downside, but geothermal activity is a straightforward energy freebie that can be easily exploited. Countries with exploitable geothermal energy are relatively few, but geothermal power plants are valuable to northern California, New Zealand's North Island, and Leyte Island in the Philippines. Geothermal Central is Iceland, where a significant amount of heating is generated this way. There are a number of unexploited sites, especially localized sites that could be developed in the future, but the really good ones are relatively few and far between.

Can we convert solar energy, one way or another, into forms that can keep our civilization buzzing? The theoretical answer is an unequivocal yes. There is more energy cascading to the earth every day than has been consumed by humans in the last century, but theory and practice are not the same thing. Renewables are the fastest growing of energy sources, but they produce only a thirtieth of our energy needs today.

When water flows down rivers and into tidal estuaries it carries a lot of kinetic energy that can be harvested for electricity generation with turbines. The use of hydropower for tasks such as the grinding of grain goes back centuries. The first hydroelectric power station was built at Niagara Falls, New York, in the 1880s. Hydroelectric plants are expensive to construct but cheap to maintain and can generate lots of electricity for a very long time. Hydro is by far the dominant source of renewable energy, and hydro projects are an extremely important source of electricity in many countries. Norway, for example, generates nearly all its electricity from hydro. The United States generates about 5 percent of its electricity from 2,400 hydroelectric dams scattered all over the country. The electric company in Canada's Belle Province is called Hydro Québec because it generates much of its electricity from a prodigious project in James Bay.

The Three Gorges hydroelectric project in central China brings back images of the Imperial China superpower that built the Great Wall. The dam is 650 feet high and a mile and half wide and has created a 100-mile reservoir on the Yangtze River. The roughly 1 billion cubic feet of concrete used to build the dam are enough to build a sidewalk that would wrap around the planet six times. It's dam big (pardon the pun) and is capable of delivering more electricity than hundreds of clunky, polluting Chinese coal-fired power stations.

Three Gorges is both a symbol of China's growth and a symbol of its deepening vulnerability. It generates enough electricity to replace hundreds of coal-fired plants, tames the dangerous Yangtze River floods that have claimed many thousands of lives, and allows the navigation of the river by oceangoing tankers clear through to Chongqing. But all sources of energy come with strings attached. One and a half million people had

**The Three Gorges Dam Project is the biggest in
the world. Photograph courtesy of Steve Hallett.**

to be relocated before their homes disappeared below the river, hundreds of thousands of acres of fertile farmland were flooded, and an entire ecosystem has been modified. The huge agricultural region downstream will no longer be replenished by Yangtze River silt.

I visited the Three Gorges Project with a group of Purdue University students recently, and we were most struck by Fengdu, a glittering town of new apartment buildings on the north bank of the river that looks like it was just unpacked from shrink wrap. The old city of Fengdu? Well, the former homes of sixty thousand people are now underwater.

My reaction to Three Gorges is strongly ambivalent. China is now capable of generating large amounts of electricity from emissions-free hydro, but the loss of farmland and the displacement of people are terrible. The control of the river floods will save many lives, and yet it is a real ecosystem-modifying force. Soil-replenishing silts will no longer wash down onto the Yangtze Plain, a farming region that is fertile only

Yangtze flood level. Signs show the winter water level on the Yangtze River west of the Three Gorges Dam. China Mobile has it all under control, locking in the perfect riverfront advertising location, but farmers taking advantage of land below the 175-meter mark need to get the harvest in before the sluices close. Photograph courtesy of Steve Hallett.

because of the flooding river. Hydroelectricity is certainly one of the cleanest forms of energy, but Three Gorges demonstrates that even the cleanest energy comes at a price.

The biggest limitation to hydro, however, might simply be that most of the best sites have already been dammed: the world reached "peak dam" about two decades ago. The big exception is the continent of Africa. The Ethiopians would love to build a dam on the Blue Nile, but

The sixty thousand inhabitants of the city of Fengdu were moved from the south side of the Yangtze River to the north. The foundations of buildings from the old city are visible each spring when the water level is dropped to accommodate flood waters. Photograph courtesy of Steve Hallett.

the Egyptians have promised to sabotage any such project (it would compromise the value of their own Aswan High Dam). Another huge project is being discussed for the Congo River.

Rivers and estuaries have provided large amounts of electricity from relatively simple projects, but much more kinetic energy rests just off-shore in the form of waves. Waves contain masses of energy, but tapping them is not as easy. Nonetheless, ambitious designs exist for a number of different types of systems that could be used to harvest wave power. There is, for example, the possibility of dropping turbines into the Gulf Stream off the east coast of Florida. Big projects such as this could deliver truckloads of electricity if we can make them happen.

Wind farms are popping up all over the developed world, and since most countries have at least some windy spots, there is lots more wind for the taking. Like water, wind is a very old source of power and requires relatively little explanation. The wind blows, turbines turn, electricity flows. Wind turbine technology has improved significantly in recent years, and turbines can now operate in a wide range of wind conditions. Large turbines can generate megawatts of electricity, but the practicalities of large-scale wind power are daunting. A windmill is still a windmill—even if you call it a turbine.

Two massive wind turbine arrays are planned for the English Channel, just east of London. The London Array will have 341 turbines over 144 square miles, and the Thanet Array will have a further 100 turbines. These two projects will generate electricity for a million homes. Impressive as this is, it will supply less than 1 percent of London's energy needs, and gives a great illustration of the disconnect between theory and practice. Oilman T. Boone Pickens touts wind energy—and confirms our worst fears about peak oil—with his "Pickens Plan." The former CEO of Mesa Petroleum is proposing an escape from America's "dependency on foreign oil"[36] through domestic natural gas and then wind energy. His proposal for twenty-seven hundred turbines on two hundred thousand

Wind turbines are popping up as vigorously as weeds in the cornfields of Benton County, Indiana. Photograph courtesy of Steve Hallett.

Wind turbine. Photograph courtesy of Steve Hallett.

acres of windy west Texas is on a scale that could generate some serious electricity, but it still falls short of a replacement technology. Thousands of other projects on the same scale would be needed for that.

Some of the really nice wind flows are found at high altitudes and far offshore, but the technology to exploit them remains embryonic. Large floating offshore platforms might return electricity via underwater cables, and massive electricity-generating kites might one day fly in the jet stream. As with the big hydroelectricity projects, I'm not counting them out, but no such project is yet scheduled for construction.

Wind energy cannot serve as a stand-alone replacement technology, but the nice thing about wind energy is that it has potential on a wide range of different scales, from small windmills to power individual homes to large arrays that electrify small towns. While turbine arrays are unlikely to service large cities or regions effectively, it may be feasible to service small towns and communities, and, in this modest role, wind energy will be extremely valuable.

The simplest and oldest methods of using solar energy are passive. Picture a snake warming itself in the morning on a sunny rock and then crawling underneath it for shade in the heat of the day. Cold climates demand heating, hot climates demand cooling, and most climates require some of each. Where I live, in northern Indiana, summertime temperatures can hit a hundred degrees, and winter cold snaps can plunge below zero, and yet I live in a plywood-and-chipboard monstrosity that leaks heat like a sieve. I have friends and relatives that live in Miami and Montreal. They live in houses built just the same way. Thanks to cheap electricity and natural gas, it's easier and cheaper to build a big, wasteful house and burn fossil fuels to make it comfortable than it is to design the thing properly in the first place.

It's a terrible shame, waste, and vulnerability that we stopped designing houses for their environment. There's a reason that the Norse lived in small stone houses with thick earth roofs and that the Mediterranean is dotted with whitewashed stucco buildings with terracotta tile roofs. These houses have been selected as the designs most suitable for controlling the inside temperature of the house as effectively as possible. Modern homes have been designed to minimize costs in an era of cheap energy. Our suburban McHouses will get very cold in winter without natural gas heating and very hot in summer if there are electricity outages. A passive solar house might cost a little more to build now, but it might be more livable through the coming energy crisis.

Incoming solar radiation packs roughly twenty watts of energy per square foot (depending on the season, altitude, latitude, etc.), and it can be harnessed and transformed directly into electricity in photovoltaic (PV) cells. These cells now achieve around 20 percent efficiency, so you can actually get your hands on about four out of those possible twenty watts per square foot, which is plenty to power a house. With the costs of PV technology declining and the costs of fossil fuel energy increasing, solar energy may play a role in the future, and further improvements in solar technology are still being made.

Solar power has rarely shown much promise on a large scale, although some efforts have been made to develop solar farms comprised of large arrays of PV cells or arrays of concentrators that focus light into centralized collectors. Many countries have large areas of arid, unproductive land that can be used for the placement of solar arrays, and there are now some quite large arrays around the world. Stirling Energy Systems is erecting an array of 20,000 curved-dish mirrors on 4,500 acres of the Mojave Desert and a cluster of 12,000 dishes in California's Imperial Valley. These are not insignificant projects, although they are far from becoming true replacement technologies. The initial capital investments and maintenance costs for these projects are high, and the evening-out of output is still a problem. An additional drawback is that these systems may need to be located rather far from population centers and the electricity wired long distances.

The biggest weakness of PV energy is the fact that the sun does not always shine, not everywhere is sunny, or that it may be sunny only seasonally. In the United Kingdom, for example, winter sunlight energy is only one-fifth of that received in the summer. Electricity is needed at night, and on cloudy days, and the problem caused by the lack of reliability of sunlight is usually solved by banks of batteries. In fact, the biggest drawback to solar power is not the advanced PV cells but the rather clunky battery technology on which they rely. Nonetheless, solar power can be extremely effective for small applications such as individual homes. Many people enjoy a fully electric lifestyle completely independent of utility companies, thanks to solar power. As with wind power, I believe small-scale solar systems will be extremely valuable to individuals and communities through the coming energy crisis, but it is unlikely that solar can generate significant amounts of electricity to feed into the grid.

The major sources of renewable energy, then, are hydro, wind, and solar.

The forests of West Africa are overburdened by a large population in desperate need of building materials and fuel. A veritable train of canoes brings wood, sand, and black-market gasoline down the So River to Cotonou, Benin. Photograph courtesy of Steve Hallett.

Each one is sorely limited but will be of value in certain situations. Each one is also capable, albeit to a limited degree, of being scaled up. But there is a fourth source of renewable energy that has been gaining significant support in recent years, and that is bioenergy. Here, alas, lies no hope at all.

Plants[37] suck carbon dioxide out of the air, mix it with water, and, with a little burst of sunlight, make sugar. They are the most efficient solar factories ever created. Strike that: *ever evolved.* The sugars made by plants in photosynthesis are then converted into wood that can be chopped down and burned, or roasted to make charcoal; fibers that can

Corncob fuel and solar water heater. Nothing goes to waste, and energy is at a premium in rural Hebei Province on the North China Plain, south of Beijing. Shucked corncobs are dried and used for household heating and cooking. Hot water is supplied by a rooftop solar heater. Photograph courtesy of Steve Hallett.

This bioethanol plant in Linden, Indiana, operated by Verasun, has a capacity of 110 million gallons of fuel ethanol per year. Photograph courtesy of Steve Hallett.

be harvested, dried down, pelletized, and burned; oils that can be squeezed out and then pumped into a diesel vehicle; and seeds and sap that can be fermented to make ethanol that burns like gasoline. Structural tissues (i.e., cell walls) can be broken down to sugars and then fermented to make more ethanol or can be heat treated and converted directly into liquid fuels. Heck, some plants can even be eaten.

In other words, plants can be harnessed as biomass or biofuels for heating, electricity, and liquid fuels. This sounds exciting but is nothing new: biomass is by far the oldest source of energy used by humankind. What is new is that we have created a complex society reliant on the consumption of huge volumes of liquid fuels, and we desperately need to find ways to make these fuels into replacements for oil.

Formula One racing cars can run on pure ethanol, which actually has a higher octane rating than gasoline. Dario Franchetti won the 2007 Indianapolis 500 in an ethanol-powered Indy car. Biodiesel, which is pretty much just vegetable oil, can be more or less thrown straight into the fuel tank of diesel vehicles. In fact, only a little basic equipment is required to make your own biodiesel from discarded cooking oil (get the waste fryer oil from the local grill and set up a small biodiesel business?).[38] Ethanol can be mixed with gasoline, and many cars can run on E85 (85 percent ethanol, 15 percent gasoline) with relatively little modification. All cars can run on gasoline with 15 percent ethanol added as an antiknock additive replacing lead or other compounds.

Hundreds of new ethanol plants are under construction in the United States, and the farmers of the Midwest have responded with record plantings of corn. Why not? Corn kernels are one of the easiest things to ferment, and the demand for ethanol has been an important factor driving up the price of corn. Midwestern politicians have succeeded in getting significant subsidies for corn ethanol, leading the business to boom. But if growing corn for ethanol seems strange to you, you are not alone.

On the face of it, you might expect the production of fuels from plants to be a winning proposition that not only will keep our vehicles running but also will reduce greenhouse gas emissions. The idea is that the carbon dioxide emitted by burning the ethanol is offset by the carbon that was absorbed by growing the plant in the first place. That seems reasonable enough until you factor in the amount of energy that goes into growing corn. Fertilizers, made from natural gas, are applied onto fields sown and harvested by diesel-powered tractors and then transported by truck to be processed at fossil fuel–driven plants. The resulting ethanol is distributed by still more trucks and, finally, burned. Much more energy goes into growing ethanol in cornfields than you get back from burning it in your car. As far as carbon dioxide emissions are concerned, corn ethanol is not a sink for carbon but a source of it. Making fuel from corn ethanol does not produce energy, it consumes energy.

There are much better crops for ethanol production than corn, such as sugarcane, from which ethanol is produced roughly eight times more efficiently. Brazil is the world's leader in ethanol, thanks to extensive plantings of this crop. Nearly all of Brazil's cars can run on ethanol, and Brazil has completely weaned itself off imported oil (Brazil also has significant oil reserves) and supplies roughly a third of the world's ethanol. Brazilian sugarcane, however, has its own serious problems. The desire to increase agricultural production in Brazil, including sugarcane for ethanol, results in the clearing of forested land. In Brazil, of course, some of this forested land is the fabled Amazon rain forest. The result is that our desire for an eco-friendly fuel promotes the destruction of rain forests and threatens to turn the Amazon rain forest into the Amazon ranch. It's hard to imagine anything more horribly backward.

Well, maybe one thing. The buzz on palm oil suddenly went sour a few years ago. For a few short years, many people thought that Southeast Asia could supply millions of gallons of bioethanol from palm trees, an energy source that would be clean, green, and would make money for struggling nations. Alas, as the ethanol began to flow the problems suddenly became obvious. The subsidies for palm oil encouraged folks to burn huge tracts of pristine forest and drain wetlands for palm plantations.

So the destruction of the Amazon rain forest for sugarcane is matched on the other side of the world by the destruction of Indonesian rain forests for palm trees. As well, the push for biofuels is a major contributor to increased food prices and is contributing to hunger around the world. The poor need to compete with your neighbor's Hummer for their share of the harvest.

It is an awfully big waste of carbon to grow crops like corn, harvest the grain or sap, and then toss away the rest of the plant. The grain comprises only a small percentage of the final biomass of the plant, so what if we could turn the whole plant into fuel? Well, we can, but it's not easy. The stems and leaves of plants are made of tough polysaccharides that need to be either broken down into simple sugars before they can be fermented to ethanol or chemically converted to more useful forms. Chemical liquefaction can be achieved through a number of processes, but specialized reactors that operate at very high temperatures are required; and these currently attain only very modest levels of efficiency.

The process of converting crude biomass into ethanol requires pretreatment with heat to begin the digestion process (some of the indigestible waste products can be dried, pelletized, and burned in the factory's furnaces to provide the heat) and enzymes to digest the material into simple sugars. These simple sugars can then be fermented to ethanol using the same process as you would use for grain ethanol. Ethanol produced in this way has adopted the name of *cellulosic ethanol*.

Easily digested plant species with relatively easily degraded polysaccharides can be selected, and it may be possible to breed or engineer plants to be more easily degraded still. Improved cellulolytic enzymes can also be engineered to break down the plant cell walls more efficiently. Nancy Ho of Purdue University has developed a genetically engineered yeast that can ferment xylose as well as sucrose, increasing the efficiency of cellulosic ethanol production.[39] Nonetheless, very little cellulosic ethanol flows yet, the technological hurdles remain high, and whatever progress may be made, turning plants into liquid fuels is a fundamentally bad idea.

Biofuels are completely outclassed by oil and natural gas and are Stone Age solutions with no prospects. What's worse is that as oil and natural gas go into decline, agricultural production, which depends on carbon-based fuels to succeed, will struggle too, and it will become obvious that this system has very limited value. It is a shame that we are creating paroxysms in agriculture, contributing to a global food crisis, and causing terrible environmental damage trying to develop an industry that is a nonstarter.

There used to be a great brasserie[40] in the town of Sainte Anne de Bellevue, on Montreal's West Island. It burned down: a tragedy, because I spent a fair bit of my life there. Occasionally, drinking up on the terrace, you might come across a guy named Roger Sampson. He was the founder of a small organization called REAP Canada,[41] a one-room operation in the back corner of a small building on McGill University's Macdonald campus. Way back in the 1980s, when the idea of harvesting biomass for heating was just a novelty, Roger would hold forth about his visions for switchgrass. Buy him an extra *pichet* of Molson Ex, and, as I recall, he'd explain how he was going to "bring back pride to the prairies," among many other things.

The basic premise is simple. There is high-quality land and low-quality land. You can produce great fruits and vegetables on high-quality land, say, in the Netherlands or Florida, and you'd be silly to waste the land raising sheep. There are other places, for example, New Zealand's McKenzie country, where sheep do OK, but you'd be crazy to try to grow corn or cotton. Extend the argument further, and you can see that we consume an inordinate number of resources forcing crops to grow in unsuitable places. Much of the Great Plains and prairies from west Texas to Saskatchewan have been forced under the yoke of industrial agriculture. Fossil fuels are consumed by the megaton, and irrigation schemes are drawing down the underground aquifers.

Simple, then: quit growing wheat and corn on the prairies and start growing prairie grasses such as switchgrass. The prairies may not be able to produce grains indefinitely, but they are very good at producing prairie. Take the switchgrass and convert it into a burnable pellet. Alternatively, simply harvest the prairies. This may seem crazy, and it certainly won't be without some negative impacts, but it would be much more productive than planting crops because it would require far fewer inputs and would cause significantly less environmental damage. Prairie plant communities are adapted to frequent disturbance in the form of grazing and fire, and, as a result, they are able to maintain significant underground storage reserves and rebound quickly. They could be mowed frequently without loss of productivity.[42]

It has been more than a century since the Western world derived a large part of its energy from agriculture and forestry, and it's hard to imagine making that transition back. Agriculture-derived fuels will be less energy dense and more costly to produce than fossil fuels, and they will be more limited to localized markets. They represent a disastrous loss of efficiency and cannot possibly fill the oil void. Biomass has potential in some areas and can, in theory, be harvested in a sustainable way, but biofuels are a quick trip to land degradation.

THE NUCLEAR OPTION

Apparently, if you are one of the world's biggest consumers of nuclear energy[43] and one of the holders of a standing nuclear arsenal, you get a bit touchy when people take an interest in your nuclear activities. If, when it is no longer *au fait* to test nuclear weapons out in the middle of the Pacific Ocean (Mururoa Atoll; French territory), and a *maudit* bunch of hippies (Greenpeace) threatens to put your *petit champignon atomique*[44] on the evening news, you might take action. That's exactly what the French government did in 1985. They took action . . . really clumsy action.

Agent secret Christine Cabon (French Army lieutenant under the alias Frederique Bonlieu) flew out to New Zealand to infiltrate the Greenpeace Organization while four French soldiers (Jean-Michel Barcelo, Roland Verge, Gerard Andries, and Xavier Christian Maniguet . . . great French warrior-heroes to a man) flew to the French territory of New Caledonia, rented a yacht (the *Ouvea*) and sailed into Auckland harbor. Major Alain Mafart, alias Alain Turenge, traveling as Swiss, and Captain Dominique Prieur, traveling as his wife, Sophie, flew into Auckland from Paris via Honolulu.

The Greenpeace ship *Rainbow Warrior* sailed into Auckland harbor and tied up to the Marsden wharf on July 7 to make preparations to sail out to protest the nuclear tests at Mururoa Atoll. Four days later, the French saboteurs attached two bombs to its hull and blew open a hole eight feet wide. The ship sank, drowning crew member and father of two, Fernando Pereira.[45]

The French plot was uncovered by the New Zealand police, and Mafart and Prieur were captured. The *Ouvea* was scuttled at sea. Mafart and Prieur pleaded guilty to manslaughter and willful damage and were sentenced to ten years in a New Zealand prison.

Now, you'd think the French would be embarrassed about being found out sending secret agents to the other side of the world to sink a ship that was preparing to sail on an environmental mission.

Apparently not.

At the news that Mafart and Prieur were to be jailed in New Zealand, the French started pushing for the return of their nationals and began organizing sanctions. They first imposed a ban on the importation of New Zealand lamb and then extended the ban to other commodities. *C'est* nutty, *non*? Give us back our murdering saboteurs or we won't eat your sheep! (you silly Kiwi k'nigh'ts!)

The United Nations agreed to arbitrate between France and New Zealand, and it ruled that France should pay compensation of thirteen million dollars to New Zealand, but that Mafart and Prieur could serve their prison time on the French territory of Hao Atoll, in the Pacific.

And then it gets really silly: Prieur's husband was made the head of security at Hao Atoll, and Mafart was released after only six months due to a stomach ailment (too many tequilas on the beach?).[46]

Rainbow Warrior: a cautionary tale of what a country will do to hide its nuclear ambitions. Do you think Kim Jong Il and Mahmoud Ahmadinejad are crazy? Well, *voyons*, they have precedent, don't they?

Nuclear energy has been extremely divisive; it is viewed by proponents as the most efficient source of energy—and nonpolluting to boot—and by detractors as insidiously dangerous. Nuclear power plants have been operating in many countries for half a century, and the leader in nuclear power, with more than a quarter of the world's installed capacity, is the United States. Nuclear power provides more than half of the electricity to some countries in northwest Europe and three-quarters of the electricity generated in France.[47] The current growth markets for nuclear power stations are in Asia with a number of plants under construction in China and India. The US company Westinghouse sealed a deal with China (to the great disappointment of the French and the Russians) to build four new plants there. China currently has more than a dozen plants under construction—the largest investment in the world.

The nuclear fuels, uranium and plutonium, are incredibly energy-dense, so much so that concerns were voiced in the 1950s that nuclear energy would be so cheap that it would destabilize the rest of the energy market. A central premise of the nuclear advocates is that nuclear fuels and nuclear reactors are extremely efficient and nonpolluting. On the face of it, this can hardly be contested, and there is good reason to view nuclear power as the most promising solution for electricity generation. Nuclear advocates also tell us that uranium is abundant on the earth, and the potential exists to make its supplies last for centuries.

But there is a lot more to nuclear power than meets the eye. The mining and enrichment of uranium and the disposal of nuclear wastes both present huge problems, and when we add them into the mix the nuclear equation looks quite different. Ignoring the mining, purification, processing, and waste disposal costs, the electricity generated by nuclear power plants can be delivered for as little as one or two cents per kilowatt hour. Fully costed, however, it is by far the most expensive source of electricity that we have.

The first misconception is that uranium is *naturally* energy-dense. Uranium is only energy-dense once it has been purified from its ores. At least 99 percent of the uranium in ores is the rather useless ^{238}U isotope.[48] Uranium therefore needs to be enriched to separate the ^{235}U from the ^{238}U, and this is no easy task—ask the Iranians and the North Koreans. Before that, the uranium has to be mined, and this is an environmental nightmare. Uranium mining in the American Southwest is a persistent pollution disaster and an unforgettable nightmare in the recent history of the Diné, who lost numerous tribal members to accidents and illness, including various cancers, in the uranium mines.

The second major issue with uranium is the problem of nuclear waste disposal, and this has become a game of "pass the radioactive parcel." No government wants to be left holding this particular political hot potato when the music stops.

France, Belgium, Germany, the Netherlands, and Switzerland currently handle nuclear waste in large, onsite pools before shipping it to a site near The Hague. Huge volumes of radioactive waste sit there today awaiting some other, theoretical, future resting place. The Americans and the Finns have come to the conclusion that the only viable long-term solution to the problem of nuclear waste is to create large repositories. This is the responsible thing to do, and credit should be given to them for admitting that unpleasant truth, but nobody wants nuclear waste in their backyard, and if you're locating a long-term repository, you'd better get it right. In Finland, the solution of choice has been a huge, deep tunnel in the granite hills at Onkalo. In the United States, it has been the controversial Yucca Mountain in Nevada.

The Onkalo site has little evidence of underground water, little risk of earthquakes, and is far from population centers. A giant tunnel spirals down deep into the rock where superstrong copper and high-tensile steel canisters will sit in networks of tunnels. Nevada is that state where you tuck away nasty stuff like gambling and prostitution, but it is proving difficult to tuck away nuclear waste even here. The Yucca Mountain project is slated to cost around half a trillion dollars over the next seventy-five years,[49] but we're just as likely to spend those seventy-five years arguing about it. During that time, we'll just keep storing it in pools and concrete boxes at nuclear power stations all over the country.

Another aspect of the nuclear equation that requires some thought is the much-parroted claim that uranium supplies are essentially unlimited, but the issue with uranium is not quantity but quality. Only a small percentage of uranium deposits will yield economically extractable ores. Some scientists argue that the availability of high-grade uranium ores may limit natural-uranium nuclear reactors within fifty years, but there is no consensus on this issue.[50] The balance of this particular savings account is very difficult to gauge, but it is quite large.

The potential limitations of uranium availability could be addressed by fast-breeder reactors that use significantly less fuel, but these reactors have proven difficult to put in place. Their construction is elaborate, and they require specialized maintenance and safety systems. The few that have been built, such as the SuperPhénix reactor in France and the Monju reactor in Japan, have been shut down more than they have been in operation. With at least fifty years of high-grade uranium ores remaining, and most people considering supplies to be much longer-lived than that, there has been little incentive to develop more efficient reactors.

Another interesting problem with the nuclear industry stems from the fact that, for a number of years now, most of the fuel used in nuclear reactors has come from decommissioned nuclear weapons. This is a great way of getting rid of dangerous weapons that could destroy us all in a heartbeat, and it has also reduced the need for uranium mining, which has reduced the size of that particular environmental disaster. As far as the nuclear industry is concerned, however, the long-term use of decommissioned weapons presents a problem. Little exploration for high-grade uranium ores has been carried out in the last decade or so, and the uranium mining industry has become largely moribund. When the uranium from warheads is used up, uranium mining will need to expand just to keep up with the needs of existing plants, never mind the supply of further facilities. This could seriously inhibit any potential nuclear comeback.

Marion King Hubbert, the peak oil guru of gurus, was a major advocate of nuclear power.[51] He argued that, since oil was running out, we needed to get the nuclear industry in shape. But this advice was given half a century ago, and, since that time, the nuclear industry has done the exact opposite. It has managed to terrify people and drive investors away.

The two major nuclear disasters didn't help. The first was the meltdown at Three Mile Island in the United States in 1979. The second was the disaster at Chernobyl in the Soviet Union (now Ukraine) in 1986 that left a swath of fallout across Europe and an intense fear of nuclear power. One could argue that the scare at Three Mile Island was not a problem at all. The safety systems ultimately did what they were supposed to—but tell that to the locals. In the case of Chernobyl, one could argue that this accident occurred under a political system that, frankly, couldn't maintain a safe television set, and to doubt the nuclear industry on this basis is irrational. But try to convince most people that nuclear countries will always be well governed.[52]

Since the disasters at Three Mile Island and Chernobyl, very few nuclear power plants have been commissioned in the Western world. Only two new plants have been commissioned in America since 1973. The last one to be completed, at Watts Bar, Tennessee, took twenty-

Three Mile Island on the Susquehanna River, south of Harrisburg, Pennsylvania, was the site of the United States' worst nuclear accident. Reactor II, which came online in December 1978, suffered a partial meltdown just three months later on March 28, 1979, as a result of a failure in its coolant system. The nuclear industry claims that neither fatalities nor injuries can be linked to the radioactive materials that were exhausted from the site, but a number of scientists recorded spikes of infant mortality, lung cancer, and leukemia in communities immediately downwind. Reactor I still operates today and is licensed to continue operations through 2034. Photograph courtesy of Steve Hallett.

three years to finish, ran billions over budget, and was completed a dozen years late. It began producing electricity only in 1996, and a second reactor at the site is still not yet up and running.

Political difficulties, unresolved problems of waste disposal, and the very long lead times before plants go into production have relegated the nuclear industry well down on the list as a financial investment over the last twenty-five years. Investors have learned to view the nuclear industry to be about as attractive as, well, radiation poisoning. The nuclear industry is notorious for paying back late, generally underperforming, and proving more dangerous than promised—and it has developed a lousy credit rating as a result. It doesn't help that a new nuclear power plant is going to require a capital outlay of about ten billion dollars, or that politicians are terrified of putting in a good word. Despite all the fear, technical challenges, and environmental risks, it might come down to this: If you want a genuinely powerful source of energy to replace oil, nuclear power might be your only choice.

There have been no major breakthroughs in nuclear technology, but there has been steady progress. The nuclear power stations currently under construction, such as those in China, are significantly improved from the clunky old monsters that were cobbled together in the sixties and seventies. They require less ore, generate power more efficiently, produce less waste, and have a range of new safety features. Despite a long, bleak winter, the nuclear industry is slowly emerging from dormancy. The Obama administration announced loan guarantees in March 2010 for the construction of two nuclear power plants in Georgia that will become the first new US plants in at least thirty years. It is far from certain that investors will be convinced to build the hundreds of nuclear power stations that will soon be needed, but, with oil and gas prices climbing, the nuclear option may make financial sense again after all. Making it happen will not be easy, but reviving the nuclear industry may be the only way to preserve our current way of life: if that's what we want to do.

ENERGY: FOR HERE OR TO GO?

We require energy for three basic things: electricity, heating, and transportation. Electricity and heating can be generated relatively easily from all energy resources, but producing energy-dense fuels for vehicles is a much bigger problem. Transportation requires transportable energy, and, without readily refinable sources of liquid fuels, keeping the lights on at the end of the petroleum interval is going to be much easier than keeping the wheels turning. Of the eighty million barrels of oil consumed worldwide per day, nearly sixty million are used for transportation. The lion's share is used to move people around (thirty million barrels). Nearly twenty million barrels are used to transport goods, and six million barrels are burned in planes.[53]

The Industrial Revolution was an era of societal transformation because coal increased the efficiency of transportation and machinery. Coal could be thrown onto the back of large locomotives or in the boiler rooms of oceangoing vessels, and it transformed societies in a few short decades.

The next great breakthrough in transportation came with oil, which enabled the distribution of huge volumes of fuels that were much more energy-dense than even coal. Tanks of diesel, gasoline, or aviation fuel provide an extremely compact form of energy that can be stored on vehicles of many different shapes and sizes, giving them huge amounts of power and a long range without refueling. A tank of gasoline is easily taken for granted, but just think for a second about the amount of power that it generates. I can put two jugs full of gasoline into my car and drive it sixty miles, taking the kids down to Indianapolis in an hour. Those two jugs full of gasoline are light enough for me to carry, one in each hand, and their weight hardly affects the efficiency of the car at all. Consider now what happens if there is no gasoline for sale in Indy and we want to get back home to West Lafayette. Think of the human energy it would take for the four of us to push the car back up Highway 65 and how long it would take. The energy contained in those two jugs full of gasoline is prodigious, and it comes in a truly user-friendly, highly dense, liquid form.

The American automobile manufacturers have really struggled over the last five years or so. They became lazy, careless, and failed to develop energy-efficient cars, partly because they were heavily subsidized by the federal government. But, in the midst of their refusal to promote energy efficiency, General Motors did a very odd thing: it created, and then destroyed, the American electric car. The EV1 electric car was not exactly a major business success. It was a GM car, after all, but many of the owners of the EV1 simply adored it. The car worked, and it was a proof of principle, hitting the market (sort of) in 1997.

The EV1 had a range of up to a hundred and fifty miles with its fanciest late-model nickel-halide batteries, but the batteries took eight hours to fully recharge, and the car was also liable to need frequent servicing and battery replacement. It was expensive, thanks to a slew of engineering features that kept its weight down, and it was a two-seater. In short, the EV1 was never a commercial winner for the general car market, but it was a major step in the right direction for new thinking in the automobile industry. Anyway, not long after its release, in 2001, GM recalled the entire EV1 fleet. The cars were impounded in Burbank, California. Protestors howled outside. The cars were then removed to a remote site in Arizona and crushed. Stranger than fiction, but there you have it.

Various companies have put out new electric prototypes in recent years that are much more promising. Tesla Motors's Roadster accelerates like a sports car and has a range of two hundred and fifty miles. That's not only extremely cool but a great sign for the future. On the other hand, it relies on not-so-standard batteries and would set you back a pretty penny. The most promising electric car coming to market appears to be the 2011 Nissan Leaf. This is a five-door, five-passenger vehicle powered by lithium-ion batteries that is competitive in price with similar-sized gas cars. The Leaf will have a range of only around a hun-

One of the fully electric shuttle buses at the 2010 Shanghai World Expo. Each bus recharged briefly at each stop, storing enough charge to make it to the next. Photograph courtesy of Steve Hallett.

This modified Smart car on display at the 2010 Shanghai World Expo is the kind of small, lightweight vehicle with which fully electric local travel is feasible. Photograph courtesy of Steve Hallett.

dred miles under normal driving conditions (not at its 90-mph top speed) and a recharge time of roughly four to six hours, so it is very much designed for only local travel.

When the costs of big, fast cars are out of reach, people may have no other choice than to use smaller, slower cars, and we may have to take a serious look at how we travel. A new lifestyle that is more localized, in which a four-hundred-mile drive at seventy miles per hour is considered unusual, will force considerable changes. Electric cars may have a significant place in these changes, but they will have to be smaller and lighter than the cars to which we have become accustomed.

The hybrid car has been a great success in the last few years. It combines the energy efficiency of an electric vehicle with the power of a gasoline engine and may serve as an effective stepping-stone away from the gasoline engine. Plug-in hybrid vehicles will soon provide a further bridge, especially those designed to recharge from rooftop solar cells or even small wind turbines while parked outside your home or office. There are certainly significant opportunities to maintain much of our car-based lifestyle without gasoline, but not every vehicle can be light, supersmall, and short-range. There's the problem of transporting freight in trucks and on ships, and the thought of flying across the Atlantic or Pacific in a battery-powered plane is not that tempting. Here is where there are high hopes for hydrogen.

First of all, let's put part of the hydrogen fuel myth to rest. Hydrogen is not a source of energy; it is a carrier of energy. There are no available reserves of hydrogen, so, before it can be used, it has to be made. Hydrogen can be made in a number of different ways, but whichever way you look at it, hydrogen does not provide energy; it consumes it. Before we dismiss hydrogen, bear in mind that electricity is not a source of energy either but merely a carrier—and electricity has hardly been a flop. An effective energy carrier is a very valuable thing, and one that is dense enough to carry on large vehicles will soon be desperately needed.

Once produced, hydrogen can be either burned directly or converted back into electricity. Both options have huge potential. Hydrogen burns very hot and very clean and can deliver the high power-to-weight ratio needed by large vehicles and planes for which electricity has never worked. On the downside, hydrogen is much harder to handle than gasoline or natural gas.

Hydrogen can be pressurized or liquefied, but, to be liquefied, it needs to be very, *very* cold, which presents significant engineering difficulties. If allowed to heat up (e.g., you leave the car in a parking lot to go shopping), the liquid hydrogen expands, becomes hydrogen gas again, and your car explodes.[54] The storage tanks used for natural gas are liable to leak hydrogen,[55] and that's not such a good thing, either. Hydrogen is also somewhat corrosive to steel, and special tanks and pipes will be needed too. Despite the problems, we will undoubtedly figure out efficient ways of handling hydrogen. There will be a few more *Hindenburgs*[56] along the way, but we had those, and still have them occasionally, with oil and natural gas.

Plants are cool. Every minute of every day, all around the world, plants are doing something that physicists and engineers can only dream of. They are making hydrogen and energy from water, and they are doing it silently, motionlessly, and without generating the slightest speck of pollution. The process is called the Hill reaction, and it's the first step in photosynthesis. All that is needed to drive the Hill reaction is water, carbon dioxide, and a wee burst of light (and a plant,[57] of course). Photons of light are absorbed by chlorophyll on stacks of membranes inside the chloroplast,[58] which undergoes a subtle change in structure that rips apart water molecules into oxygen and hydrogen. The hydrogen atoms power the production of a high-energy chemical (ATP), the production of sugars, and the growth of the plant. How cool is that! If only we were as smart as plants.

OK, so we're not as smart as plants, and we can't make hydrogen fuel effortlessly, but we have figured out a few different ways. Prodigious volumes of hydrogen are generated for the production of fertilizers during the Haber process,[59] and for other chemical processes. Nearly all this hydrogen is produced from natural gas, however, so alternate methods of producing hydrogen had better be feasible if the hydrogen economy is going to last longer than our reserves of natural gas. Just like plants, we can zap water with some electrons (electricity) and separate oxygen and hydrogen in a process called electrolysis. It's actually not that big of a deal, and electrolytic cells can be made relatively easily. A second cell— a fuel cell—can then collect the oxygen and hydrogen, reverse the reaction, and make electricity. The only by-product is water.

Although it ultimately wastes energy, the electrolysis–fuel cell combo is very exciting because the intermediate—hydrogen—can be used as a transportation fuel. The same electrolytic cell can be used to both produce and consume hydrogen, so hydrogen can be synthesized in a stationary vehicle and then consumed to make it go. Hydrogen technology is not ready yet, but it shows promise to play a significant role in the future. Hydrogen is an extremely energy-dense, nonpolluting fuel (of course, if you burn fossil fuels to get hold of it, that rather destroys the nonpolluting aspect), and it is one of the relatively few substances that we may be able to get our hands on for transportation.

Experimental hydrogen-powered cars are under development by all the big automakers. The Mercedes Necar can zoom you along at a smooth seventy miles per hour and has a range of 450 miles, although it's jam-packed full of cells and fuel canisters, so don't try to take the family camping in it. The GM Sequel is a prototype fuel-cell vehicle that gets forty miles per gallon equivalent from hydrogen and can accelerate from zero to sixty in less than ten seconds. You can get your hands on one of these beauties for just a few million or so.

A number of hydrogen filling stations also now exist in various parts of the world. The first such station was built in Iceland and was used for filling up a handful of special-order city buses. The Icelanders deserve lots of credit for being first-order reformers. Iceland has its sights on becoming the world's first hydrogen economy—and why not. Iceland:

It's a Niceland.[60] Significant research and development is still required to make affordable fuel cells that are sufficiently compact and powerful to be incorporated into production-run vehicles. While I expect that many advances are still possible, it is worth remembering that fuel-cell technology is now a hundred and fifty years old.

The biggest problem with hydrogen technology for transportation, however, might not be the scale of the remaining needs for technological innovation but the scale of the needed transition. Converting our transport systems to hydrogen will require changing vehicle designs, gas station designs, distribution systems, and power-generation systems; and the size of the required infrastructure makeover is huge. The entire transportation fleet and its supporting industries—trillion-dollar industries—will need to be replaced. That's a billion gasoline-powered cars and the industries that support them. As the Jewish saying from the Great Depression has it: "If I had some ham, I'd have a ham sandwich, if I had some bread."

THE PLATTER OF OPTIONS

The last century has been an era of astonishing human development, and we credit ourselves with great ingenuity to have tamed this world so completely with comfortable homes; to have shrunk it so dramatically with planes, trains, and automobiles; and to have harvested it so efficiently with fertilizers, pesticides, and agricultural machinery. Only a century ago we were a largely rural population traveling and trading mostly locally, and now we are a predominantly urban, global community. We should not credit our ingenuity too much. None of this would have been possible without oil.

Our world has been transformed by oil, and the rate of transformation has been matched by the rate of production. So much has been possible these last hundred years because we have had vast, and constantly increasing, amounts of energy at our fingertips. The next hundred years will be very different: we have withdrawn too greedily from our savings of this transformational source of energy. We have used roughly half of our accessible reserves of oil, and it will become increasingly difficult and expensive to pump out the other half.

Our astonishing global economy relies on constant supplies of energy. We will pump as diligently as we can, and yet our supply of petroleum will decline through the next century as surely as it rose through the last. We are at the peak of the petroleum interval, and, a century from now, the petroleum interval will be over. As we pass the peak, we will attempt to save our economies in the face of soaring oil prices and declining oil supplies. How we handle the coming energy transition is one of the great questions of our time.

Our energy platter has grown in leaps and bounds since capturing fire and burning wood, and its offerings have become ever more efficient. When our most advanced societies sit down at the energy table, a grand feast is laid out before them. They have gorged themselves to the point of bellyache, and yet the platter has always been refilled. But the cook is returning from the energy pantry with a worried look on his face. The restaurant is full, and the guests are hungry, but the choicest morsels are gone.

The nuclear industry is offering up some dishes, but for now there is no certainty that more than a few sample platters will reach the table anytime soon. People are reluctant to choose these dishes anyway, remembering the food poisoning they suffered last time. Huge amounts of energy can come from nuclear power if the industry is developed methodically, but it is unlikely that this will happen quickly.

Coal is still on the menu, but, in the food analogy, coal is baked beans. Not good eatin' and bad for the environment.

There can be little doubt that the sun, the moon and the spinning earth offer a supply of energy far in excess of our needs. There can also be little doubt that humans are more than ingenious enough to figure out ways of harvesting a good portion of it. There are, however, a number of reasons to be extremely pessimistic about our ability to get this done on a big enough scale. Civilization's sources of energy have come in increasingly compact forms, and stepping backward into the future does not seem feasible. Weight for weight, oil stores twice the energy of coal, and coal stores twice the energy of wood. Solar, wind, and wave energy are even less compact.

One of the biggest difficulties with many energy sources is that while they can be easily converted into electricity they are harder to convert into transportation fuels. Putting effective options on the energy platter that can replace petroleum-based liquid fuels will be particularly difficult. The loss of petroleum products marks the loss of not only our most efficient form of energy but also our most versatile.

Perhaps the biggest frustration will be trying to reach our renewable energy potential without oil itself. When we smile at the clean energy generated by wind turbines we forget the huge tractor-trailers that transported the pieces across the country and the cranes that assembled and erected them. The next Hoover Dam may have to be built like the last: by thousands of workers with picks and steam shovels. The construction of solar panels demands advanced plastics and heavy metals that are the products of energy-intensive industries. We could have invested our oil endowment into the creation of its replacements, but, so far, we have not.

The new energy platter is decidedly *nouveau cuisine* compared to the supersized fossil fuel feast on which we have been gorging for the last century. It is difficult to see how we can avoid economic disaster as oil declines because the alternatives are not good enough. But the new energy meal is the only choice we have, so we had better start stocking the pantry and coming up with recipes. It's going to be a tough transition, but, as unappetizing as it currently looks, the new energy platter is more varied than the last one, slightly healthier, and it's on the table.

CHAPTER 6

THE ECOLOGICAL DEBT

I f you borrow money you have to pay it back, and if you accumulate too much debt you may go into bankruptcy. The same applies to the environment. If you borrow from the environment, you accumulate an ecological debt that needs to be paid down. In agriculture, for example, crops withdraw nitrogen from the soil, and that nitrogen must be replaced to secure productivity for the next year. Over a longer period of time, agriculture may deplete the structure of soils and make them liable to erosion. This can cause a much more serious ecological debt that may threaten your farm. A farmer who has pushed her land too hard may find both yields and the value of the farm going into a downward spiral, and so her yield losses and the declining assessed value of the farm might serve as a crude measurement of the ecological debt she has accumulated. Eventually, it may be impossible to sell the unprofitable farm because of the damage caused to the land.

Witness the great hardships endured by American farmers during the Dust Bowl. Farming expanded dramatically across the Midwest and Great Plains in the late 1920s when diesel-powered machinery rolled onto the land. The rich prairie soils poured out food but were over-worked and left exposed. Few windbreaks were maintained to protect the huge, flat landscape; the land was depleted by thirsty crops, pulverized by John Deere's steel blades, and left bare each winter. The dust bowl had been inevitable for years, and it finally arrived when the soil was lifted into the air on hot, dry winds.

A dust storm in 1934, lasting four days, removed an estimated three hundred million tons of soil from the farms of the Great Plains. The plume of dust was so large that it obscured the sun in New York City and deposited a layer of dust on ships in the middle of the Atlantic Ocean.[1] The date of April 14, 1935, was named Black Sunday when another huge dust storm turned day into night. The dust cloud was centered in north Texas, Oklahoma, and Kansas, but it extended from the Rockies to Ohio and Canada. The Dust Bowl and its aftermath are vividly described in John Steinbeck's *The Grapes of Wrath*: "Houses were shut tight, and cloth wedged around doors and windows, but the dust came in so thinly that it could not be seen in the air, and it settled like pollen on the chairs and tables, on the dishes."[2] The first mechanized farmers of the Great Plains accrued an ecological debt that is still being paid down generations later.[3]

The Dust Bowl was merely a sign of things to come. As the petroleum interval shifted into high gear, we accelerated our drawdown of resources all over the world. Forests are shrinking while deserts expand. Ocean fish populations are crashing, and freshwater supplies are collapsing. As serious as these ecological debts are, however, the fastest path to bankruptcy comes not from the drawdown of resources but from damage their consumption can cause.

Economists have a wonderfully neutral word for this damage: they call it an *externality*. Any economic transaction between two parties may have impacts on a third party. This impact may be positive—for example, fireproofing your house protects your neighbor for free—but most externalities are negative. Your purchase of a car benefits you and the vendor, but it adds a vehicle to the roads, which increases everybody's rush-hour misery. That car also consumes large volumes of resources when you drive it, and, most important, it causes pollution—externalities—with every mile you drive. The greenhouse effect has become the great externality in the sky. Global climate change is an ecological debt of planetary proportions.

THE GLOBAL COMMONS[4]

A community that shares a common resource must find ways to cooperate. Failure to do so may result in the tragedy of the commons, depletion of the resource, and ruin for all. A common resource may be a small
village grazing commons, a massive ocean of fish, an immense forest, a
mine full of coal, an aquifer of freshwater, or a planet's endowment of oil.
The commons can also be cut two ways. In the same way that competing
consumers can empty a commons of a limited resource, competing polluters can fill the commons with their wastes. A potential polluter may be
reticent to pollute his own land because the costs would be his to bear,
but if he can discharge his mine wastes into a Montana stream, his sulfur
dioxide into the air to fall as acid rain on a distant forest, or his millions
of tons of electronic garbage onto a Chinese town, well, that's a good
deal. Some of these malfeasants even drive around in cars and let carbon
dioxide spew into the great global commons in the sky.

Any commons can become a tragedy when the rate of resource
extraction is unsustainable—its size is irrelevant. The skies above
America's eastern deciduous forests were once filled with the most
numerous species of bird on the continent: the passenger pigeon. Its
flocks were so vast and dense that they could block out the sun for minutes on end as they swarmed by, and yet the passenger pigeon was
quickly bundled into extinction by axe and shotgun when the Europeans
arrived. The bird lost much of its habitat when forests were cleared for
farming and then was shot whenever it dared to approach the crops.
Anything that seems safe because of its abundance is probably nothing
of the sort.

Resources are safe only if they are extracted more slowly than they
can recover. The immense forests of the Mediterranean were safe for
hundreds of millennia because they could easily recover from the relatively benign impact of bands of hunter-gatherers, but they fell disastrously at the onslaught of Roman industry.

Common-pool resources have become so threatened in the last half century that maintaining commons has been increasingly seen as a vain utopian ideal of a bygone era. Avoiding commons tragedies has become one of our most urgent needs. The main solution in our prevailing era of free-market capitalism has been to remove common-pool resources from the control of the communities that use them—to privatize the commons—and this has resulted in significant improvements for many resources.

The most well-known exposition of this concept comes from Nobel laureate Ronald Coase. The Coase theorem states that the assignment of ownership to any good will allow bargaining between interested parties and that this will be beneficial no matter to whom ownership is assigned. As an illustration, consider the example of a river (as the good) that is subject to pollution. The parties are the public that uses the river for recreation and a factory that pollutes it. Ownership of the river by either party may be preferable to maintaining the river as a commons.

If ownership is assigned to the public, it will charge the factory for discharging pollutants and will likely extract a punitive price to ensure the cleanliness of the river. This would seem fair to most people, but even the other scenario where ownership is assigned to the factory may be better than no ownership at all. One might expect that were the factory to own the river it might simply discharge more pollutants, but this outcome can be countered by the willingness of the public to pay for nonpollution, perhaps through fees for recreational services.

The two parties are able to enter into negotiations because ownership and rights are clearly assigned. Payment for nonpollution will flow from the public to the factory commensurate with the demand for use of the river, and pollution may be curbed if the factory rationalizes that this benefits its bottom line. The payment for nonpollution may not be fair, and in this case it certainly is not, but the outcome is better with respect to the cleanliness of the river.

That's all well and good, and the remediation of the river is a good thing, but repeated applications of the simple logic of the Coase theorem to resource after resource leads us down an even uglier slope. What happens when all our rivers are owned by factories?

The petroleum interval and the global economy it has spawned have turned the world into a great global commons. As localized as any particular resource may seem, it may still be sought by many people. It may not be immediately obvious, but if you buy, say, a piece of furniture from a midwestern Wal-Mart, you are an unwitting part of a cascade of events including traders, shipping companies, and Chinese factory workers that may strip the forest surrounding an impoverished Indonesian village. Just as farmers can degrade a pasture by the simple—and rational—act of increasing their flocks, so nations anywhere in the world can degrade a rain forest, deplete an ocean, or empty an oil field by the simple—and rational—act of increasing their wealth. We can expand on the famous Garrett Hardin quotation thus: "Ruin is the destination toward which all nations rush, each pursuing their own best interest, in a society that believes in the freedom of the Global Commons."

THERE ARE PLENTY OF FISH IN THE SEA

> Do we countenance such loss because fish live in a world we cannot see? Would it be different if, as one conservationist fantasized, the fish wailed as we lifted them out of the water in nets? If the giant bluefin lived on land, its size, speed, and epic migrations would ensure its legendary status, with tourists flocking to photograph it in national parks. But because it lives in the sea, its majesty—comparable to that of a lion—lies largely beyond comprehension.
>
> Fen Montaigne, "Still Waters: The Global Fish Crisis"[5]

The mighty bluefin tuna once existed in great abundance and poured into the Mediterranean Sea from the Atlantic Ocean each spring to spawn. In 1864, using land-based nets, the fishermen of Favignana, near Sicily, took over fourteen thousand bluefin, averaging more than four hundred pounds each. In the last few years they have barely captured a hundred, weighing in at a scrawny average of sixty-five pounds. The world's appetite for tuna, and the efficiency of tuna fisheries, is driving the species toward extinction.

You know something is wrong when the United Kingdom and Iceland go to "war," but that's exactly what happened in the 1970s during the "cod wars." It all got rather nasty for a while as the mighty British trawlers battled the fearless Icelandic navy for the right to devastate a fishery. Ah, I remember the halcyon days of battered cod, soggy chips, and mushy peas from the chippy on Thompson Lane. Cod was the staple of the Great British chippy because it was cheap, and it was cheap because it was abundant. Cod was once so abundant that it served as the main protein source for the Caribbean slave trade. Cod is now so expensive that salmon, once a rare luxury, can be produced more cost-effectively in river estuary fish farms. But battered salmon sucks, especially with mushy peas.

You can't build a fence in the ocean, and it's hard to put up a "no trespassing" sign. It's a shame, really, because that might have helped. The world's fisheries are in a very sorry state and have been suffering serious declines for years. Fisheries have been forced farther out to sea, and into deeper waters. Many stocks are in danger of collapse nonetheless.

The prodigious efforts of the Japanese and their apparent bid to vacuum the oceans clean of fish are worthy of special recognition.[6] I wandered into a supermarket on a recent trip to Tokyo to see what was for sale. The food looked great: the Brie was straight from France, the Emmentaler from Switzerland. The beef—extremely expensive—was fresh off the boat from Australia. And then there was the fish: a huge double aisle of perch, trout, salmon, mullet, flatfish, char, sardines, tuna, shark, and dozens of others. Japan takes roughly 15 percent of the world's catch of ocean fish (and continues to do "research" on an inordinate number of whales). Fisheries are very important to Japan because it sorely lacks agricultural land.

It might seem logical for a deeply fish-dependent country like Japan to find ways to ensure the sustainability of fisheries. But rather than taking action to limit fishing, they seemed to have settled on the tried-and-true tragedy of the commons: get what you can while the getting's good before anyone can take it from you. Even better, you might be able to convince your government to pay you to do it—and all in the name of free-market economics. Many countries, including Russia, the United States, China, Korea, those of the European Union—and Japan is the worst—don't try to limit fishing at all; they promote it with huge subsidies to their fishing fleets.

Significant changes are needed in the fishing industries to reduce pressure on fish stocks, but the overwhelming force is for the pressure to continue to increase. There are a few very positive exceptions, such as rules against drift netting that have limited losses due to by-catch,[7] and some fisheries have been managed better in recent years.

Two nations, Iceland and New Zealand, are worthy of particular praise for developing systems to sustain their inshore fisheries. Both these countries have operated versions of a tradable permit system that has reduced commons tendencies and stabilized fish stocks. These systems have not been without problems. In Iceland, for example, many small fishermen have been rapidly bought out by larger companies able to monopolize the permits, and the fishing industry is in some degree of disarray as a result. Nonetheless, the outcome with respect to fish stocks has been very positive. There are still fish in the waters off Iceland, even some cod.

How can we be so shortsighted as to ruin such a valuable resource? Actually, it's difficult to grasp the fact that we are even capable of it. One of the world's great truisms is "there are plenty of fish in the sea," and you can be sure that the optimist who devised that one would be nonplussed. Perhaps it is the fact that fish are hidden in the water, as Fen Montaigne suggests, that makes fish particularly susceptible to overexploitation, but fish are hardly the only tragedy of the global commons. We have sent numerous species to extinction—and decidedly visible ones, to boot.

Humans have driven many species to extinction by overexploiting them directly, but, in the last few centuries, we have accelerated the process by destroying their habitats as well. Another cause of extinctions is invasive species that have been foolishly established in many places. The British thought it would be a hoot to introduce foxes into Australia for hunting. We should insist that they finish what they started because the foxes have been wiping out Australia's marsupials ever since. The brown tree snake is probably the most memorable invader. It extirpated dozens of species of small animals within a few decades after its arrival in Guam in the 1950s. Guam's tropical forests, once home to a diverse array of chirping tropical birds, are now silent, thanks to a massive population of silent but ravenous brown tree snakes.

Paleontologists describe five major geological epochs during which huge numbers of species went suddenly extinct. The paleontologists of the future will describe a sixth: the Great Holocene[8] Extinction. They will record the sudden disappearance of the North American megafauna, the oversized marsupials of Australia, and the giant flightless birds of Mauritius and New Zealand. But their records will be much more troubling than this. Over a period of little more than ten thousand years, the thinnest sliver of rock in the fossil record, they will record the extinction of a good part of the earth's species. Just how many remains to be seen.

MISSING MOUNTAINS AND PLASTIC OCEANS

In his spectacular book *The World without Us*, Alan Weisman presents an ingenious thought experiment that asks: How would the world change if humans were suddenly removed?[9] He explains the weathering that would bring about the demise of cityscapes, the vegetation successions that would return farmland to forest, and the impact of radioactive waste that would endure for millennia. He exposes a vast array of human legacies and asks which might be transient and which might persist. Even in a world without us, our mark on the landscape—made indelible through the petroleum interval—would surely be detected by some hypothetical visitors from space, even a hundred millennia hence. The legacies that will persist long after we are gone might warrant special attention.

High on the list is global warming. The planet might breathe a sigh of relief if our species were suddenly removed—but would it cool? Well, yes, it would, but not for more than a century. The sudden silencing of vehicles and industry would prevent the release of gigatons of carbon from fossil fuels. The removal of carbon from the atmosphere would begin quickly too, as weeds flourished on farmland and pushed their way through sidewalks. Many ecosystems would begin to recover immediately. The consumption of carbon dioxide from unconstrained plant growth would increase as soon as we were gone. The warming would continue for a while, however, and there would continue to be important consequences. Were the arctic tundra to release its trapped methane, a greenhouse gas more potent than carbon dioxide, a further flush of warming would occur. It is possible that we have triggered a warming chain reaction that might persist for many centuries, or our removal today might be just soon enough. Our removal would not quickly reverse our impact on the oceans, however. Warming of the oceans has begun its slow expansion, and, whether or not we are here, sea levels are destined to rise for a millennium.[10]

What would hypothetical alien archaeologists visiting in the future make of those strange-looking flat-topped mountains in Appalachian coal country? "Why are they so flat?" they might ask. When their studies revealed that the rubble in the valleys had been displaced from the tops of the mountains, they would conclude that it had been shaved flat by a former civilization: but why? They might also find unusually high concentrations of heavy metals—at which point they would probably put on hazmat suits to continue their work. Perhaps some kind of religious ritual carried out here required a large plateau elevated toward the gods?

We might ask why we remove the tops of the Appalachian Mountains ourselves, but why bother? Mike Yeager, a Keystone Industries employee, has given us the answer: "Right now all they're looking at is trees. When we're done they can look over and see grass and animals running. That's a whole lot prettier than trees."[11] And, in any case, it's all for the best, as Bill Caylor, the president of the Kentucky Coal Association explains: "To imply that we're flattening Appalachia is so untrue. We're creating level land for Appalachia."[12]

The Industrial Revolution began our harvesting of fossil fuels and their legacies of global warming and pollution. It is through the petroleum interval, however, that we have found the most powerful ways of converting the landscape to energy and waste. Appalachia would probably be delighted to see us spirited away and our incessant trampling ended. Trees would soon grace our shameful artificial plateaus; wind, rain, and snow would gradually bevel their edges; and, come the next ice age, the mountains would be reshaped anew.

Imagine that our alien archaeologists visit from a watery world and set up camp, ten thousand years from now, in the middle of the Pacific Ocean. Surely they would find no trace of our long-gone civilization there? They would analyze the water: salty, full of wonderful, bizarre organisms; some of them rather intelligent. And plastic: lots of plastic. Imagine the confusion that would cause. What are these complex hydrocarbons doing in the ocean? How did they get here? Would these future archaeologists conclude that an ancient civilization had put billions of tons of persistent, chemically and biologically impervious molecules into its oceans? Coming from a watery world, they surely would be unable to imagine that a civilization could be so stupid as to poison the stuff of life.

THE GREAT CORN LAWN

> **Nature will condemn artificial manure [chemical fertilizer] as one of the greatest misfortunes to have befallen agriculture and mankind.**
> Sir Albert Howard, British agronomist, 1873–1947

Nitrogen has been a limitation to crop production since the origins of agriculture because, although plants are supremely efficient at grabbing carbon out of the atmosphere (as carbon dioxide), they are unable to grab nitrogen. Nitrogen is a key component of proteins[13] and the fourth most abundant element in all living things—including plants—so this might seem like a significant evolutionary oversight. But the plants are not alone in natural systems. Some plants, notably the legumes, form a symbiosis with nitrogen-fixing bacteria. Most plants acquire their nitrogen fix from bacteria in the soil.

The management of farmland has always had the maintenance of soil fertility, particularly nitrogen, as one of its most essential activities, and, for thousands of years, fertility was maintained with manure from farm animals and the rotation of nitrogen-fixing legumes. The classic "three sisters" production of corn, squash, and beans of Mesoamerica exemplifies this system. It can sustain high levels of productivity without fertilizer because the beans replenish the nitrogen depleted from the soil by the corn and the squash. Corn, beans, and squash also provide a well-balanced diet; the corn and the squash provide a good carbohydrate source, while the beans furnish protein. Ancient agriculture in different parts of the world incorporated peas with wheat in west Asia and soybeans with rice in China to provide a similar balance.

Fritz Haber was awarded a Nobel Prize in 1920 for the invention of an industrial process for fixing nitrogen—which must surely qualify as an evolutionary-level invention. The first major application of the Haber process was not in agriculture, however, but in warfare, and Fritz Haber has a very nasty legacy. Cut off from dwindling supplies of Chilean guano[14] when war broke out in 1914, the German Empire used the Haber process for the production of nitrate for bombs and then for the synthesis of chemical weapons in the trenches. Later, Haber would participate in the manufacture of Zyklon B, the poison used to murder millions in Nazi concentration camps. When the Haber process became the mainstay of the fertilizer industry, however, we conveniently overlooked his contributions to genocide and lobbed a tainted Nobel Prize at him.

The Haber process uses natural gas as a feedstock for the production of ammonia, binding it, at high temperature and pressure, with nitrogen from the air. Thousands of cubic feet of natural gas are consumed to make each ton of fertilizer, but the Haber process is extremely cost-effective because natural gas is plentiful and cheap—so much so that we produce more than one hundred and fifty million tons of nitrogen fertilizer per year.

At first blush, making fertilizer from natural gas seems like a relatively modest proposition, and not at all like a process that could change the world. But the consequences of the Haber process have been profound. Consider that fully one-half of the nitrogen taken up by crops around the world now comes from the Haber process, and that half of the world's food production depends on it.[15] Billions of lives trust to the steady flow of calories from natural gas.

The widespread adoption of synthetic fertilizers in the middle of the twentieth century brought immense changes to agriculture. Coupled with the adoption of diesel-powered tractors replacing horses, agriculture became much more efficient and achieved new economies of scale. Farms were expanded and simplified by eliminating their horse pastures, which were converted into more grain fields, and then by eliminating their cattle pastures and chicken pens (cattle and chickens could be more efficiently raised in CAFOs [concentrated animal feed operations]), and even more grain fields were planted. Agricultural landscapes changed from quaint rural scenes to vast lawns of grains. The American Midwest has become the great corn lawn.

This is how we feed ourselves. This ammonia plant at Ince in England's rural Cheshire produces approximately a million tons of ammonium-based fertilizer per year from natural gas. As Britain's supply of North Sea gas declines, the plant finds itself at the end of a very long pipeline—the last stop from the gas fields of Siberia, five thousand miles to the east. Photograph courtesy of John Hallett.

The consequences of industrial agriculture have been both wonderful and disastrous at the same time. By increasing farm productivity, millions who could not otherwise be fed have been fed. It's hard to see this as a bad thing, as long as the productivity can be sustained. But *sustainable* is the last word I would use for industrial agriculture. Farmers have been forcing huge yields from the land but have not been giving enough back, and soils in many parts of the world have become degraded and eroded. Agriculture has also demanded increasing volumes of water to irrigate these expanded areas of high productivity, and rivers, lakes, and aquifers have been depleted or are under threat.

Diesel engines and synthetic fertilizers dramatically increased the productivity of agriculture, but a farm is no longer a place where crops and animals are raised using the power of the sun, diligently managed soil, and the sweat of a farmer's brow. A farm is now a place where calo-

Cargill corn silos. Most westerners' view of agriculture remains that of quaint rural scenes—farmyards replete with clucking chickens and gamboling newborn lambs. This Cargill grain silo in central Indiana, however, is probably a more representative image. Photograph courtesy of Steve Hallett.

ries are generated from the sun, oil, and natural gas. We are, in a very real way, eating fossil fuels,[16] and, as Milton Friedman put it: "There is no such thing as a free lunch."[17]

DEATH BY OVERPOPULATION

> The power of population is so superior to the power of the earth to produce subsistence for man that premature death must in some shape or other visit the human race.
>
> Thomas Malthus, British scholar[18]

There are many disastrous legacies of the petroleum interval, from global warming to traffic jams, but none is capable of inflicting more environmental devastation and human misery than overpopulation. The size of the world's population is without precedent and has more than tripled in just the last century.[19] This massive population growth is a direct result of the increased food production and energy use that has been made possible by oil and natural gas. The first century of the petroleum interval has made it possible for the world to support a population of seven billion. It is not clear, however, that this population can be supported beyond the petroleum interval.

It's no big secret that the world is filling up with people, so let's not dwell on that; still, it's worth remembering just how recent this growth has been. It's also important to recognize that population growth around the world has been very uneven. Some countries have now managed to arrest population growth, especially in western Europe and Japan. The vast majority of the growth is in poor countries, especially in Asia.

The global population grew over tens of thousands of years to one billion around 1800 and then doubled in a century and a quarter to two billion in 1925. The next two billion people were added in only half a century, resulting in a global population of four billion in 1975. The next increase of two billion occurred in little more than two decades, resulting in a population of over six billion by 2000. Projections put the global population at around nine billion in 2050. More than half of the annual increase in global population is currently accounted for by six countries: India, China, Pakistan, Bangladesh, Nigeria, and the United States.

The migration of people into towns, and the growth of towns into cities, has been going on for hundreds of years, but urbanization also accelerated rapidly in the twentieth century. The urban population was only 2 percent in 1800 and 12 percent in 1900, but more than half the world's population now lives in cities. Nineteen cities contain more than ten million people, and fifteen of them are in poor countries. While the global population is projected to reach about nine billion by 2050, the world's rural population is projected to remain roughly constant, at three billion. Big urban centers are massive resource sinks. They consume enormous amounts of energy and put enormous strain on food production systems and other resources. The problems occurring in the countryside are much harder to see from the city.

It is important to note the difference between a projection and a prediction. Projections are simply extrapolations of historical and current trends. Predictions are more complex and consider factors that may change in the future. If the limits to the growth of the human population were to be relaxed by, say, a new agricultural technology, these projections may be underestimated. Alternatively, if there are new limits to growth, these projections may be overestimated: perhaps grossly.

One of the biggest problems of poverty is the inability to afford adequate healthcare and adequate nutrition. In many poor countries around the world there is little of either of these. Poor healthcare and poor nutrition result in increased infant mortality, and, fearing that their babies will not survive into adulthood, women tend to have more pregnancies in the hopes of increasing their chances of successfully raising a child. These additional pregnancies, of course, make women even more vulnerable and exacerbate the problem sometimes referred to as the fertility trap. In addition, there are cultural biases in many countries toward male children that exacerbate the pregnancy rate. As well, some cultures may have religious beliefs that encourage population growth.

There are a number of diseases that we think of as "plagues of the past," and Westerners fret much less than they used to about the risks of infection. Death in the West is no longer caused primarily by disease, but many plagues of the past are very much plagues of the present in poor countries.

Disparity in health is largely a result of disparity in wealth. Medical care, including preventive healthcare, is efficient in the Western world but extremely inefficient in many poor countries. Ditto the availability of effective waste management, clean water, and adequate nutrition. Poverty and disease are indelibly linked, and while people in the richest nations can expect to live roughly eighty years, people in the poorest nations can expect to die in their midforties. With wealth comes an abundance of clean water and a never-ending supply of uncontaminated food, ambulances, and hospitals with machines that go "bleep." With poverty comes a scarcity of water, perhaps contaminated; and food, often nutritionally inadequate; and death, for the lack of a fifty-cent shot of penicillin.

The most common reaction of the rich to the horrendous health problems of poor countries is to feel terrible and powerless all at the same time. It might be more enlightening to think about a future in which your country is no longer rich and falls increasingly vulnerable to the fertility trap and a lack of adequate healthcare.

Overpopulation is one of the most pressing problems of the world, and yet it has no obvious solution. If birth rates cannot be reduced, then millions will continue to die young, hungry, and from preventable diseases. The most frightening problem of our overblown population, however, is that we may not even be able to maintain the population we already have. The current population is fed by crops grown on soils that are declining in productivity, irrigated by collapsing aquifers, and fertilized with ammonia —which is synthesized from natural gas, which will soon be running out.

Garrett Hardin pointed out that "[n]obody ever dies of overpopulation."[20] Something else is always to blame. When a cyclone strikes Bangladesh and hundreds of thousands die in the ensuing floods, it is the cyclone that is blamed for their deaths, not the overpopulation that led them to live so densely in a flood-prone river delta. When a hurricane lingers over Honduras, rain turns hillsides to mud, and when thousands are killed in landslides in Tegucigalpa, we blame the weather, not the overpopulation that caused millions to be crowded into a denuded mountainous landscape. A million people die of tuberculosis every year. A million die of malaria. Millions more die of cholera, influenza, and measles. Wars break out and people die. In Rwanda, eight hundred thousand people were killed in six weeks by machete during a horrific genocide. Not by overpopulation. Nobody, apparently, ever dies of overpopulation.

People can fall into the trap of blaming the poor of developing countries for the problems of the world since it is poor countries that have these massive, ballooning populations. It is true that overpopulation in poor countries exacerbates the living conditions in those countries, but bear in mind that the average middle-class citizen of a Western nation consumes more than a hundred times the volume of resources of the average poor citizen of a developing nation.[21] Armory Lovins calculated that the average American consumes 250 times the resources of the average Nigerian.[22] This means that the United States has the global impact of seventy-five trillion Nigerians. I'll go one step further: I'll bet American citizens consume more Nigerian resources than Nigerians themselves.[23]

CHAPTER 7

THE VIEW FROM MAUNA LOA

Most of the observed increase in globally averaged temperatures since the mid-twentieth century is very likely[1] due to the observed increase in anthropogenic greenhouse gas concentrations.
Summary Statement, Intergovernmental Panel
on Climate Change Report, 2007[2]

I'm conflicted. It's 1:00 a.m. on the sixteenth of December in northern Indiana,[3] and it's 60 degrees outside (around 15° C). Now, I'm not one for nasty cold winters and feet of snow on the road, and we all had a nice day outside in the warm weather, but it still feels rather

Blue Glacier, Olympic National Park, Washington. The
glacier has shrunk by hundreds of yards since I took this
photo in 1991. Photograph courtesy of Steve Hallett.

197

strange. Indiana seems to be turning into Arkansas, and I can't see how that can possibly be a good thing.

I have vivid memories of making snowmen as a child in northwest England in the early 1970s. The snowmen used to sit in the backyard for weeks, and we often had good snow cover for Christmas. My mum still lives in the same house, and she tells me there hasn't been a "snowman year" for more than a decade. Last year I saw corn growing in a number of fields around Lancaster. When I was a student there in the 1980s, all I remember was barley. That's quite a change. In 2004, I stood in a cornfield near the town of Maramba in northeastern Tanzania with my colleague,

The Tibetan plateau—the roof of the world—has been called the third pole because of the vast amounts of water locked in the region as snow and ice. Five of the world's most important rivers flow off the Tibetan plateau: the Brahmaputra (its tributary, the Tsangpo river, is pictured here), which joins the Ganges and flows into Bangladesh; the Salween and the Mekong, which pass through Southeast Asia; and the Yellow and the Yangtze, which pass the breadth of China. Increased melting on the plateau as a result of global warming threatens the flows of these rivers along which hundreds of millions of people live. Photograph courtesy of Steve Hallett.

Ambonesigwe Mbwaga. It was raining, the field was soggy, and our boots were caked in mud, but the rains had only just arrived to end a drought that had lasted about a week too long. The corn had died during the drought, and the rain seemed to be mocking us as it splashed off the dried-up stalks. The farmer took us through her dried-up field, and we picked half a dozen shriveled cobs. This was the third time in succession that the rains had come so late, she said, and she would not be growing so much corn next year. As I recall, she said, "The weather has changed. We cannot change it back, so we will plant more sorghum next year, but the sorghum is not as good."

We are beginning to face the most giant ecological debt of them all, and this single debt may be large enough to send us into bankruptcy on its own. It is a debt we will be paying for centuries, at least, and a debt that continues to accumulate. We have been able to purchase fossil fuels from the environment at bargain-basement prices because we have paid only a minuscule part of the cost. We have paid to find, refine, and burn fossil fuels, but we have not paid for waste disposal: we have simply dumped our wastes back into the environment as if the planet, especially its atmosphere, was a massive landfill. But the ecological debt is huge, and the planet has called its collection agents.

All the ski slopes in Indiana have been closed: no snow. Polar bears were recently recognized as an endangered species. Islands in the Indian and Pacific Oceans are sinking under the waves. Not to worry: new islands have appeared in Greenland beneath the receding ice.[4] The Alpine glaciers are disappearing. The Sahara and Gobi Deserts are trudging south. Bark beetles moved into the Rockies a few years back. No longer confined by the cold, they are killing millions of trees. Melting ice on the Tibetan plateau is affecting the flows of the great rivers of Asia—the Ganges, the Brahmapurta, the Salween, the Mekong, the Huang He, and the Yangtze—threatening the lives and the livelihoods of millions of people. The Dutch are building floating houses on the polders. The hottest year on record was 2006. The collapse of seabird colonies in Scotland is attributed to decreased fish populations in unusually warm sea water.[5] Thousands died in the European heat wave of 2004. The West Antarctic ice sheet is beginning to fracture. The snows of Kilimanjaro are almost gone.

You probably have your own stories. People are really starting to notice climate change, and the phenomenon has finally been widely accepted as human-caused. Anecdotes are not enough, of course, and some people continue to believe that modern climate change is part of a natural variability. They are nutters, of course, but let's take a closer look. Have we really been able to change the weather of the entire planet?

IT'S A SMALL WORLD AFTER ALL

James Lovelock's *Gaia*[6] took an unusual view of the earth, suggesting that the earth is not just a planet with living things on it but a living planet. Rocks such as limestone and chalk, for example, were once the shells of marine creatures. As they are weathered, they become incorporated into the bodies of living things again and, in many ways like this, living and nonliving things are one and the same. All living things are built from the nutrients of the earth and the gases of the atmosphere and then returned: ashes to ashes, dust to dust.

A great place to look for signs that the planet is truly alive is in the atmosphere. The planet breathes. It exhales carbon dioxide in the northern winter and inhales it in the summer. Its atmosphere has held steady for millions of years, with animals and plants exchanging oxygen for carbon dioxide and the oceans trading water with the land. Whether or not you choose to take Lovelock literally, *Gaia* posits an interesting way to look at things.

The temperature of the biosphere is determined by the amount of light reaching the earth from the sun and the amount of heat bouncing back out into space. Figuring out the energy balance of the planet seems like it should be pretty straightforward, but there are lots of things that can affect both the amount of sunlight received and the amount of heat retained. Volcanoes throw dust into the atmosphere that can block incoming sunlight, causing cooling. Continental drift can shrink or expand landmasses, having multiple effects. Eccentricities in the earth's orbit can increase or decrease the amount of light energy reaching the planet.[7] There is, of course, another factor that has a powerful influence on the earth's energy balance, and that is the chemical composition of the atmosphere. It is here that humans are exerting their disastrous influence.

Incoming sunlight passes through the atmosphere more easily than outgoing heat, which is trapped by a number of atmospheric gases. The atmosphere behaves like the glass in a greenhouse, allowing light in but restricting the escape of heat, and so the earth warms up.[8] A large number of different atmospheric gases contribute to the greenhouse effect, and they do so to differing degrees.[9] Nitrogen and oxygen, which form the majority of the atmosphere, are not greenhouse gases because they do not absorb any of the reflected heat energy. Heat trapping falls to some of the less common gases.

Water vapor is actually the most abundant of the greenhouse gases. Even on a clear day it represents more than half the greenhouse effect, but only a small increase in the concentration of water vapor has been measured in the atmosphere over the last few decades. The effect of water vapor (the invisible gas) and water (as droplets, clouds, mist, etc.) on the climate is complex. Different types of clouds, for example, cause very different patterns of light reflection and absorption. Thick, low clouds reflect incoming light, causing cooling, and thin, high clouds absorb outgoing heat, causing warming. Altered hydrologic cycles may have a significant impact on climate, but it is extremely difficult to predict the relative outcomes of the various heating and cooling effects. (Which, I suppose, all goes to show that we've looked at clouds from all sides, but we still don't know them at all.[10])

Methane (CH_4) is a gas of great significance both as a major fossil fuel (natural gas) and as a major greenhouse gas. The atmospheric concentration of methane began to rise with the advent of agriculture thousands of years ago, particularly as a result of an increased number of belching and farting cattle and the cultivation of paddy rice in east Asia.[11] Methane concentrations have increased from 700 ppb (parts per billion) to 1,750 ppb over the last 250 years, as estimated from ice cores. Methane is a particularly scary greenhouse gas. Its concentration in the atmosphere is much lower than that of carbon dioxide, but it has more than twenty times the ability to absorb heat.

A large number of minor contributors to the greenhouse effect include nitrous oxide released from fertilized agricultural land and the synthetic chlorofluorocarbons that are also responsible for the destruction of the stratospheric ozone layer, but the most important greenhouse gas is carbon dioxide.

Carbon dioxide (CO_2) is numerically less important than water vapor in the overall greenhouse effect, but is the second most abundant greenhouse gas in the atmosphere. Carbon dioxide has undergone the biggest human-caused changes and is therefore the principal greenhouse gas of concern. Concentrations of carbon dioxide have increased from roughly 280 ppm (parts per million) to 390 ppm in the last century and a half—an astonishing increase of 40 percent. Take a moment to grasp the enormity of the earth's atmosphere[12] and then consider the effort that has gone into increasing the concentration of carbon dioxide throughout that massive volume of air.

The concentration of carbon dioxide in the atmosphere can be increased in two ways: either more can be released or less can be removed. The constant flux of carbon among the land, sea, and atmosphere was in balance for millions of years, but in our brief tenure on the planet humans have decreased the amount locked up in the land by deforestation and increased the amount released directly into the atmosphere by the combustion of fossil fuels. Deforestation is estimated to be decreasing sequestration by about 1.6 gigatons of carbon per year. A further 5.5 gigatons of carbon are released each year by burning fossil fuels.[13]

Our first inkling that humans were increasing the concentration of greenhouse gases in the atmosphere, that this would cause global warming, and that the global climate would change, came in the 1950s when scientist Charles Keeling began his meticulous experiments at the desolate peak of Mauna Loa, Hawaii, in the middle of the Pacific Ocean. He recorded the first steady but ominous increases in the atmospheric concentration of carbon dioxide. Those same measurements continue to this day, and the gradual enrichment of carbon dioxide in the atmosphere continues unabated. The view from Mauna Loa is not good.

THRESHOLDS AND FEEDBACKS

The basic global warming story is straightforward: the concentration of carbon dioxide and other greenhouse gases in the atmosphere increases, more heat is trapped in the troposphere, and the planet gets warmer. There is no great confusion here. As a result of this warming there are various changes that should be expected, such as more rapid evaporation from water bodies, faster melting of ice, the modification of weather patterns, and the expansion of the oceans. These changes have their own knock-on effects, however, and so predicting the detailed outcomes of global warming is extremely difficult. By increasing the concentration of greenhouse gases in the atmosphere, we have set in motion a palette of changes that we can predict only with uncertainty and over which we have virtually no control.

A feedback is a cause-and-effect scenario. A negative feedback is like a thermostat: the effect reacts to reduce the cause and therefore keeps the system in equilibrium. An increase in the temperature of your home flicks on the air conditioner, resulting in cooling. Once your house is cool, the air conditioner switches off, and so the temperature inside remains comfortable.

A positive feedback response has the opposite effect. Here, two factors reinforce each other in a vicious cycle. Positive feedbacks take systems out of balance, cause instability, and can be disastrous. Imagine an increase in the temperature of your home switching on the heating instead of the air conditioner. There are a number of climate systems that have the potential to be set into positive feedback by global warming, and these are particularly scary.[14]

The first dangerous feedback event is already under way in earnest in the Arctic, where sea ice is melting. Since water is darker in color[15] than ice, it absorbs more sunlight than ice. Consequently, the disappearance of ice sheets results in warming, which, of course, causes more ice to melt. Melting begets warming, and warming begets melting.

Another Arctic feedback involves the gargantuan volumes of methane trapped beneath the permafrost that may be released as the permafrost thaws, turning global warming into a very rapid, very scary global cookout. This seems improbable, but a group of Norwegian scientists believes that a sudden methane hydrate release caused a mysterious mass extinction event fifty-five million years ago.[16]

On a local scale, warming can interact dangerously with careless land use, particularly overgrazing or deforestation. There is significant concern that the logging of the Amazon rain forest may result in drier weather throughout Amazonia because less water evaporates from deforested land than transpires from rain forest trees. The ensuing drier weather may put stress on the rest of the forest, closing the feedback loop, so even the areas of forest that are not logged may be threatened. It seems beyond the imagination that the destruction of the Amazon rain forest could come about as a result of global warming and partial logging, but I guess that depends, somewhat, on the scope of your imagination. Donald Hughes suggests that similar deforestation by the ancient civilizations of west Asia, Egypt, and the Mediterranean may have played a significant role in the creation of the deserts of the Middle East and North Africa, including the mighty Sahara.[17] Meanwhile, overgrazing of marginal lands in China and Africa is accelerating the expansion of the Gobi and Sahara Deserts still more.

A last, rapid climate change feedback involves the Atlantic Ocean circulation. Milan, Italy, is at the same latitude as Montreal, Canada, but is much warmer because the Gulf Stream brings warm water into the North Atlantic from the tropics. The heat from the Gulf Stream modifies the climate of Europe, bringing warm, moist air. As the warmed water of the Atlantic evaporates, it becomes colder and saltier—and therefore denser—so it sinks and circulates back to the south at depth. The cycling of the Gulf Stream in the North Atlantic is called a thermohaline pump—a circulating pump driven by changes in temperature and salt concentration.

The fear that ocean circulation may be affected as a result of freshwater influx and increased ocean temperatures has received considerable media attention from former vice president Al Gore's book *An Inconvenient Truth*.[18] Scientists believe that the North Atlantic thermohaline pump can be "disconnected" by significant changes in ocean temperature and salinity and that changes such as these may have been involved in the initiation and termination of ice ages in the past. If such a disconnection of the thermohaline pump were to occur, it would not be warming that would concern Europeans but the onset of the next ice age. Support for this theory is mixed, and a complete shutdown of the thermohaline pump thankfully seems reasonably unlikely in the next few decades.

These dangerous climate feedbacks will be triggered as carbon dioxide concentrations and temperature increases reach threshold levels, but estimating those thresholds is little more than educated guesswork.[19] The scientific community has adopted a benchmark threshold of 400 ppm atmospheric carbon dioxide, which, it is generally agreed, would make a dangerous temperature increase of two degrees inevitable. We are already missing this target. The only question is whether or not this threshold is a good prediction for the point at which our capacity to mitigate global warming basically ends.

The importance of feedbacks in climate systems cannot be overstated because they contradict the assumption that global climate change will be slow and gradual. It may turn out to be no such thing. Certain threshold changes in temperature may trigger sudden feedback events, and climate change is likely to combine an overall pattern of gradual warming and gradual sea level rise, but it may also be punctuated by other disruptive changes that occur much more rapidly.

THE LONG-RANGE WEATHER FORECAST

The long-term weather forecast is generally for higher mean temperatures, more extreme hot days, and fewer extreme cold days, with the biggest temperature changes occurring at the poles and the smallest temperature changes in the tropics.

Rainfall patterns are expected to change in many ways, and predicting rainfall changes is more difficult than predicting temperature changes. Many land areas are likely to experience increased rainfall because of increased rates of evaporation from the oceans. This will not be the case in the semiarid tropics, however, where rainfall will probably decrease. At midlatitudes, increased precipitation may be quite seasonal, increasing in winter and decreasing in summer. The Hadley Center at the UK Meteorological Office predicts rainfall in the British Isles to increase in the winter and decrease in the summer.[20]

Hurricanes and cyclones have claimed much media attention because they are among the most dramatic potential consequences of global warming, and global warming may result in an increased frequency or intensity of these events, although the data and conclusions on this subject are mixed.[21] The power of hurricanes and cyclones is determined by the distribution of warm water in the oceans, and since both phenomena develop only in surface water warmer than about 80 degrees (26.5° C), this condition is likely to be met much more often in the future.

There will probably be many other climatological outcomes of global warming. Disturbing the movement of air and water around the troposphere will cause unexpected changes. Some of these changes may serve to minimize the worst impacts, whereas others may create problems we have not yet even considered.

Various components of the global climate have considerable momentum. Even if carbon dioxide emissions are reduced in the next few decades, the atmospheric concentration of carbon dioxide will not stabilize for at least a century. As a result, the global temperature will not stabilize for at least two centuries. From the carbon dioxide that we have already released into the atmosphere, sea levels will now continue to rise for at least a millennium. Melting ice currently contributes the most to rising sea levels, but over the next centuries, the major component will be thermal expansion, as the oceans simply enlarge and then spill onto the land as they warm.

We have set in motion a sequence of events that we can no longer control and the outcomes of which we can barely predict. Meanwhile, the weather will continue to change in a range of predictable and unpredictable ways, and the earth will bear the legacies of the petroleum interval for a thousand years.

IMPACTS ON THE LANDSCAPE

Major impacts on the landscape are likely to occur as a result of global warming, including rising sea levels, expanding deserts, and melting ice caps. Glaciers all over the world are retreating at dramatic speeds; by the end of this century, there will be virtually no glaciers at all in the Alps. As Al Gore has quipped: "Glacier National Park will soon need to be renamed 'The Park Formerly Known as Glacier.'"[22] Who says he has no sense of humor?

The consensus that the land-based ice caps of Antarctica and Greenland would melt only very slowly is beginning to splinter as fast as the ice caps themselves. Glacial "earthquakes" can be detected in the Greenland ice cap as it melts and shifts more rapidly, and its glaciers are calving (large pieces are breaking off) twice as fast as was expected. Scientists studying the melting of the Greenland ice are beginning to think that a rise in sea levels by feet rather than inches may occur in the next few decades. Meanwhile, on Greenland's southwest coast, where once was only pasture, farmers have been planting barley!

Some of the world's most important ecosystems are recognizable as landscape features because plant communities are adapted to their own particular temperature regimes and rainfall patterns. The deciduous forests are creeping farther north into the boreal zone, and the boreal forests are migrating into the tundra. Wildlife that relies on boreal and tundra ecosystems is under threat. As the planet warms, many other ecosystem changes are to be expected, such as the timing of various life-cycle events like flowering, bird migrations, breeding dates, insect emergence dates, and the encroachment of invasive pests and weeds. Farther south we are seeing a general increase in the ranges of subtropical grasslands, scrublands, and deserts. Many of the dry environments of the world are likely to get even drier—and hotter—and may suffer changes such as increased fire frequency.

Major changes are expected in the oceans, including sea level rise, water temperature increases, and altered circulation patterns. Seawater is also becoming more acidic as a result of absorbing increasing amounts of carbon dioxide, and some marine species may struggle to adapt to this change.[23] Coral reefs around the world have been suffering from bleaching in the last two decades, and scientists are now convinced that this is due to increased water temperatures. The bleaching is due to the loss of photosynthesizing microbes (zooxanthellae, affectionately known as "zooks"), with which many corals form a symbiosis. When water temperatures increase, the corals expel their zook symbionts and turn white. Large areas of reef have already been lost in this way.[24]

Rising sea levels are having multiple impacts on estuarine systems, salt marshes, and mangrove swamps; and they are causing significant shoreline erosion during storms, which now deliver larger wave impacts farther inland. Although some coastal ecosystems may be able to adapt in time, others will undoubtedly be damaged. Mangrove swamps, in particular, may be threatened since they are located in the shallow interface between freshwater and salt water and may not have the capacity to "creep upstream" as sea levels rise. In some areas, mangroves are likely to be extirpated and wetland ecosystems lost. The effects of global climate change on ecosystems are legion, and it seems that a new report hits the news almost every day.

THE HUMAN LANDSCAPE

> It has been pointed out many times that we are engaged in a titanic global experiment. The further it proceeds, the clearer the picture should become. At age seventy-one, I'm unlikely to be around when it resolves to everyone's satisfaction—or dissatisfaction. Many of you may be, and a lot of your descendants undoubtedly will be. Good luck to you and them.
>
> James E. Hansen, head of NASA Institute
> for Space Studies and adjunct professor,
> Earth and Atmospheric Science Department,
> Columbia University

Our modern civilization is a ridiculously recent thing. It feels old and stable, but it has never been tested with environmental change on a planetary scale. Most people seem to view the disintegration of society as an impossible, even laughable, scenario. It has, however, been the most common outcome of societies to date. Our history has been written in a world with a stable climate, but our future will be written during times of change. The adjustment will be difficult. When times change, simple societies can break camp and move. It's going to be hard to break a camp of twenty million people.

Discussions of the impacts of global climate change often begin with sea level rise, perhaps largely as a result of Al Gore's *An Inconvenient Truth*, in which he presents some truly disturbing models for the drowning of parts of cities such as New York City and San Francisco. The actual rate of sea level rise is hard to predict, but we do know that it is irreversible and will afflict our societies for at least a millennium. By the end of the millennium, Al's predictions will seem trivial.

A sea level rise of one meter (about forty inches) will be enough to flood more than 10 percent of Bangladesh: the 10 percent occupied by much of its population. The same sea level rise will make the Pacific island nation of Tuvalu essentially uninhabitable; plans for the evacuation of its population are already under way. Next up might be the Bahamas (the beaches will get narrower with less space to put down your towel) and other low-lying island nations. Even small island nations with land at high elevations tend to have their major cities beside the sea, and even if they do not officially sink below sea level, they become increasingly vulnerable to tsunamis and storms. Much of Polynesia and Micronesia, home to a rich diversity of cultures and histories, is in great peril. By the end of the millennium, many societies will have ceased to exist. Since many of them are thousands of years old, we tend to assume that the locations of our cities will be viable in the long term—but we no longer live in a static world.

The biggest impact on the lives of people, however, will not come from the direct effect of sea level rise, flooding rivers, or more violent storms on our towns and cities, but rather will occur in our agricultural regions. Many an impact will be dramatic, but even the moderate ones felt everywhere will be troublesome. Reduced rainfall is forecast for a number of regions that are already suffering water scarcity, and the farmers of these regions will struggle the most.

Over the last fifty years, growing seasons have lengthened by at least a few days in most of the Northern Hemisphere and by more than two weeks at high latitudes.[25] Canadian, Russian, and Scandinavian farmers are probably licking their chops expecting longer, warmer growing seasons with less risk of drought. Even northern farmers will have to make significant adaptations, however, such as to the shifting patterns of pests and diseases.

The farmers of eastern Canada may be able to switch to longer-season varieties of soybeans and corn, such as those currently grown in the midwestern United States, but midwestern farmers may not be happy if they need to switch from growing corn and soybeans to growing cotton. For many farmers, it may be possible to modify planting dates, harvest dates, and production practices, but others, especially those at more southerly latitudes, will see growing conditions worsen, often dramatically.

Decreased rainfall and the possible increased prevalence and intensity of El Niño events may make agriculture much more difficult in Australia, a country that has suffered drought conditions for most of the last decade already. Similar problems are coming to the Great Plains of the United States, where massive acreages of irrigated corn may struggle as the Ogallala aquifer shrinks, fertilizers become more expensive, and the climate brings more heat and less rain. We might see more prairie and more cowboys. Not to worry, that's all part of the American dream, and we can sit around campfires under the stars singing yippee-ay-aye.

The biggest problems for agriculture, however, will undoubtedly be seen in the semiarid tropics. In some areas, crops are already grown at the very limits of their temperature tolerance,[26] and decreased rainfall, where that occurs, may make many areas increasingly unsuitable for cultivation. The combined impacts of decreased rainfall and increased rates of evapotranspiration[27] will be devastating. Since many areas are already suffering from chronic food shortages and periodic famines, increased malnutrition and starving should be expected. Many of these areas will be in Africa, on the southern fringes of the Sahara Desert. Other regions of major concern are the Indian subcontinent and the Middle East.

Two major breadbaskets are under threat in China. The erosion-plagued Loess Plateau and the North China Plain are both projected to see significantly reduced rainfall. The North China Plain is already beginning to struggle from both the loss and degradation of farmland and the depletion of freshwater aquifers in a region that is likely to get drier still.

MITIGATE, ADAPT, OR SUFFER

A considerable range of possible outcomes is encompassed by the various climate change predictions that have been made. Carbon dioxide concentrations may increase by a further 20 percent by the end of the century, or they may more than double. The resulting temperature increases may be a modest additional half a degree or a whopping six degrees—or even more. The outcomes predicted by the most modest temperature increases are bad; the worst-case scenarios are horrifying. What makes prediction difficult is the fact that many changes may not be gradual but decidedly abrupt.

The awareness of climate change has increased over the last few years, and this has been quite inspirational, with people all over the world calling for action. But what, really, do people think can be done? The president of the American Association for the Advancement of Science, John Holdren, suggested that "[w]e basically have three choices: mitigation, adaptation, and suffering. We're going to do some of each. The more mitigation we do, the less adaptation will be required and the less suffering there will be."[28] I'm afraid we have less chance at mitigating global climate change than we are encouraged to believe, and we will have to adapt to a series of unavoidable changes. In many cases we will not be able to adapt, and suffering is inevitable.

Global climate change will be the enduring legacy of the petroleum interval. Deforestation has reduced the amount of carbon dioxide removed from the atmosphere, and our fossil fuel feeding frenzy has returned gigatons more that had been locked away millions of years ago. The worst impacts have come in the last century as the global population has tripled and our emissions have skyrocketed. The petroleum interval is entering its second phase, and the end of fossil fuels is in sight, but the passing of the petroleum interval will not mark the passing of global warming. Our disastrous two-hundred-year glitch may tip the planet into an extended tropical era. Our great geologic inheritance, with which we opened our account in the fossil fuels savings bank, could have been invested—but it was simply spent. The enduring legacy of this remarkable historical era may not, as we might have hoped, be the enduring society that ended conflict and hardship but rather the biggest ecological debt ever created.

Global climate change is already in full swing, and the impacts have already begun. More—and worse—will be coming around for scores of generations of our descendants. Global climate change will affect many of our activities as we struggle with the end of the petroleum interval and will continue to drag us down as we attempt to recover. We tend to speak of global climate change as some future that must be avoided. This is not the case. It is one of the serious here-and-now problems that sets us on a collision course with an uncertain future.

PART III

THE WEALTH OF NATIONS

T he passengers and ship were the stuff of legend: leaders of industry and commerce aboard the largest and most luxurious ship ever built. The unsinkable *Titanic* began her maiden voyage from Southampton, bound for New York, on April 10, 1912.

At 11:30 p.m. on the fourth night, seamen Fleet and Lee were freezing in the lookout's cage fifty feet above the fo'c's'le (forecastle), peering into the icy dark. It might have helped if the binoculars had been brought along, but, in the last of a hundred fatal errors, they had been left behind in Southampton. Fleet stared into the distance and then instinctively pulled the alarm bell. Lee reached for the telephone.

"Iceberg—right ahead!"[1]

First Officer Murdoch threw the ship hard-a-starboard and full-astern. But, as the iceberg loomed into full view, the ship would not turn. A smaller or slower ship might have turned, but not the *Titanic*. The crew tried frantically, and in the last agonizing seconds before impact the ship began to veer away. Perhaps the momentary drama would end in nothing more than a near miss? No: the ship scraped along the edge of the iceberg, and her hull was pierced below water.

The *Titanic* foundered in the icy North Atlantic for hours as she slowly filled with water. The bow of the ship began to sink. People scrambled to the stern as it lifted high into the air, and then the great ship plunged to the bottom of the ocean. The next morning the liner

Carpathia rescued seven hundred survivors from their lifeboats, but more than fifteen hundred had perished.

The most important lessons from the *Titanic* are not related to maritime navigation or the avoidance of shipwrecks. Ship happens, after all. The *Titanic* was important for the lessons we can learn about culture and human nature in the face of risk and disaster.

First of all, the probability of being saved from the *Titanic* was not a matter of random assignment, and death was not democratic. First-class passengers were given first priority in the lifeboats, many of which drifted away only partially full. Selfishness and fear kept the lifeboats at a distance from the masses crying for help as they died in the water. Third-class passengers were much more likely to lose their lives, as wealth and power played their winning hand even on a sinking ship in the middle of the North Atlantic.

The *Titanic* disaster was completely avoidable. Any one of a number of things might have prevented the disaster; the iceberg itself was so nearly avoided at the last moment that perhaps only a few more feet would have made all the difference. A smaller hole in the hull might not have sunk the ship. A little less speed? More lifeboats (there was plenty of time to fill them before the ship sank)? Perhaps just those damned binoculars would have made all the difference.

In another sense, however, the disaster was completely inevitable. Cultural factors played an important part, and it is more than simple irony that the ship was sailing from England (a fading power) to the United States (a rising power) in the early years of the petroleum interval. The ship's designers, owners, and even its captain were guilty of complacency and overblown pride.[2] Repeated warnings went unheeded and a disastrous chain of events took place. The whole endeavor was a demonstration of wealth and power: the fastest, biggest, most luxurious ship afloat, and yet, out of arrogance, the flood control design was inadequate and lifeboats were insufficient. The ship was traveling too quickly following a particularly cold winter, and icebergs should have been expected. Not enough lookouts were posted. The *Titanic* represented a whole culture that thought it was unsinkable.

So are we on a planetary *Titanic*? Have we miscalculated the environment? Do we have too much momentum? Are we too proud of our world to recognize that it may be vulnerable?

Pick up the binoculars, and you'll see the iceberg—right ahead.

CHAPTER 8

COLLISION COURSE

THE HARSH LIGHT OF MORNING

> Industrial societies have been flourishing for
> roughly 150 years now, using fossil energy
> resources to build far-flung trade empires, to fuel
> the invention of spectacular new technologies, and
> to fund a way of life that is opulent and fast-paced.
> It is as if part of the human race has been given a
> sudden windfall of wealth and decided to spend
> that wealth by throwing an extravagant party. But
> soon the party will be fading into memory—not
> because anyone decided to heed the voice of mod-
> eration, but because the wine and food are gone
> and the harsh light of morning has come.
>
> Richard Heinberg, *The Party's Over:
> Oil, War, and the Fate of Industrial Societies*[1]

We face a whole range of problems in the modern world, but
the biggest one is that all these problems are coming
together on a collision course. This should be no surprise: they are all
symptoms of the same oil-induced disease.[2] Environmentalists seem to
think of oil depletion as a minor issue. First, they are unlikely to have
read much about oil and its associated industries. Their reaction might

be "Well, good. Running out of oil might finally reduce carbon dioxide emissions." I think they underestimate the consequences. Peak oil pessimists tend to think of global warming as a secondary issue. They see a worldwide economic collapse as a result of oil depletion and figure "What could possibly be worse than that?"

The fuses attached to each colliding factor have been lit, and the fireworks will explode at various times over the coming decades. The opening salvos have already been heard—heatwaves and extended droughts, gas price spikes, crumbling ice sheets and disappearing glaciers, food riots, and an unexpected economic downturn—but this is just the warm-up.

As the global economy staggers out of one beating, it will stumble into the next, and the coming decades will be characterized by a sequence of economic slumps. Each slump will seem to be the nadir, but the floor of the economy will keep sinking away until the fundamental problems of energy availability, food production, water supply, and population control are sufficiently well corrected. We are entering a period of global economic contraction: the great recession.

Hurricane Katrina blew a huge sign of global vulnerability ashore in New Orleans on August 29, 2005. It was a big storm that caused extensive damage and loss of life; but much more than that, it showed how poorly a rich country can respond to a catastrophic disaster.

My family took a vacation to New Orleans earlier that month. We hung out in the French Quarter, took a steamboat ride on the Mississippi, strolled down Bourbon Street, quaffed a few hurricanes (!), and bought trinkets on Canal Street. As we were returning home to Indiana, Hurricane Katrina was forming over the Bahamas. It rounded the Florida Keys, gathered strength in the warm—too warm—waters of the Gulf of Mexico, and swept past the city. The levees broke and the city flooded.

Maybe Katrina was a forewarning of catastrophes to come as a result of global warming, but that's not really my point here. The take-home message from Katrina—not a message we seem to have heard—was that even a great, modern American city can dramatically descend into chaos.

The next day, as the storm receded and the city stood in oily water, everything began to go wrong, and a terrible storm became a civic crisis. People were trapped in their attics as the bloated bodies of their neighbors floated through the streets. By nightfall, gangs began to roam the streets as cops abandoned their posts. Hospital workers deserted their patients. As the response failed, the city became violent and lawless. The next day shots were fired at the (inadequate number of) rescue helicopters that plucked desperate people from their rooftops.

New Orleans had become one of the most corrupt cities in the country, and government failed at all levels. The Federal Emergency Management Agency (FEMA) had been neglected by the Bush administration, and when talented, levelheaded people were needed, panic reigned. At one ridiculous moment we watched a top official on CNN saying, "There are no people at the convention center," even as we watched literally thousands of people on our television screens fighting for their lives at that same convention center. First, Bush was congratulating FEMA director Michael Brown with the famous "Brownie, you're doin' a heck of a job." Next, the administration was running for cover.

New Orleans had always been a disaster waiting to happen. There was the ever-present chance of a powerful hurricane, and many doubted that the levees would hold. Ecologists had warned for years that the degradation of the southern coastline had compromised its ability to slow down advancing storms. New Orleans was also a disaster waiting to happen on a social level. It was a city deeply divided by race and wealth, a city of apparent opportunity but also a pervasive poverty trap. New Orleans was home to a local government and local services, especially the police force, which were known for inefficiency and corruption.

And so it happened. An extreme weather event struck a poorly governed population living in a precarious environment that had been degraded. The area was overpopulated, leading many people to live in vulnerable areas, and the society was deeply divided by race and wealth:

the perfect storm. The world watched as the most powerful nation on the planet panicked, fumbled, and dropped the ball.

By the harsh light of morning, many parts of the world might look something like this.

DISRUPTION IN SUPPLY

There is a high level of optimism that new technologies will extricate us from our oil addiction. I do not doubt that new technologies will come—eventually—but that is not the crux of the issue. The crux of the issue is whether or not they will come in time. Any lag in the replacement of oil with other sources of energy will put our global economy in jeopardy. The juggernaught of civilization set in motion by the agrarian revolution and accelerated through the Industrial Revolution cannot be slowed or stopped. But, if its thirst for energy cannot be slaked, neither can it be maintained.

The powerful economies of the Western world have climbed the ladder of development from agrarian economies through industrial and manufacturing economies to economies dominated by services and technology. Having reached the top of the ladder, they have been able to invest significant resources into social welfare systems and environmental stewardship. They have done this with democratic systems of government and regulatory systems that have helped to protect, at least in part, their environments. Other countries are on different rungs on the ladder of development; the poorest countries appear unable even to climb beyond the first rung. The poor countries of Southeast Asia and South America are nervously climbing up the bottom half of the ladder. China and India are climbing rapidly but have not yet reached the top and have not yet been able to invest back into environmental protection.[3]

This view of development supposes that economies can be stimulated to a certain point from which they will have the momentum to continue the climb to the top of the ladder on their own—like a space-ship attaining escape velocity from the earth's gravity. If sufficient propulsion is supplied, the spaceship will have enough momentum to head out into space, and, once in space, it can glide along, silently, on small jets. This was the model of economic growth for the Western world, but the feat has not been repeated of late.

Many economists seem to think that the same type of economic momentum will carry us through the coming energy transition. They see a shining future of abundant, nonpolluting renewable energy. Having attained escape velocity and developed a technologically advanced society, they now expect that more technologies will arrive, on demand, to solve whatever supply problems we might have. There is an engineering solution to every environmental problem, right?

Dramatic economic transformations do occur. Take cars, for example. From being a mere curiosity—even laughable "horseless carriages" at the turn of the twentieth century—they became commonplace in little more than a decade, despite the immense amount of retooling effort that was required. So why can't such a huge retooling effort occur now, to lead us into, say, a new nuclear-hydrogen economy?

I think there is a big difference. At the time of Henry Ford and the emergence of the automobile, rapid change represented rapid progress. Back then, horses were replaced by cars because they were much more efficient, and the economy boomed because of it. It was an era in which a massive and rapidly growing new energy capability had been unleashed. We are in a very different position now: we need to replace cars with other types of transportation and gas stations with other types of refueling stations. We are facing an era of regress, rather than progress, and an era of shrinking energy availability, rather than growing, and the response must be slower. When folks make a lifestyle change, they generally want to trade up from a compact to a midsize. There is little enthusiasm for trading down. Before big changes can be made, I think we first have to pass through a protracted recession. Only once we have done this—when the current models are no longer usable—will we be able to make progress with new cars and new refueling stations that use new sources of energy.

There is a problem of asset inertia at many levels. The current energy model has required massive capital investments to explore, discover, produce, refine, and distribute oil, and these assets are difficult to let go of. Although BP touts "beyond petroleum" to promote an eco-friendly image, it is actually extremely difficult for such a company to switch from oil to, say, wind or biofuels. Asset inertia will continue to delay transitions from oil to energy alternatives, and the transition cannot happen proactively. Alternatives will come online only when they are not alternatives at all, but the only option.

Numerous problems have emerged as our swollen population has depleted essential resources and polluted the environment, but the rot will set in most disastrously as we begin to run out of fossil fuels and the mad scramble for alternatives begins. Perhaps this mad scramble has already begun. The United States is busily securing Middle Eastern oil with its disastrous adventure in Iraq; Brazil is planting sugarcane on the back forty of the Amazon ranch; and China is squabbling over Sudan and Iran, building the huge Three Gorges hydroelectric project across the Yangtze, and digging out coal, coal, and more coal.

The price of energy will climb even as its availability falls, and the immediate responses will create their own disastrous problems. The world's capacity for generating energy from nuclear power and renewable sources is extremely small, and there is simply no way for the world to maintain its current energy supply from these sources without disruption. The size of the infrastructure adjustments required is too large and will be especially daunting during a long recession. The only possible conclusion is that the nations of the world, as they descend into recession, will suffer an epic disruption in supply. They will attempt to minimize this disruption with whatever sources of energy they can get their hands on. For most, this will be coal.

The end of the petroleum interval may seem like a good thing to some people, seeing it as finally heralding the dawn of a new era of renewable energy. They perhaps view reduced oil consumption as a good thing, expecting reduced carbon emissions. But it is this period of transition that frightens me. It will not be a smooth transition from the bad old days into an environmentally conscious future. Rather, it will be a terribly dangerous and uncomfortable transition scarred by many serious impacts stemming from a disruption in the supply of energy.

I'm not sure people will easily recognize the energy crisis as a fundamental force. They will experience various struggles in different industries and periodic economic failures, but the realization that the root cause is an energy shortage will come only when we are well past peak and into the decline.

Oil cost less than $20 per barrel[4] until the end of the 1990s. Even as recently as 2004 we thought of $40 per barrel as a high oil price, and at that price it was inconceivable that significant efforts would go into the production of alternatives. We quickly got used to the idea of a reasonable oil price being at least $70 per barrel in 2007, and since then, the price of oil has become extremely volatile, but it continues to climb. As oil prices pass the $200 per barrel mark, there will be money to be made from producing the crappiest stuff the ground has to offer. I can't see this doing much to delay the inevitable. Frantic investments will certainly flow, but prices will continue to rise.

The oil business will do very well for a few years on revenues from high oil prices, but soon enough, as the oil begins to disappear, the oil companies will lose their core business. This will likely catalyze another round of mergers. When BP merges with Shell, and ExxonMobil merges with Conoco Phillips, you should take it as a sign. When the US Congress, in desperation at the lack of oil, approves a large program to start uprooting the Rockies to dig out the oil shales, you'll recognize that we are in major trouble.

A prolonged global recession will result from high prices and fuel shortfalls and will cause economic stagnation with high inflation. The economic decline will reduce the demand for oil, which will cause prices to fluctuate violently, and repeated contractions will occur, deepening and lengthening the recession. The key word for the coming decades will be *stagflation*, an economic term conflating *stag*nation and in*flation*. In order to combat stagnation, economists generally call for the releasing of credit and the injection of liquidity into markets to make them grow. With a pervasive energy crunch and lack of resources, however, this growth will be unattainable. In order to combat inflation, economists generally call for fiscal restraint and control over economic growth to avoid the increase in commodity prices. But it will be impossible to control the costs of energy, and commodity prices will continue to climb as a result.

Stagflation cannot be cured by normal market forces when the supply of an essential resource is depleted. Stagflation will be curbed only when a substitute is put in place. Since replacements for the current energy model and other resources are not in place, the release of stagflation will come from decreased demand—a global contraction. Only when replacement technologies are in place can the global economy finally recover.

James Howard Kunstler coined the term *the long emergency*[5] for his vision of the troubles afoot at the end of the oil era, and I think he has it just about right. The next great economic downturn will be a long, stifling contraction, and it will take decades for the global economy to come out on the other side. When it does, many things will look very different.

Previous depressions and market collapses have all begun with a main panic followed by mild recoveries and further panics. On the whole, however, the economic damage has been done within a matter of a few months, and the recovery has never taken more than a few years. But these previous shocks were based primarily on irrational investments caused by a rapid market overcorrection. The Great Depression, for example, corrected a period of irrational exuberance in the early days of a US economic expansion. The dot-com debacle of the 1990s corrected a period of irrational investment in all things mysteriously technological. The "credit crunch" of 2008 leading to the current recession was largely the correction of thoughtless lending and borrowing in a housing market that was supposed to somehow miraculously expand forever (even though most of the houses concerned were made of matchsticks, chipboard, and staples). The current recession was exacerbated by the government's slow realization that the world's megabanks and megainsurers were in on the scam.

The coming crisis will be much more severe and protracted because it will require more than the simple removal of a few unrealistic companies and the restoration of investor confidence. It will require a significant overhaul of societies at fundamental levels. Economies will rebound from one crash, only to fall into the next. More than once we may think the economy has bottomed out, only to watch it fall further as the gravity of the situation gradually sinks in. As the shockwaves of oil depletion begin to settle, more will come from the depletion of natural gas and then coal. The contraction of the global economy, stemming from a fundamental failure and long-term decline in its energy sectors, will continue for decades.

SHOCK AND AFTERSHOCKS

The immediate shocks to the global economy will come from industries that are direct consumers of oil.[6] The airlines are already in big trouble; more will go out of business, and the mergers among the survivors will continue. Flights will become increasingly expensive. The automobile industry will also be sent through repeated paroxysms as people trade in their gas guzzlers for smaller models. Cars will get smaller and less powerful but more expensive. But the energy crisis will cause inflationary pressures to spread into all sectors of the global economy, causing aftershocks. All products and services are either directly or indirectly affected by energy prices.

One of the most pervasive aftershocks will be in the price of food, which is susceptible to a number of dangerous trends. Food production, especially highly productive Western agriculture, is dependent on the consumption of large volumes of diesel for land management and distribution systems, and on natural gas for fertilizer. As the costs of diesel and fertilizer increase, so will the price of food. The price will increase further only if we insist on the folly of using agricultural land to grow fuel.

The threats to agriculture are broad and include land degradation and the loss of water for irrigation. Much of this degradation, of course, is the direct result of unsustainable farming practices that have become the norm in the era of cheap fuel and fertilizer. Global warming is also taking a bite out of some agricultural areas, bringing more food insecurity. Food production is further jeopardized by the continued collapse of ocean fisheries.

Expensive corn makes for expensive chickens, and expensive chicken makes for expensive chicken vindaloo. All sectors of the food industry will feel the tremors. Meanwhile, as the global population continues to climb, the demand for food will continue to grow, especially in Asia.

It's wonderful that millions of people in China can now afford a healthier, higher-protein diet, but chicken, pork, and beef production uses land much less efficiently than wheat and rice production—yet another upward pressure on food prices. Add to this the fact that the world is rapidly losing agricultural land. The most obvious damage to the global economy will come from transportation failures, but the greatest human suffering will come from increases in the cost of food. While the average American family may spend only a tenth of its household budget on food, food is the primary expenditure of billions around the world.

Much of the pressure on food production around the world is a direct consequence of agricultural policies in the West. While touting free trade, the West goes to great lengths to prop up its farming sector, and European and American farmers find themselves in the embarrassing situation of getting a large part of their income directly from the government. This enables them to make a living selling agricultural products for less than it actually costs to produce them. It also enables agribusinesses to make very tidy profits processing supercheap agricultural commodities. It also makes the fattening of animals in CAFOs (concentrated animal feed operations) much more cost-effective than raising them in a sustainable and ethical way. Crops are produced at low financial cost but at an exorbitant environmental cost.

The biggest losers from subsidies to Western farmers are foreign farmers because they cannot compete on this uneven playing field. In Central America, for example, land is acquired by multinational companies to produce vast acres of soil-sapping commodities like bananas or pineapples for export. After the land is destroyed by these hungry monocultures, it often suffers severe erosion problems and is no longer suitable for local food production. None of this should come as a surprise in the era of globalization. Former US secretary of agriculture John Block once commented, "The idea that developing countries should feed themselves is an anachronism of a bygone era."[7] Quite. Why should they worry about their land when we can "take care" of it for them?

As the petroleum interval comes to a close and agriculture suffers paroxysms and production failures, this path we have trodden of intensifying agriculture into a set of unsustainable industrial processes will come back to haunt us. As we demand ever more food from the land, it will no longer be up to the task.

Eventually the realization will come that the world is changing, that the petroleum interval is on its way out, and that the recovery is going to be traumatic. Exactly when that realization will come is hard to say, but I think it will come much too late. We are, after all, in the middle of the petroleum interval, not at its end. There is a lot of oil still in the ground—about half, in fact. But economic disruption will come as soon as we can no longer continue to increase oil production. A simple flattening of oil supply will be disastrous, even before the long decline begins. Our global economy will be traumatized long before the end of oil, just as the Roman Empire was destroyed long before the end of wood. Our environment, through the depletion of many resources and global warming, has been brought to crisis through our massive oil consumption just as Roman farms were degraded by overproduction and deforestation. Peak oil marks the middle, not the end, of the petroleum interval, but it marks the beginning of the great recession.

I had an interesting discussion about this with my uncle Deryck, now eighty years old, who recounted how he was taught, at a British public school in the 1940s, that the British Empire was the greatest empire the world had ever seen and was "the empire upon which the sun would never set."[8] It seems that the whole nation felt this way. Winston Churchill, just a few years earlier, had proclaimed: "I did not come here [to Parliament] to preside over the dismantling of the British Empire."[9] To the vast majority, the British Empire seemed to be at the height of its powers, and yet within a few short decades it had been reduced to the British Isles, the Falkland Islands, and the Rock of Gibraltar. Within the life of one person, the invincible fell and the impossible became inevitable.

My children are in American public schools right now, and they are being taught a distressingly similar story. Although they are being taught that we face significant environmental problems, the overwhelming message is that the sun will never set on an all-powerful America—a growing world filled with opportunity. They will be eighty around 2070 and will look back on a world that has gone through monumental change.

I wonder if people will recognize the oil peak as the cause of the great recession. If they do, then they will hopefully understand that the solution lies in the development of sustainable food and energy systems. If they do not, then what, or whom, will they blame? Well, history has a long and glorious portfolio to choose from: communists, the poor, liberals, foreigners—yes, always foreigners, especially those who are supposed to supply unlimited volumes of cheap oil.

World events are about to take a turn for the worse. As the oil squeeze is applied, it will catalyze all sorts of mayhem. The Great Depression resulted in two fiercely contrasting historical outcomes. In the United States, it resulted in FDR's New Deal and the emergence of a superpower. In Germany, it resulted in Adolf Hitler's Nazi Party, one of the world's worst genocides, and the world's worst conflagration to date. Regional conflicts are likely in many parts of the world, particularly in the Middle East, and if these occur, they will deepen the crisis even more.

OIL SKIRMISHES, OIL WARS[10]

> In dealing with foreign policy, because we mess up our energy policy, we have this so-called great need to defend our oil, and it drives our foreign policy. Whether it is in Colombia to protect a pipeline, whether it is in Venezuela to have our CIA involved, whether it is in the persistent occupation of the Persian Gulf (which does not serve our interests), whether it is in the expansion of our occupation of central Asia, whether it is our control of where and how the oil comes out of the Caspian Sea, and possibly our presence in Afghanistan, may all possibly be related to energy.
>
> US congressman Ron Paul[11]

The First World War was not initiated on the basis of competition for oil—the importance of oil had not yet been fully understood—but it was the first war in which access to oil became an important strategic consideration. America had lots of oil, and Britain had secured access to its supply in Arabia and Persia. Germany became depleted of oil while the Allies retained uninterrupted access. Incidentally, Winston Churchill was Lord of the Admiralty in Britain prior to the First World War, and his championing of the conversion of the Royal Navy from steam to diesel gave British ships a huge advantage over the clunky old German ships when war broke out.

After losing the First World War, Germany was constrained to an oil-deficient region with much weaker access to oil than most other rich nations. Germany was demoralized, geographically limited by the Treaty of Versailles, and did not accept the new world order in which it perceived that its rightful place as a dominant power was being denied. Lacking needed resources and control of significant colonies, its power was impaired. The Nazis, and all their evil supremacist and genocidal agendas, needed offshore resources to fulfill their dreams of leading an Aryan world. The situation of Japan was not dissimilar; it was a disenfranchised nation with a sense of superiority but a lack of resources. The Germans and Japanese believed that they were racially superior and therefore had the right to expand their territories and access to resources. By the 1930s, the key global resource was oil.

In the Pacific, Japan needed to secure oil supplies from Indonesia, a treacherous 2,500 miles of ocean to the south. They attacked the US Navy at Pearl Harbor on December 7, 1941, to ensure safe passage of their tanker fleet, but the Americans recovered, gained control of the Pacific at Midway in the summer of 1942, and began to choke off Japanese oil supplies. By 1944, Japanese oil tankers were being sunk at will, and the outcome of the war in the Pacific was no longer in doubt.

In Europe, Hitler was forced to push east into Russia to secure oil from around Baku. Embroiled in brutal fighting at the battle of Stalingrad, he would fail. By the time the Nazis reached the northern edge of the Caucasus in the summer of 1942, the oil wells had been sabotaged under the orders of Joseph Stalin. The Germans never pushed on to Baku and never secured the oil they so desperately needed. Meanwhile, Erwin Rommel, the Desert Fox, was speeding across North Africa intent on securing the Suez Canal for oil shipments to Germany. After Rommel was stopped at the battle of El-Alamein, Winston Churchill commented: "Before Alamein we never had a victory. After Alamein we never had a defeat."[12] Britain's oil was being supplied by its oil-rich ally, the United States, and despite sending thousands of U-boats out into the North Atlantic, the Germans could not sink enough oil tankers. Britain and America had all the oil they needed. Germany ran short.

The Second World War made it abundantly clear that access to oil was a key strategic objective. It should be no surprise, then, that so many of the conflicts of the last half century have involved oil. In the 1950s, the attempts of Egypt's prime minister Gamal Abdel Nasser and Iran's premier Mohammad Mosaddeq to nationalize their oil industries were met with strong resistance from the West. Nasser survived, but Mosaddeq was overthrown during Operation Ajax, conceived by Britain's MI6 and carried out by America's CIA. (Only later, when confronted by Ayatollah Ruhollah Khomeini, would they wish they had not interfered.)

The oil producers formed OPEC (Organization of the Petroleum Exporting Countries) in a bid to avoid outside manipulation. OPEC was tentative at first, and in its early years it saw the CIA-encouraged ouster of Iraq's Abdul Rahman Arif by the secular-socialist Baath Party (in which Saddam Hussein was a major player), but it did not remain a pawn for long. Frustrated by the West's support of Israel during the Six-Day War (1967) and the Yom Kippur War (1973), OPEC imposed the 1973 oil embargo. This was the first major negotiating statement made by the oil producers that they would not be manipulated by the oil consumers, their customers.

OPEC cut oil production by five million barrels per day, and the price of oil skyrocketed. OPEC was in control of the world's oil supply, and the West was suddenly faced with defiant, unified oil producers. The shah of Iran (considered an ally until this point), declared: "Of course the price of oil is going to rise. Certainly! You increased the price of wheat 300 percent and the same for sugar and cement. You buy our crude oil and sell it back to us, refined as petrochemicals at a hundred times the price you've paid to us. It's only fair that, from now on, you should pay more for oil. Let's say ten times more!"[13] The Saudis eventually ended the oil embargo by increasing oil production, probably because they were concerned about a global depression affecting their sales. As Ahmed Zaki Yamani (considered the lead figure in the 1973 oil embargo) put it: "If you go down, we go down."[14] Having barely recovered from the oil embargo, the world was hit with oil shocks again as a result of the Iran-Iraq War in 1979. Lines grew at the gas pumps once more, but this time the recovery came from new discoveries in the North Sea and Alaska.

At the end of the Second World War, the two oil-producing giants, the United States and the Soviet Union, embarked on the great battle of ideals between communism and capitalism known as the Cold War. Despite the supposed ideals, however, the Cold War was really fought on two classic battlefields: competition for resources and economic productivity. President Ronald Reagan, spurred on by Prime Minister Margaret Thatcher, decided to take on the Soviet economy and outspend it, but Reagan's principal weapon against the Soviet Union was oil. As long as oil prices remained high, the Soviets were able to fund their arms race and subsidize their industries, but they had little else to use for cash. The high oil prices of the 1970s lulled them into a false sense of security, and they overextended in various ways.

The Soviets' biggest mistake was invading Afghanistan at the end of 1979. Not only did this draw the Soviets into an expensive, protracted battle in a country renowned for its difficult terrain, but it also mobilized Saudi Arabia against them. Osama bin Laden (a Saudi Arabian) and his CIA-funded cronies established a mujahideen resistance in the mountains of central Asia, and, much more important, Reagan persuaded the Saudis to remove the infidels from Arab lands[15] by increasing oil production. The Saudis flooded the market with oil, the price of oil plummeted, and the Soviet economy was crushed from the lack of oil revenues. It also didn't hurt that the American economy was boosted by the low cost of oil, a commodity that was now being imported in great volumes.

Ever since the industrialized world committed to an oil-based economy, it has made sure that oil was freely available. This has involved abuse of power, including direct and indirect assault, political bullying and manipulation, undermining governments, and occupying producer nations. Hostile oil negotiations have been raging between the oil consumers and the oil producers for most of the petroleum interval. The negotiations simply concern access and price. The US military is deployed around the world with the clear goal of protecting oil supplies. Protecting them from what? Well, protecting them for sale, at a reasonable price, to America and the West. Perhaps we should think of the defense budget as the "Pentagon Tax" on oil.

The world settled into an oil-transporting economy in which all players understood their positions. This persisted until 1991, when Saddam Hussein made the miscalculation that would eventually end him. Saddam wanted to control his country's oil. That had always annoyed the West, but when he also attempted to capture the oil fields of Kuwait, he finally fell afoul of his former allies. President George H. W. Bush hesitated for a while but eventually decided to send a strong reminder to the oil producers of the world: threatening the supply of oil to America will not be tolerated.

Operation Desert Storm became the first major oil skirmish, taking place in Kuwait in 1991. The West slapped sanctions on Saddam, sanctions that were easily justified now that his despotic credentials and genocidal tendencies had become clear; and when he acted out again, Bush Junior, egged on by neoconservatives Dick Cheney, Donald Rumsfeld, and Paul Wolfowitz, came back to finish the job. America finally had a major police station in oil country, and Saddam was dragged from his hole and hanged by the neck.

The oil crises that we have endured so far began as turf wars among producers and then became hostile negotiations and skirmishes between producers and consumers. So far, however, these crises have either been nonviolent or one-sided contests in which powerful countries have exerted their influence over much weaker adversaries. The real trouble will come when the powerful consumers begin to squabble among themselves. As oil supplies decline globally and there is not enough oil to go around, things will get much more dangerous. China and India have arrived in the market to join Europe and the United States as major customers to the Middle East, an area that, while rich in oil, is largely defenseless. The price of oil was the major issue in the producer-consumer skirmishes of the first half of the petroleum interval, but through the second half, access to oil will become the major issue. The danger is much greater, and consumer-consumer competition could expand beyond skirmishes into wars and proxy wars and major standoffs among global powers.

THE GLOBAL ECONOMY AS AN ECOSYSTEM

> **In the end, it may be impossible for even a single nation to sustain industrialism as we have known it during the twentieth century.**
>
> Richard Heinberg, *The Party's Over:*
> *Oil, War, and the Fate of Industrial Societies*

The world is about to be visited by economic hardship and all the other problems that will flow from peak oil: resource depletion, environmental degradation, overpopulation, and global warming—but which parts of the world will struggle the most? One concern is that, since the world is now so intimately linked in its economic dance, perhaps the problems of the world will be visited, catastrophically, on us all. The fate of one nation can have a disastrous impact on many others. On the other hand, some economies remain isolated. A loss in one part of the global economy might cause losses elsewhere or might be corrected by gains elsewhere, but it is too simplistic to say that the global economy is either dangerously interdependent or robustly self-balancing.

The interactions among global economic systems are extremely complex, but we can borrow from a field of study that has looked at complex relationships in great detail. Ecology has developed into a comprehensive science that may serve as a suitable analogy to the global economy here.

Frederic E. Clements, who was instrumental in developing the field of ecology in the early twentieth century, proposed the concept of an ecosystem as a superorganism.[16] His premise was that an ecosystem was reliant on all its component organisms and that the loss of any species could dramatically alter the structure and function of the ecosystem. Ecologist Henry A. Gleason disagreed, arguing that an ecosystem is merely a neutral collection of organisms that could be relatively easily interchanged without the ecosystem losing its essential structure.[17]

Clements and Gleason were both partially correct, and a more sophisticated view now incorporates both concepts. Take a rain forest, for example, which is home to a myriad of different species. For a rain forest to maintain its structure, a large number of canopy trees must collect energy from the sun and carbon from the atmosphere by photosynthesis. A range of organisms that can extract nitrogen from the air must also be present, as must a range of herbivores that can convert plants into other forms of biomass. A complement of decomposers is needed to recycle dead organic matter back to the plants. The most basic elements of an ecosystem, then, are *producers*, *consumers*, and *decomposers*. Lacking any one of these elements, the ecosystem will fail, but the relative abundance of different species within each element can often be switched around. One anteater can be replaced with another, ants still get eaten, and the rain forest is still a rain forest.

There are some organisms, however, that are entirely dependent on others. Without bamboo there is no hope for China's giant panda; without gum trees there is no hope for Australia's koala. There are also some very clear examples of mutual dependencies: many species of hummingbird are dependent on the nectar from single species of plant, which, in turn, are entirely dependent on the hummingbird for pollination. The loss of either one dooms both.

Predicting the far-reaching consequences of changes in an ecosystem, then, is extremely complicated. An impact on one species may affect many others—or few. Some impacts may have consequences that are difficult to detect, such as a shift in the composition of microbial species in the soil; or the consequences may be obvious, such as the extinction of a colorful bird. One thing is certain, however, as per the second law of ecology: you can never do one thing.

The impacts that affect whole guilds of organisms are the really dangerous ones and can be irreversible, such as the sudden removal of large numbers of trees from a rain forest or changes in the climate. Following the logging of a rain forest, a plethora of tree-dwelling organisms—from monkeys to bromeliads and lianas—lose their homes. The understory plants, now exposed to full sun, wither. Rain penetrates to the forest floor, and when the soil is washed away, the landscape is pervasively changed.

So how do ecological systems serve as analogies to the global economy? Well, we might compare the major economies of the world with the major guilds of organisms in an ecosystem. The main resources that go into the economy are energy, water, food, and mineral resources. Various nations, then, are primary producers. Other nations serve as manufacturing centers that convert these primary resources into products. The rich service and technology centers add value to these products and serve as the dominant consumers. The global economy has relatively little that resembles the decomposer cycle, which, of course, is one of its inherent weaknesses. Without decomposers, an ecosystem would quickly run out of resources and fill with trash.

The producers, manufacturers, and service providers are linked in a range of relationships that might be either intimate or casual, but the overall sweep of globalization has been to make them more intimate. This has all been made possible by a high level of primary production and the linking of geographically separated economies with oil-based transportation systems.

Viewed, then, as a set of energy flows around the global economic ecosystem, we find that the success or failure of certain economies can have either minimal or far-reaching effects on others. The economic failure of a small island nation in the South Pacific may affect its neighbors but would not likely affect the rest of the world. The economic failure of a large but somewhat isolated nation such as India may have severe consequences in South Asia and send ripple effects around the world, but its global consequences may be short-lived. An economic failure in China, the United States, or the European Union, however, may cause the entire global economy to contract.

The price of oil is akin to an ecosystem-level energy flow. An increase in the price of oil causes cash to be transferred from oil consumers to oil producers. A decrease in price causes the cash to be "returned." Many factors can affect the energy flow among the different players in the global market, and this can affect the relative health of each, but the real agent of change in the global economy—like the rain forest—is a change in environment or in energy input. An increased input across the board will enable the global economy to grow, and this is what has happened, more or less, throughout history. The terrifying opposite, of course, is a decreased energy input that will cause the entire global economy to contract. As oil depletion begins to bite, it will be like dimming the sun over the global economic rain forest.

Oil depletion will have impacts that seep down through the economic guilds. As the energy industry goes into decline it will infect agriculture and manufacturing. Failing manufacturing in east Asia will affect exports to America, Europe, and other places. The contraction of the American and European economies will impede the functioning of service economies, such as outsourcing to countries like India. Agricultural failures will cause great hardship across the global economy, hitting the poorest first and hardest.

The oil-producing nations will be the keystone species[18] of the next decade or so, with the whole global economy relying on them for energy input. Soon, however, they will go into irreversible decline. Their loss will be like a massive die-off of trees in the forest, and we will be trapped in a long recession.

The global economy will begin to unravel, and economic activities will become increasingly localized. Countries that are dependent on others for goods and services will need to find alternate suppliers at home. Those that are able to function on the basis of their own production, manufacturing, and services will fare the best, as the global economy reverses its trend of *globalization* into a new era of *localization*.

There are a million symbiotic business relationships in the global economy that rely on the outsourcing of labor-intensive manufacturing tasks to poor countries in order to supply merchandise at competitive prices in rich countries. All these relationships are reliant on the fact that rich countries have wealthy consumers, that poor countries have natural resources and cheap labor, and that merchandise can be moved large distances cost-effectively. This model is exemplified by the relationship between China and the United States, and by one company in particular: Wal-Mart.

Wal-Mart seems invulnerable, but watch out for bad news from Bentonville, Arkansas. Wal-Mart has been both one of the major beneficiaries of globalization and one of its architects, but trouble is brewing.

The Wal-Mart business model has created the biggest retailer in the world with a dominance based on vast economies of scale and a fine-tuned distribution system. Bear in mind that Wal-Mart manufactures absolutely nothing. All it does is collect, organize, and distribute goods—but it does this on a scale, and with a degree of efficiency, that is almost beyond comprehension. But localize the world by increasing the price of oil, and just about everything related to Wal-Mart becomes more expensive. The price differential between imported and locally produced goods decreases, and the cost of shipping goods from overseas increases. The model of moving goods around the country from centralized distribution centers, operating a nonstop, just-in-time rolling warehouse, becomes less efficient. Let's call this the Smal-Mart Effect.[19]

The decline of retailers such as Wal-Mart will herald far-reaching changes. Much of the basic structure of America, and other countries to a lesser extent, has been rearranged by the big-box retail system. Wal-Marts have been placed out in suburbia's cheap land, and plenty of shoppers are to be found there. In response, of course, suburban lots increase in value when a Wal-Mart is built nearby, and new subdivisions spring up around it. Suburbia and the big-box companies have grown symbiotically in recent decades, and the 'burbs will be less and less appealing when the big-box stores begin to close.

The depletion of oil will be a fundamental force that will affect all economic activities, but it is hardly the only inevitable threat. Many other resources are falling into short supply, huge ecological debts are accumulating, and all these problems are on a collision course. Some impacts will be modest and delayed, but others will be severe and will happen soon, and different impacts will be felt in different places. The impact of oil prices will be the first and most obvious one in the West. The repercussions of freshwater scarcity, agricultural failures, and collapsing fisheries, however, will be the principal concerns elsewhere, and they will add to the burden everywhere. And as if this were not enough, it will all happen against the backdrop of global climate change. Impacts from changing weather conditions not only will strike during the great recession but also will impede our attempts to recover.

Another great challenge for ecologists is to recognize not only the complexity of how ecosystems are structured but also the complexity of the changes they undergo. There has been a tendency to view large, productive ecosystems as successful and depleted ecosystems as failed, and yet it is quite natural for ecosystems to pass through repeated cycles of growth and collapse. The great grasslands of the world, for example, are dependent on fire. When we see flames sweeping across the prairies we are tempted to view this as destructive, but grasslands need to burn. Without periodic fires, grasses tend to be outcompeted by longer-lived species, and grasslands are replaced by scrubland or forest. Although the grasses burn to the ground each time a fire sweeps over the prairie, they recover quickly. Their competitors, the trees, on the other hand, suffer much more pervasive harm. Neither the landscape of flowing grass nor that of scorched earth is more successful: both are parts of a necessary cycle.

In attempting to understand complex systems, then, we are ill-advised to consider any particular stage of their development as desirable over another. Even more important: perhaps we should resist the temptation to maintain ecosystems in any given permanent state. To understand this, we might consider Smokey Bear and our management of the forest ecosystems of the American West. "Only you can prevent forest fires!" claims Smokey—but prevent them from doing what, exactly?

The wildfires that ravage the West make spectacular viewing on the evening news every summer. They cause terrible loss of life and destruction of property, and we spend millions of dollars preventing them and trying to extinguish them. But one of the reasons we have such destructive fires is precisely because we attempt to prevent them. It is natural for many types of forest to burn quite frequently.[20] Fires burn off the herbs, shrubs, and fallen tree limbs that accumulate as fuel on the forest floor, and when fires are frequent, the fuel load of the forest floor remains small—and so does the fire. When Smokey Bear prevents fires, he encourages the accumulation of fuel on the forest floor. The probability of fire may decrease, but its destructiveness, when it happens, will be much greater. By preventing fires, then, we make them much worse.

It should be no surprise that we see some of the worst fires in the outer suburbs of cities such as Los Angeles because it is there that fire prevention is most keenly promoted. Once we have planted houses in the forest, our fear of forest fires becomes more intense—as do the fires when they occur.

An important aspect of ecosystems, then, is not just their beauty and complexity at any one time but also the ways in which they change through time. Examining ecosystems this way, ecologist Buzz Holling pioneered the analysis of ecosystem resilience.[21] He defines resilience as the ability of an ecosystem to respond to disturbance, and he has found that this resilience changes through time in important ways. America's western forests, for example, are at their most resilient when they are in the process of regrowing after fire. Young forests are affected relatively little by most impacts, but as they age and mature they lose their resilience, as is demonstrated by wildfires.

Resiliency thinking can be applied to social systems as well as to ecosystems, and perhaps it gives us some further insight into dramatic civilization collapses of the past. The Roman legions were sent to the edges of the empire to prevent any brushfires that might be ignited by the surrounding barbarian tribes, and they built giant colosseums to douse the discontent that was smoldering among their citizenry. They drained their resources in the process and turned the Mediterranean basin into deadwood. The Roman experiment lacked nothing in complexity, productivity, and beauty, but it lacked everything in resilience. When it finally burned, it was consumed.

And where do we stand today in our own complex, productive, and beautiful modern society? The armies of the world: military, economic, and environmental are busy putting out fires everywhere you look—but the deadwood is accumulating nonetheless.

DIMINISHING MARGINAL RETURNS

Imagine you are the planet's equivalent of *Titanic*'s seaman Fleet, peering into the darkness, looking for icebergs. What can you see? Are there any signs that tell us when the major upheavals will begin?

The Romans appeared to be at the peak of their powers with their empire extending from Britain to the Middle East when Rome was sacked and all bets were off. Likewise, the Maya built their biggest pyramids just before collapse, and the Easter Islanders were still carving their biggest Moai even as the last tree on the island—which might have been used to move it—was felled. The apparent power of these near-collapse civilizations was masking diminishing marginal returns from their economic fundamentals. These societies were no longer powerful but were simply putting on a brave face.

The last half century has seen the world's most remarkable expansion. In the West, the standard of living and material wealth of individuals have grown enormously, and most people would conclude that we are still making considerable progress—especially in the broad area of "technology." I'm not so sure. Recent technological advances seem to me to have been mostly cosmetic, and we appear to have done little in the last few decades that will help us address the immense problems we are about to face. Are we experiencing the same type of diminishing marginal returns that presaged the collapse of past societies? Are our apparent technological wonders really setting us up for a robust future, or are they simply latter-day Moai on a global Easter Island?

We perceive an ever-progressing world driven by redefining advances in technology, but I think it is worth taking a look at our "new technologies" from another perspective. Consider these factoids: humans have not stepped on the moon since 1972.[22] The air speed record has stood since 1976, the land speed record since 1997, and the water speed record since 1978.[23] The fastest passenger jet, the Concorde, first flew in 1969 and was scrapped in 2003. Nuclear power, the presumed savior of the energy world, went out of vogue decades ago; no nuclear power station has been commissioned in the United States since 1973. Fuel cells, the next savior of the energy world, are a 150-year-old technology. What is the technology that you rely on the most? It's probably your car, a machine that was invented a century ago and has not changed in decades, except for what might be considered minor tweaks.

The modern era has not really been made possible by brilliant, transformational technologies at all. It has, in a much more fundamental way, been just a logical extension of what was possible for a civilization powered by fossil fuels. New technologies have added significant "comfort features," but the basic model is the same. We live in the petroleum interval and depend on oil for energy and technology. But the petroleum interval is passing its peak.

If diminishing marginal returns is an early warning system for a civilization's collapse, then our sirens should be blaring right now because wherever you look, it is getting harder and harder to get ahead.

CHAPTER 9

AROUND THE WORLD IN EIGHTY DEPRESSIONS

THE NEXT HALF CENTURY

> **Prediction is very difficult, especially about the future.**
>
> Niels Bohr, quantum physicist[1]

It is impossible to predict exactly how the decline of oil will play out as we pass the peak of the petroleum interval over the next few years, and it is impossible to predict all the consequences of global climate change and when they will strike. Ditto the effects of freshwater shortages and other resource shortages: fisheries, agricultural productivity, and all the rest. The global economy may grow for a few years and then gradually contract, it may grow strongly for decades more and then collapse suddenly, or it may begin to contract again very soon, extending the current recession indefinitely.

This uncertainty is inevitable because, although we would like to be able to pinpoint these events to within the nearest year or two, we are attempting to analyze a civilization-level event, and this is unrealistic. Even now, when we look back on the fall of the Roman Empire, we argue about whether we should mark its fall in 410 with the sacking of Rome by Alaric the Visigoth, in 447 with Attila the Hun, or perhaps as early as the death of Marcus Aurelius in 180. The moment that would really interest us would be the tipping point—the point at which a change of course might have saved the Roman Empire—but we can't say when that tipping point was reached, even with the benefit of hindsight. Our fall is as inevitable as Rome's because our inputs cannot support our demands. Still, the epidemiology of our fall will be every bit as confusing.

This chapter examines some of the problems that are likely to occur in different countries and regions over the next half century or so. It operates on the broad assumption that the global economy will stagnate over the next decade or two and go into a long, deep recession. It considers the apocalyptic view of total collapse within that time frame unlikely, but who knows?

THE OIL PRODUCERS

History teaches us that men and nations behave wisely only once they have exhausted all other alternatives.

Abba Eban, former Israeli foreign minister[2]

The Middle East, once the cradle of civilization, has repeatedly become civilization's graveyard. The core of the region—Arabia, Iraq, and Iran— is the global center of oil production, and the region as a whole is heavily reliant on oil revenues. Without oil, the region will more or less hollow out and collapse. The peripheries of the region—North Africa and "the Stans"[3] are already poor and are likely to suffer further gradual declines through the end of the oil era. The countries with the biggest oil reserves, namely, Saudi Arabia, Iran, Iraq, the United Arab Emirates, and Kuwait, will generate enormous wealth while prices are high but will burn out as their reserves fail. The rich will move to London, Paris, and New York, and they will take their fortunes with them. When that happens, it will become obvious that they have not invested one brass razoo

into the development of sustainable futures for their countries.⁴ The
countries themselves will hollow out and die, and the folks left behind
will need to take camel riding lessons.

Water is extremely scarce in the Middle East, and agriculture is difficult. The region is likely to become significantly warmer and slightly
drier over the coming century, and its support structures beyond oil are
likely to decay significantly. Water has been an issue in the region since
its population was one-tenth what it is now, and conflicts over water are
likely to intensify.

The Middle East is notoriously volatile, with historical conflicts
among Arabs, Persians, Berbers, Turks, Kurds, Sunni, Shia, Uzbeks,
Tajiks, Taliban, Pashtun, and Jews. Under conditions of economic
depression it seems hard to imagine that the lid will stay on all these
rivalries. Meanwhile, relations between the Middle East and the West
have been strained ever since the Crusades, and they remain tense. As oil
reserves become increasingly concentrated in the Middle East, the powerful oil consumers will have an increasing stake in maintaining their
control over their preferred parts of the region. Trade conflicts and
proxy wars seem inevitable. Direct conflict among oil consumers in the
region cannot be ruled out and could be disastrous.

Improvements in the economic sustainability of the region, particularly its agricultural sustainability, are urgently needed. Governments
need to plan for a challenging future, but it is not clear how much can
be achieved, especially as the political climate degrades. The Middle
East is overpopulated, even considering oil revenues, but it is still experiencing significant population growth. I fear that it will seem grossly
overpopulated quite soon.

Iran has a broader range of resources than most countries in the
Middle East, but it is also dependent on oil revenues. It will not be long
before Iran declines into oil-deficient obscurity, but the big questions
are, what will that decline look like? and will Iran take anyone down
with it? Iran's current leadership includes the rather nutty Mahmoud

Ahmadinejad, who is having delusions of adequacy while oil prices are high. Inflation and unemployment are rising, and folks are getting very restless with their (probably illegitimate[5]) government. When oil depletion starts to really bite, Iran's economy will fold like a house of cards.

Iranian agriculture is already suffering from water scarcity. The hitherto productive northeastern Chenaran Plain suffers from collapsing water tables and crop failures. Iran's ill-maintained infrastructure will not hold up, its water-deficient agriculture will struggle, and the people of Iran will be ready for another revolution. The new Iran might be best called Iranistan, because it will soon look a lot like its neighbors to the north and east: degraded countries lacking oil.[6]

> **Egypt will never go to war again, except to protect its water resources.**
>
> Anwar Sadat, former Egyptian president, on the occasion of the 1979 peace treaty with Israel

There are some significant cities and population centers in North Africa, and nearly two hundred million people live on the south side of the Mediterranean Sea. That's odd, because from my Western world perspective, it always seemed like the Mediterranean had people to the north but only desert to the south. So who are all these people? Well, to start with, eighty million people live in Egypt (more than sixteen million in Cairo alone). Algeria and Morocco each have populations over thirty million.

North Africa is a relatively homogeneous region in many ways, with a relatively similar standard of living and similar social and environmental issues across the region. It is moderately poor, with around a fifth of its population living below the poverty line. There are considerable reserves of oil and natural gas, although the production of all countries is well past peak, especially for oil, and only Libya and Algeria continue to be significant exporters, a fact for which Spain and Italy are particularly thankful.

North Africa does not seem prone to a dramatic crash in the near future, but with few opportunities for the replacement of declining oil revenues, its economies will contract considerably. Agriculture seems to be maxed out and susceptible to decline, and yet populations are climbing steadily. Global warming is likely to increase the difficulty of agriculture in this already marginal region by delivering more heat and less rain.

Freshwater is considered scarce in all of North Africa with the exception of Egypt, whose water comes from the mighty Nile. Egypt has made it abundantly clear that it will tolerate no interference with this supply. Ethiopia's analysis of potential dam sites on the Blue Nile (which carries the majority of the flow into the Nile, joining the White Nile in Sudan) was greeted with the stern warning that Egypt would destroy any such dam. Ethiopia, of course, suffers many deaths from floods on the Blue Nile, has great need of water for irrigation in a region of notoriously unreliable rainfall, and could use all the extra electricity generating–capacity it could get. A significant dam project would ameliorate all these problems. Egypt's stance, however, has made such investments impossible. Egypt generates 16 percent of its electricity from the Aswan High Dam.

Meanwhile, Muammar al-Qaddafi, de facto leader of Libya, has nearly completed the eighth wonder of the world or—depending on your point of view—unleashed Libya's great national fantasy.

The biggest desert in the world was once a region of temperate grasslands supporting vast herds of wild animals. Early civilizations found significant resources here before the Sahara Desert claimed most of the northern half the African continent. In a great scene from the Miramax film *The English Patient*, archaeologists find the Cave of Swimmers in the middle of the Libyan Desert, at the Gilf Kebir: *"Maddox! Maddox! Come quickly, I've found something. . . . My God, they're swimming!"* Beneath the sands of the Sahara lies the giant Nubian Sandstone Aquifer System, in which millions of gallons of freshwater have been stored for more than forty millennia.

Drilling for oil in the 1950s, oilmen repeatedly hit water. This was a great disappointment at first, but it eventually fueled Qaddafi's great dream. His first idea was to move thousands of Libyans out into the desert to farm. There was little enthusiasm for this idea, so, in 1984, Libya began construction of the Great Manmade River. Thousands of miles of pipelines accessing more than a thousand wells, many more than five hundred meters deep, now run beneath the Sahara, bringing water to Tripoli and Benghazi. Now that the water is flowing, fast, and fresh, the plan is to build a new Libyan agricultural economy and export food to Europe.

So is this the eighth wonder of the world or Qaddafi's pipe dream? That, of course, depends on just how much water there is in the Nubian Sandstone Aquifer System, and for how long it can be accessed. There is certainly a heck of a lot of water, and even a grandiose irrigated agriculture system can be run for a while, although the estimates of "centuries," reported by the Libyan government are at odds with the estimates of "decades" reported by geologists and engineers. The Great Manmade River also requires huge amounts of energy. Although the water comes at much lower costs than desalination plants (the only other alternative), it takes each drop roughly nine days to make it from aquifer to faucet, propelled over some significant elevations by a series of powerful pumps. Whether or not the Nubian aquifer runs dry, however, may be moot. When the pumps run short of oil, the water will stagnate in the pipes.

Nonetheless, of all the countries in North Africa, Libya is the one with a significantly brighter few decades to look forward to. As the rest of North Africa becomes increasingly parched, this country of four million people will spend a few blissful years swimming in an abundance of freshwater. As North Africa continues to slide into poverty, Libya is likely to look decidedly odd—a little green oasis on the southern banks of the Mediterranean. A temporary one, alas.

If the Arabs were to put down their weapons today, there would be no more war. If Israel were to put

down its weapons today, there would be no more Israel.

Benjamin Netanyahu, Israeli prime minister

A thousand pundits in every country from Albania to Zambia would like to know what the future holds for the little chunk of land on the eastern shores of the Mediterranean Sea. This is without doubt the most politically volatile region in the world. The supposed clash of the Judeo-Christian West and Muslim East, in its many real and perceived forms, has its epicenter in the struggle for the Holy Land. Ground zero is the Temple Mount in Jerusalem, but let's not even bother with the history; it's been a mess since the winners of the Second World War decided that Palestine would be a good location for a sovereign Jewish state, whether or not that was a good call. Let's not play the politics game; let's play the resource distribution game.

Among Lebanon, Syria, Israel, Palestine,[7] or Jordan, none of these countries has anything much in the way of resources. Syria is the only one with oil, but it is barely a trickle. There are few minerals; hence, there is virtually no mining. Agriculture is found in various pockets, but arable land is lacking, so broad-acre agriculture is virtually nonexistent and there is little grain production. All countries produce a wide variety of fruits and vegetables such as citrus, tomatoes, and olives. Israel has very advanced agriculture and is a significant exporter, but it uses huge amounts of water and energy. In fairness, Israel has the most water-efficient agriculture in the world, but large volumes are consumed nonetheless, and water is extremely scarce in the region. The fabled River Jordan has a very limited flow and represents the classic zero-sum game. If Israel takes more water, Palestine and Jordan get less. Israel, controlling the headwaters in the north (the Golan Heights, taken from Syria after the 1967 war), does indeed take the lion's share. The Arabs see this as Israel "stealing Arab water," and, along with the land itself, they would like it back.

So, if the squabbling states of the eastern Mediterranean have no significant agriculture, virtually no fossil fuels, and only a miserable trickle of muddy water, what do they have?

One thing: buddies.

Israel is backed by the West, especially the United States. It is a developed nation, and yet it receives in the order of 2.5 billion dollars per year in US aid.[8] Palestine and its neighbors are backed by North Africa and the rest of the Middle East.

Israel is in need of all the help it can get. It is a tiny pocket of land with a population of only six and a half million surrounded by many people who would like to see it destroyed. There is little doubt that some of Israel's neighbors would be rid of it given half a chance, and I'm concerned that they might get their chance. Israel is afraid, too, which is why it invests an eye-popping 7 percent of its GDP in military hardware and has mandatory military service. Israel receives many weapons from friendly countries, and it has nukes.

So what will happen on this famous strip of land in the decades to come? It's hard to say, but bear in mind that Israel imports the following: oil, grains, raw materials for its technologically advanced industries, weapons, and cash. It is essential to Israel that these resources—all of them—keep coming in. It is not clear, however, that this can be ensured. Israel's reliance on oil is particularly bad news. Its neighbors attempted to pull the oil rug out from under Israel in 1973; it was saved by emergency shipments from the United States, but similar saves may not be possible forever. Back then, less than a fifth of the world's oil endowment had been consumed, and America was still a major producer. We are now at the point of peak oil, the United States is a much less important producer, and the Middle East, once again, sits atop the world's oil supply.

My prediction is that the Arab world will continue to pressure Israel, and it's hard to see how Israel can stay afloat forever. As Israel's major backers struggle with their own woes, the Arab world may have another serious crack at Israel sometime in the next decade or so, and it could go either way. The presence of nuclear weapons makes the equation significantly more precarious. If its conventional forces are not up to the task of defending it, what other choices will Israel have but to either succumb or launch?

> **Today, August 17 [2007] at 00:00 hours, fourteen strategic bombers [armed with nuclear warheads] took to the air from seven airfields across the country, along with support and refueling aircraft. From today, such patrols will be carried out on a regular basis. We hope that our partners will treat this with understanding.**
>
> Vladimir Putin, former president and current prime minister of Russia[9]

Understand this: Russia is back.

Russia has gone though enormous economic and political changes in the last century, being, in its turn, a cultural center and economic power and a cultural desert and economic basket case. Russia was a testing ground for the world's first massive experiment in communism and became the political giant and oppressor that annexed large areas of eastern Europe and central Asia as the Soviet Union. The Soviet Union was a huge machine and an undoubted, and feared, world superpower. Hardship and economic collapse came as the Soviet Union was squeezed by its arms race with Ronald Reagan and a foolhardy military adventure in Afghanistan, was drained by two decades of low oil prices, and eventually crumpled under the weight of its cumbersome bureaucracy.

Former Soviet president Mikhail Gorbachev saw it all coming and eased the transition as best he could. Poor old Boris Yeltsin, Gorbachev's successor, tried to make admirable social changes, but the economic train wreck that had recently trampled his country had not yet moved on. In 1998, Russia suffered a severe financial crisis, and the rest of the world looked on (a little too smugly?) as the former superpower floundered in debt and struggled with Mafia-style corruption and violent crime. Deep in debt, the country needed an influx of cash.

That cash finally came in the form of high oil and natural gas prices. Vladimir Putin took over Russia at the right time when oil and natural gas prices were climbing and the reserves of many countries were in serious decline. Russia is back in the money, and Putin is seen as a megastar.

Russia is a huge country covering ten time zones from Europe to east Asia, and it has enormous underground wealth. Although most Russians remain moderately poor (those with big houses in London notwithstanding), its middle class is growing rapidly. Russia borders the West at both ends, with Europe at one end and Alaska at the other (I understand you can even see Russia from Sarah Palin's place). To the south, it borders the Middle East and China. Russia is a hugely important country. Its oil and gas are concentrated in three areas: the Caspian Sea region (oil), geographically in the Middle East; the middle of nowhere, Siberia (predominantly gas); and off Sakhalin Island on its Pacific coast, north of Japan (oil and gas).

When it comes to oil and intrigue, you can't beat the Middle East, but the fun and games do not end there. Russia has a long and painful legacy of battles over oil. Millions of Russians died at the battle of Stalingrad and then blew up their own oil fields around Baku to keep them from the Nazis during the Second World War. Four decades later, the Soviet Union was nailed to the wall by US and Saudi manipulation of oil prices during the Cold War. Russia has learned enough lessons about the importance of oil and is unlikely to forget them.

Russia was desperate for investors in the 1990s and needed foreigners to kick-start its moribund oil industry, but now that the cash has begun to flow, it is taking back control. Shell and its Japanese partners Mitsui and Mitsubishi drove the development of Russia's Sakhalin projects for more than a decade, at great cost, but when they were ready to produce oil, licking their chops at high oil and gas prices, they suddenly reduced their shareholding. Russia's state-owned Gazprom now owns 50 percent plus one share, for which it paid well below market price. You can only imagine that they got an offer they couldn't refuse.

Another case was that of the oil company Yukos and its CEO Mikhail Khordokovsky, once one of the most powerful men in Russia. He was accused of embezzlment and exploiting the natural resources of Russia for personal gain. When it suited Putin to have assets developed, he let Khordokovsky stretch out his leash, but when Putin wanted control back, Khordokovsky was packed off to jail. It seems that Putin's Russia[10] will take whatever measures are necessary to renationalize its oil industry. Russia's economic outlook has improved steadily in the last five years and its middle class has grown dramatically, so it is not surprising that Vlad the Gasman remains popular despite his systematic reassertion of state control over Russian industries.

We can probably expect Russia to become increasingly wealthy, powerful, and influential. As the world's oil and natural gas become concentrated in fewer and fewer countries, Russia will be one of those countries, and it will continue to be the biggest producer of natural gas until the gas has sputtered out. Russia will get wealthier even as some of its neighbors get poorer. If it is wise, it will start investing in other, more sustainable activities now, but it will be a powerhouse for some time, thanks to its endowment of fossil fuels.

Russia is reliant on oil and natural gas for hard currency, but Russia is not the Middle East. It has a range of other natural resources, including good soils in a number of areas, timber, and lots of coal. Russia also gets fully one-fifth of its electricity from large hydro projects in the Far East.[11] Another option for the Russian energy portfolio is nuclear power, and a number of new reactors are planned.[12]

Russia is a country of a hundred and forty million people with a solid natural resource base and a recent memory of being a world superpower. Problems will come to Russia relatively late, and as the world slides into the great recession, Russia will ride high. While it may be possible for the United States, Europe, Japan, and China to squabble over oil reserves in the Middle East, they will not mess with Russia. There's that small matter of the thousands of nukes.

THE FIRST-WORLD CONSUMERS

> **Peak Oil may be written into history books beside the Second Iraq War as the beginning of the end of the American Empire.**
>
> The author

North America used to be a very long way from both Europe and Asia. It was colonized from the west more than twelve thousand years ago but then sealed off from the rest of the world as the Bering Straits flooded. Native Americans had migrated from east Asia and had been cast adrift in the American lifeboat until it was disastrously rediscovered by a second wave of people, this time coming from the east. These easterners—the Europeans—displaced the first Americans with a genocidal cocktail of guns, germs, and steel.[13] Under their tenure, the continent gradually became an integral part of the trading world and, eventually, its dominant military and economic force.

The second colonization of the Americas by Europeans occurred under a different set of rules than had the first. The new colonies were established under slave power, and then coal, and then came into dominance in the twentieth century powered by oil. With abundant fossil fuels, hitherto uninhabitable areas became desirable places to settle. The Great Plains yielded water from underground aquifers, and the herds of roaming buffalo were destroyed to make way for cattle, and then corn. The deserts became retirement homes. The mountains became ski resorts. Energy was poured into the land to bend it to the will of progress.

Powered by oil, America was rapidly transformed from the status of a developing nation to become the world's sole superpower in less than a century. America was built on black gold. As the oil in its own territory went into decline, America found a range of different ways to secure access to oil from around the world, and the dream surged on. But there is great danger. America has been designed around the oil economy of the twentieth century like no other and is exquisitely vulnerable to the end of oil. As the world reaches peak oil and America struggles with its energy future, the land will begin to push back. This huge nation, shrunk by planes, trains, and automobiles, will expand again. This distant continent, brought closer to the rest of the world by tankers, freighters, and cheap intercontinental air travel, will grow more distant.

As the world's biggest consumer and importer of oil, the United States is deeply affected by the price of oil. As a paying customer, purchasing roughly thirteen million barrels of oil per day is very expensive. At 1990s prices of $20 per barrel, this costs roughly $100 billion per year. At $200 per barrel, the price tag shoots up to a cool trillion. America has an enormous stake in the price of oil, and its heavy reliance on black gold is gradually eroding its position of global dominance.

Americans also use a huge amount of natural gas for heating and electricity generation, and North America will be the first continent to run up against significant natural gas shortages. North America will need to significantly expand its production of gas from shale deposits, but it is unclear just how much gas can be extracted economically. We will also need to bring tankers across the Atlantic and Pacific Oceans, but this will also come at ever-increasing cost. The most fundamental civilization-level resource of all is energy, and, for America, this means oil. As the invisible hand of nature reaches out and removes this resource, America will have some huge adjustments to make.

Despite its lack of access to oil and natural gas, America does have a number of viable alternatives for electricity generation. As has already been discussed, America has huge reserves of coal, and coal-fired power plants can be constructed quickly, so this will keep the lights on for some time. We also have a reasonable nuclear capacity and an abundance of suitable sites for wind turbines and solar arrays. These sources of energy are not without significant problems, but electricity generation will not be America's biggest energy conundrum, and keeping the lights on will be significantly easier than keeping the wheels turning.

The United States is a huge country spanning a wide range of different ecosystems from desert to tundra and grassland to forest. Parts of the country are resource-poor while others are resource-rich. Some regions are only sparsely populated while others are highly developed. The difficulties faced by the various corners of the country will be very different. At the end of the oil era there will be parts of America, such as the resource-poor Southwest, that will drain the economy, whereas others, such as the resource-rich Midwest, will be pivotal to its recovery.

Of all the parts of the world that have been put to the yoke of human determination, there is nowhere that can compare with the American Southwest. This is a region of severe ecological fragility and old, weathered soils. Rivers are few. Gullies and gulches (and Grand Canyons) attest to the active water erosion of the landscape, but if you're out visiting for a week, odds are you won't see rain. Even more striking than the dryness is the size of the place. The American Southwest is spectacularly empty, and then suddenly you hit a city of four million people (Phoenix), one and a half million people (Las Vegas), or sixteen million people (Los Angeles).

Perhaps one of the most bizarre experiences you can have on a road trip is arriving in Las Vegas from the east. Drive in from Phoenix, three hundred or so miles away, to escape the hordes of retirees, zoom past the south rim of the Grand Canyon through desert, desert, and more desert. You can fill up with gas and get a burger at various dusty towns along the way. Eventually, you round the last curve in the hills and get your first glimpse of the glittering city in the desert.

The mountains frame Las Vegas like a film set backdrop. The Mandalay Bay and the Luxor shine like gold at the south end of the Strip. There are two trails of planes in the sky; one leading in and one leading out. Vegas, especially as you emerge from the desert, is a truly crazy, but amazing, place. Vegas is the home of gambling and prostitution. In fact, lax laws in Nevada basically created the place for that purpose, but it's a gamble that is poised to fail this quintessential prostitute to oil. Without oil, there will be no Vegas. The city sits on fragile land with limited water[14] and no other resources.

In the era of cheap oil, this has all been eminently possible—easy, even. Fresh lobster from Maine (or even Australia—heck, why not?!), caviar from Russia, steak from Texas, oysters from Louisiana, salmon from Alaska (baked beans and Marmite from England?), and a myriad of other treats are flown in fresh daily. Building materials are brought in on a never-ending conveyor belt of trucks that ply the desert highways. Water is piped across the desert from Lake Mead. And then there are the people; millions of them each year. They fly to Vegas to play. Well, why not? Airfares and hotel rooms are cheap, and Vegas has anything you could possibly want (and an abundance of things you should probably not want . . . "what happens in Vegas, stays in Vegas").

But without oil, there will be no Vegas, and as oil prices continue to rise, Vegas will begin to struggle. The rot is already beginning to set in with deflation of the American housing bubble in early 2007 hitting Vegas hard, and other symptoms will follow. The price of aviation fuel will hit travelers directly in the pocket, and the number of visitors will decline. The price of fuel will also affect the price of lobster, caviar, steak, oysters, and salmon; and the famous Vegas seafood buffets will start to look more and more like Atlantic City fish-and-chips. As revenues fall, maintenance will decline, and the Bellagio and the Wynn will look increasingly like overblown Super 8's. Cheap accommodation will become plentiful as the hotels become desperate to fill their rooms, but this will not bring back the good old days. Once its mystique has been lost, Vegas will decline into a decrepit middle-of-nowhere sleaze joint with cheap whiskey in the saloon, hookers upstairs, an out-of-tune piano playing in the corner, and Josey Wales striding to the bar chewing a cigar.

The decline of Vegas, a weird but distinctive American city, will make a great *60 Minutes* episode. The troubles in other parts of the Southwest, however, will be much more disturbing. The desert has been tamed so completely by the oil era that places like Phoenix have become the destination of choice for retirees from colder climates to get away from it all in the sunshine with their swimming pool, 24/7 air-conditioning, and overirrigated golf courses.

Los Angeles, the glittering city of movie stars, is in real trouble. If there is any city designed for the oil era, it is this one, in the arid landscape of Southern California. Public transport in Los Angeles is about as effective as camels in the Arctic. Pollution is chronic. A dysfunctional city is ringed by gridlocked highways as people scuttle around from air-conditioned suburban enclave to air-conditioned workplace in oversized, gas-guzzling, air-conditioned cars.

The Southwest presents a bad combination of prodigious, empty distances conquered by cheap and efficient transportation. It does not help that the region is also highly vulnerable to climate change. It is, by far, the most vulnerable region of the United States in the coming decades—but the Southeast may not fare much better.

The disaster and ensuing debacle brought on by Hurricane Katrina in New Orleans revealed something that we already knew about the Deep South. Despite its apparently miraculous development in the last twenty-five years, it is a region of racial division and extreme weather. The South is now a booming region of suburban sprawls punctuated by rundown towns separated by long expanses of empty space. The recent growth of the region has been largely due to a single, dominant industry: real estate, and the new prosperity of the old Confederacy is another product of the oil age. Sealed-up, air-conditioned box homes have replaced airy, sprawling houses with large verandas and the famous Southern front porch. The elements are excluded, and defeated, by an air-conditioned lifestyle. Walt Disney chose Florida as the oil-tamed dreamscape for Mickey and Minnie.

The prognosis for Miami is particularly bad. This is one of the most divided cities in the world, characterized by great wealth, sprawling suburbs, fancy yachts, racial tension, and crushing urban poverty. Miami will get even hotter and more prone to hurricanes; its water table will be contaminated with salt water, and many low-lying areas will be increasingly vulnerable to flooding as sea levels rise. The collision of oil depletion and global climate change has nothing but misery in store for Miami. For a sign of things to come, Miamians should look to New Orleans and understand the lesson of Hurricane Katrina: there should not be a big city at this location.

The future looks much more promising in the Northeast, the Northwest, and the Midwest than it does in the Southwest and the South. Resources are much more abundant and include freshwater and farmland with a classic temperate climate characterized by hot summers and cold winters. Agriculture will need a makeover, its scale and productivity will decline, and a much larger agricultural workforce will be required, but the resources are, for the most part, available.

The Northeast and Midwest have many small towns scattered across the landscape that will support a significant revival. The medium-sized centers will lose their Wal-Marts, Targets, and Home Depots, but the small towns will regain their mom 'n' pop groceries, hardware stores, and butchers. On the whole, this transition, painful though it will be for many, is not entirely a bad thing. This, however, is not true for urban and suburban areas.

An amazing strip of real estate stretches as a more or less unbroken three-hundred-mile urban ribbon from Washington, DC, through Philadelphia and New York to Boston. The Northeast Corridor,[15] as it is called, contains more than fifty million people. If there is an economic and technological center of the world, this is probably it, but this global nexus will face serious problems.

Suburbia drives me crazy at the best of times, when the so-called good life consists of shutting your doors and windows to lock out the elements, turning on the heat or air conditioning, as appropriate, to maintain perennial spring, and avoiding your neighbors by never setting foot in the neighborhood. You reverse your car out of the garage (make sure to check as you go—more kids get killed by cars in suburban driveways than anywhere else) down the driveway and nip off to the "nearby" Wal-Mart to get all the goodies you need. You can have a nice house out in the 'burbs, where land is cheap, and you can zoom off to your office job in the city in your gas guzzler. Upon your return, you simply drive back into the garage, and the automatic door closes behind you.

My mum had quite a shock when she first visited West Lafayette, Indiana. I had told her how conveniently located we were; close to the kids' schools, close to work, and close to the shops. So the first morning of her visit I headed off to work, leaving her at home, nice and snug, with the AC running, plenty of Floridian vegetables for a salad, and California strawberries for a snack. I showed her how to work the television: "Channels 34 and 51 are news, Mum. Stay away from channels 260–300" . . . you know the drill. What more could a girl want?

Well, apparently (crikey, the English—what are they like?!), she wanted to go for a walk. I had told her that the shops were nearby, so she went off to find them. On foot. On foot! What was she *thinking*? Eventually, she made it back home. Hot and bothered, but home. "It's hot here, in't it, luv?" Yeah, Mum, it can be. A few people had stopped on the side of the road to check on her. "You all right, ma'am?" Oh, yes, she was fine, she explained, and pottered along. She had been a little annoyed that there were no pavements (sidewalks) and that she had to walk on the edge of the road. It seems that she had walked in a sort of zigzag search pattern looking for the shops, and had covered about six miles or so. Thankfully, she eventually stumbled into the local gas station and stopped for a bottle of water, a Mars bar, and a nice sit down. They told her the quickest way back home.

Of course, I was highly amused and not in the slightest bit sympathetic. But it made me look at where I live in a different light. It *seems* convenient: but only by car. Without a car, the place is a disaster. It's about three miles to Wal-Mart and a reasonably complete range of other shops, including hardware stores, restaurants, and the like; about four miles to the kids' schools; and about five miles to work. All in all, I have it cushy, suffer no major commute, and live the easy life. But take away the car and my lifestyle is turned upside down—and I live in West Lafayette, shop in West Lafayette, send the kids to West Lafayette schools, and work at Purdue University in West Lafayette, which is a town of barely fifty thousand people.

Magnify that to the Northeast Corridor.

Now take away the oil.

A major key to survival in the suburbs will be securing access to modes of short- and medium-distance transportation. Fuel-efficient hybrid cars are a good start, but folks will increasingly need to turn to even more efficient options. Public transportation systems will need to be redesigned and dramatically expanded. Living out in the suburbs will be less appealing as the commute becomes even more annoying. There will also be less convenience in the suburbs as the big-box stores move out. The revival of mom 'n' pop stores will contribute to the survival of some communities, but the economic transformations required in suburban America at the end of the oil era will be painful.

The other major weakness of the Northeast is the big cities themselves. Take Manhattan, for example. The centerpiece of modern civilization is a massive black hole for resources. To get a feel for the quantity of resources used, consider what becomes of them. Manhattan sucks in resources from all fifty states of the union and all nations of the world. What resources does it return? Let me know if you think of one.

This is actually a rather contentious subject since many people claim that city dwellers have a smaller ecological footprint than folks living out in the countryside. In fact, I think the contradiction is quite easily explained by the fact that suburbia is often conflated with the country-side. The claim that city dwellers have a smaller footprint than subur-banites is true. High-density housing within the cities promotes a popu-lation that walks or takes public transport to most of its destinations, cutting out much of the suburban gas guzzling and occupying less land. On the other hand, cities have a huge ecological footprint. Also bear in mind that most city folk do relatively little that is productive.

Manhattanites are the top echelon of society, making the big bucks while being in the privileged position of being required to produce zero food and zero fuel. At the very pinnacle of society (in a roundabout sense) are the cadres of bond traders, hedge fund managers, stockbro-kers, and all those other "money types" who not only don't have to pro-duce anything but, frankly, don't even have to value-add to anything. They simply trade whatever they can to make a profit. Supposedly, they keep the markets ticking and healthy by winnowing out the poor per-formers like predators taking out the antelope with the bum leg.

Filled with people like these, and the people who feed them, clothe them, and teach their kids to play the harpsichord—and the harpsichord salesmen, I suppose—big cities are a huge sinkhole for resources, and they are critically dependent on the continued availability of those resources. I'm afraid we won't be able to support quite so many nonpro-ducers in the coming years. It might be time to bob down to Wall Street and offer out some farm implements and maps showing Dorothy the way back to Kansas.

The economic prospects for the United States are extremely compli-cated. The world's (current) sole superpower possesses some of the biggest opportunities to make an effective transition through the end of the petro-leum interval. It is the most technologically advanced nation in the world and has access to significant resources and wealth—and significant devel-opments should be expected in alternative energy, among other things. The country also has a very strong agricultural base and significant oppor-tunities exist for the maintenance of effective food production systems.

But at the same time that we enjoy some of the greatest advantages, we are also saddled with some of the biggest problems. Much of our population and infrastructure is located in inhospitable and resource-poor regions, many areas are vulnerable to climate change, and America is by far the world's biggest consumer of liquid fuels. Its growth and economic dominance has been built around the availability of huge volumes of these liquid fuels at low cost. The cost is climbing, the supply is about to go into decline, and the American dream is in peril. The United States will remain a powerful and important country into the foreseeable future, but President Obama and his successors had better get things right or the American dream will increasingly become the American nightmare.

The Canadians are the designated drivers of North America. When the Americans rush off to war, the Canadians stay sober so they can drive them home.
John Rogers, former theoretical physics student
at McGill University[16]

Canada and the United States are culturally quite similar and their lifestyles are much the same, except that Canada is politically the "grown-up"[17] and produces all the best hockey players. Canada has a much bigger landmass than its southern neighbor but has only one-tenth its population. The two countries share a four-thousand-mile border and are, economically, tightly interwoven. There are some huge differences between them with respect to their access to energy and their vulnerability to global climate change. In short: Canada, the baby brother, is in much better shape than its big brother to the south.

Canada has an excellent energy portfolio. With huge dams in British Columbia and Quebec, it is the largest producer of hydroelectricity in the world, derives nearly two-thirds of its domestic electricity from hydro, and is an exporter of electricity to the United States. Canada also has a modest standing nuclear capacity and has large reserves of oil and natural gas, making it the biggest exporter of hydrocarbons to the United States.

An additional Canadian ace in the hole is the fact that its principal reserves of oil—the Alberta tar sands—are almost unlimited in size. Being hard to extract and refine, Canada's steady production of oil will continue long after reserves of conventional oil have completely dried up. Canada will be able to keep the wheels turning much longer than most.

The impacts of global warming will also be rather mild in Canada, with the exception of the southern part of the prairies. Global warming will increase the yield potential of a broader choice of crops, for example, as most of its agricultural regions enjoy longer growing seasons.

Another advantage in Canada is a more versatile political system that is likely to be more effective in directing the emergence of a new economy. With good government,[18] limited impacts from global warming, and one of the most robust energy portfolios in the world, Canada should do well through the great recession. Canada will likely fare much better than its big brother to the south and might want to think about hiring a few extra border nannies.

> **By means of steam, one can go from California to Japan in only eighteen days.**
> Townsend Harris, first consul to Japan (1858)[19]

I get the sense that the Japanese are a tad annoyed by all the attention given to the Chinese economy these days. Japan, after all, still has the second-biggest economy in the world and is still ahead of China (by a hair's breadth). All seems relatively well in this country of a hundred and twenty million well-to-do people with a minuscule infant mortality rate, excellent overall health, and the highest life expectancy in the world: over eighty-two. But Japan is in serious trouble; the country is like a ship that has sprung a leak—and nobody seems to be bailing.

Middle-aged Japanese are horrified at their youngsters, who they see as terribly lazy and decadent (Westernized?), and there is a subtle sense of societal decay in Japan.

Following the Second World War and the horrific nuclear demonstrations at Hiroshima and Nagasaki, Japan was assisted back into the global economy by the international community—and it bounced back extremely quickly. Closely knit manufacturing groups provided an efficient, motivated workforce, and Japan's superefficient industrial sector rapidly developed into a superefficient high-tech center. Many factors contributed to this astronomical growth, but a major factor was abundant, cheap oil.

It has been a terrible disappointment to the Japanese that they have struggled so badly in the last decade—sometimes referred to as "the lost decade"—and Japan has endured a long and painful recession already. But the problem with Japan is its basic economic model. It suffers from a serious lack of access to base resources, and so things are likely to get much worse. Japan is the only global economic power that is completely reliant on the importation of fossil fuels. It is also highly dependent on the importation of a large proportion of its food.

Japan is self-sufficient for rice and guards its rice production very carefully. Farmers have tightly set quotas that ensure Japan produces exactly the volume of rice it needs, and neither imports nor exports. The Japanese would not want to compete on the open market for rice with any of their neighbors. Japan has a surprisingly weak agricultural sector and imports grains, fruits, vegetables, and meats. Japan is also the world's largest fishing nation, taking roughly 15 percent of the world's catch; and the news from the fisheries is a disastrous story of collapsing stocks.

Japan is the world's second-largest importer of oil. It is very active overseas, especially in the Middle East and Caspian Sea region, and has significant interests in the Russian Far East. The protection of these resources is proving difficult, however, as recently demonstrated by Russia's forced downsizing of Japan's role in the Sakhalin Island projects (particularly annoying since Japan owned Sakhalin during its imperial expansion days only seventy years ago). Japan also imports all its natural gas, and does this at enormous expense on tankers from Indonesia, Australia, Malaysia, and Alaska. Even worse, Japan lacks coal and brings huge quantities into the country every day on massive ships.

The fossil fuel situation is not good, and yet Japan generates nearly two-thirds of its electricity from fossil fuels, produces steel from imported coke, and drives a massive industrial machine. It is in an extremely weak position with respect to the geostrategic resource basics.

All in all, Japan is the epitome of the modern global economy. It is a huge importer and exporter, playing the resources and value-added products game with the rest of the world. It gets its hands on plentiful supplies of cheap raw materials, including oil, natural gas, and coal, and it converts them—with great skill—into valuable, exportable items. But the efficiency of this model is eroding. As the costs of its imports skyrocket, and the demand for its high-tech goods plummets, Japan is in a very big mess. Of all the industrial nations, Japan will be the one taking the biggest economic nosedive in the next few decades. This, of course, is no great prediction; it's already happening.

On a positive note, albeit a rather small one, Japan is probably the world leader in wind energy, has been instrumental in research and design, and is beginning to install a fair amount of electricity generating–capacity wind turbines. This type of development will be essential to the survival of an industrial economy in Japan.

And one last note: fully thirty million people live in Tokyo/ Yokohama, a city that is slowly sinking into the sea.

Europe must lead the world into a new, or maybe one should say, postindustrial revolution, the development of a low-carbon economy.

José Manuel Barroso, leader of the
European Commission, at the unveiling of the
European Union's energy policy, 2007

Western Europe is one of the major global hubs, but it has very small reserves of fossil fuels and acquires its share through trade. Low oil prices are always a benefit to Europe, and high prices a problem, because Europe is almost exclusively an importer.

Europe has a landmass that is about the size of China and a population around seven hundred and fifty million carved up into forty-two to forty-nine[20] sovereign nations. Western Europe contains all the former colonial powers that once ruled the world. Although they have now lost their colonies and have shrunk back into their home territories, they are still benefiting from the global trade that was established under their leadership and by many of their companies. Germany, the United Kingdom, France, Italy, and Spain are among the world's top ten economies when comparing their respective gross domestic products. Add the Netherlands, Belgium, Turkey, Sweden, and Switzerland (in that order), and the combined GDP is equal to that of the United States. There is great wealth in western Europe,[21] but Europe as a whole is not uniformly wealthy, not by a long shot.

We often refer to the Americas as the New World and to Europe as the Old World, and the long tenure of dense population centers and industrialization in Europe has had important ramifications. Europe has been repeatedly upgraded over a long period of time in ways that the Americas have not. Europe is, after a fashion, a product of the Dark Ages.

One of the most important characteristics of Europe is the existence of many borders. Europe has become increasingly unified in an effort to increase economies of scale and become more competitive in the global economy. Its fragmentation is generally viewed as a weakness, but it will be a benefit through the great recession. This political and cultural fragmentation has contributed to the maintenance of a complex landscape characterized by strong local markets and will become increasingly valuable as the world suffers from a lack of transportation capacity, reemerging inefficiencies of long-distance trade, and the localization of markets.

Europe is an old center of civilization and has gone through a number of far-reaching societal transformations. As a result, it is an extremely unnatural place. Even its so-called natural areas are so heavily influenced by human activities that they are largely artificial. This is a terrible shame, and the truly wild places in Europe are now very few and far between.

There is no more wonderful place to go hiking than the English Lake District. Park at the Olde Dyngeon Ghyll in Great Langdale, grab a pint of Old Pec[22] and head off up the fells. Walk through the sheep pastures and climb the wooden styles over the dry stone walls up the Band onto the Crinkle Crags. It feels like you're in a really wild place, but you're not. It's undeniably beautiful and one of my favorite places in the world, but you are passing from a human-made environment into a human-degraded one. Part of the beauty of the Lake District is the way the green valleys transition seamlessly into high sheep pastures and then into peaks. But this once was forest. It is not a wild place at all. Most of Europe is like this, in one way or another.

Since most of this degradation is fairly ancient, however, the environmental depletion of Europe has already had most of its impacts on

societies. The European landscape has been relatively stable with land use patterns more or less unchanged for half a century. What's more, Europe has maintained a more or less stable population throughout that period.

Considerable differences also exist between Europe and the United States in the organization of agriculture. Although still extremely oil-intensive and using large quan-

Great Langdale. Most of Britain's wild places were deforested thousands of years ago and have been extensively managed by people ever since. Great Langdale, in the English Lake District, is certainly beautiful, but wild and untouched it certainly is not. Photograph courtesy of Steve Hallett.

tities of fertilizer, mechanization, and pesticides, agriculture in most European countries is much more localized than in America. Fields tend to be smaller, and agricultural regions are much more diverse. The distribution of agricultural products in Europe is much more complex, and many more products are distributed and sold locally. The European Union has done much to streamline the distribution of products around Europe and support larger-scale production, but this change has been only partial. The diverse and localized agriculture of Europe may seem inefficient to bureaucrats, but it will be significantly easier to maintain than the vast US industrial agriculture systems. The failure of the European Union to "Americanize" agriculture is a good thing, and I, for one, hope they continue to fail.

The European Commission's latest energy policy, unveiled in 2007, has the goal of reducing carbon dioxide emissions by generating a fifth of its energy from renewable sources by 2020.[23] This is clearly not enough and is probably unrealistic, but it may encourage progressive policies and investments. Europe's action toward the installation of alternative energy technology is light-years ahead of anyone else's and could spark the competition that countries like the United States need.

It would be easy to give the Europeans a nice pat on the back as the do-gooders of the world, but the renewable energy call to arms in Europe is an act more of necessity than of altruism. Europe has very little oil or natural gas on its territory and is becoming increasingly aware of its vulnerability as an oil and gas importer. The need for increased energy security is becoming glaringly obvious, partly thanks to its political squabbles with energy company Gazprom and Vladimir Putin. America has yet to be frightened by the end of oil, but, thanks to Vlad the Gasman, Europe is getting the message loud and clear.

Economic development in Europe through the twentieth century presented particular challenges that were not seen to the same extent in America. Developers found it difficult to redesign cities, towns, and transportation systems on a network that was initially designed to support small populations with horses and carts. In the next few decades, however, this will work in Europe's favor. Whereas the United States has largely been constructed through the petroleum interval, Europe has merely been renovated. America has been the better performer through the century-long rise of the petroleum interval, but Europe is much better suited to withstand the challenges of the impending century-long decline of oil.

The most obvious difference between Europe and America is the layout of their respective cities. Nearly all American cities sit on a classic grid pattern with wide roads suited for large numbers of vehicles, and their residential areas are primarily outside the city in suburbs. Public transport in American cities is either bad or hopeless, whereas European cities have retained much more functional bus and light rail systems. Far more residential buildings are embedded within European cities, and they retain much more effective, multifunctional communities. European cities tend to have scatterings of small shopping areas and large numbers of small grocers, butchers, bakers (and candlestick makers?), compared to the American "big-box" model of Wal-Mart, Target, and Home Depot stores in the 'burbs.

As a result of their cramped style with smaller roads (cities like London, Paris, and Stockholm have a myriad of winding lanes even in their very centers) and smaller traveling distances, Europeans have tended to go for small fuel-efficient cars such as the Austin Mini or Renault Clio. A Toyota Corolla, Honda Civic, or Ford Fiesta is considered a decent-sized car in Europe (and Japan) but a compact in most of America and, frankly, a wimp's or ecofreak's car south of the Ohio River. One can imagine many Europeans being able to dump their gasoline-powered car for a supersmall electric car even if it only had a range of a hundred miles or so. They might not be delighted about it, but most could make the change and still go about their daily lives. Such a change would be much harder in America.

Western Europe represents the epitome of petroleum interval economics. It has been possible to maintain massive productivity and a high degree of economic dominance by importing an abundant supply of cheap energy. This energy has been used to power a vast capitalist machine. Possessing advanced technological capabilities, the nations of western Europe have been able to convert cheap, imported energy and raw materials into valuable products and services for export. Low transportation costs for both the acquisition of raw materials and the distribution of products have made the model even more efficient—but it will erode through the second century of the petroleum interval as the costs of energy, other imports, and distribution rise.

Europe is reasonably rich in coal, although most of its reserves are concentrated in the east. Europe also has a significant standing nuclear and hydro capacity. The energy situation in Europe is extremely complex and quite different in each country.

Britain has perhaps the most vulnerable energy portfolio in Europe, having ridden high in the last few decades on healthy oil and natural gas revenues. The economic resurgence in the Thatcher years and into the Blair years was widely attributed to good governance, but the underlying principal was really the North Sea, which enabled the country to increase its economic output even as its coal mining decayed. Although it is still the largest oil producer in Europe, Britain is facing steep production declines, and its exports are now very weak. Britain recently became a net importer of natural gas and suddenly finds itself at the end of a very long pipeline from Siberia. The country has a long history of fossil fuel use and has never developed much hydro or other renewable energy capacity. By European standards, it has only modest nuclear capacity, from which it generates roughly one-fifth of its electricity. Much work needs to be done in Britain to modernize its energy portfolio and find ways around its dependence on both the consumption of oil and natural gas and the revenues from them. Prime Minister Tony Blair tried to jam new plans for nuclear power stations through the House of Commons before his departure in 2007, but he was rebuffed by the courts. Although Britain is currently one of the strongest economies in Europe, its long-term outlook is weak.

France, by comparison, has a much stronger energy portfolio, thanks to a large nuclear capacity from which it derives three-quarters of its electricity. France is a significant exporter of electricity and has made major strides in the last quarter century, reducing its oil dependency by half. Nonetheless, France is still a huge consumer. Like most other western European countries, France's oil comes from all over the world, including Norway, Russia, Saudi Arabia, and anywhere else that its oil companies have a foothold.

Germany has struggled to secure adequate supplies of oil for a century, first in Romania during the First World War and then in Russia in the Second World War. It is the largest economy in Europe and the biggest consumer of oil and natural gas, yet Germany has no reserves at all. It imports a third of its oil from Russia, Norway, and the United Kingdom, and the remainder in dribs and drabs from the rest of world. Germany is the third-biggest user of natural gas in the world, with most of its supply now coming from Russia. Germany could have been in a stronger position, like France, with a larger nuclear capacity, but the political opposition to nuclear energy in Germany has been, and remains, vociferous. The country produces roughly a quarter of its electricity from nuclear power, but virtually no investment has been made in the last decade or so. Only recently, with the German energy predicament becoming more obvious, is the nuclear debate even back on the table.

Germany is a world leader in the development of renewable energy, and its support of alternative energy industries has been a model to the world. Germany has shown that renewable energy can be promoted by progressive government policies, but, if the truth be told, it has also shown their inadequacies. Renewable energy still contributes only a tiny fraction of Germany's energy supply.

Spain and Italy are in a similar bind to Germany, finding it increasingly difficult to get their hands on energy. Both countries import nearly all their fossil fuels, with their natural gas coming through long pipelines under the Mediterranean Sea from North Africa. Despite their dependency, Spain and Italy continue to generate nearly all their electricity from coal, oil, and natural gas. Recently, like other Western nations, they have been switching from oil to natural gas, which is more efficient and reduces carbon dioxide emissions, but this energy mix cannot last.

Scandinavia stands out in the world as a region of unsurpassed beauty and stable, well-organized social-democratic governments. Its countries cover large landmasses, sustain small populations, and appear to be the place to be in the middle of the twenty-first century. The impacts of global warming look as though they will be particularly kind to most of Scandinavia. Parts of Denmark may be increasingly vulnerable to flooding, but agricultural production in the region will become more versatile with longer growing seasons. Scandinavia utilizes a high proportion of hydro power and nuclear power. Finland uses a significant volume of wood for heating and achieves this in a sustainable way; Iceland is a leader in geothermal power; and Norway may have the best energy portfolio in the world.

Of the scores of nations blessed (or cursed) with oil reserves, Norway seems to be the only one that has genuinely recognized that the resource is finite. Norway has been careful not to overexploit its oil or natural gas, ensuring that supplies will last. This oil-rich country derives nearly all its electricity from hydro, with just a small number of natural gas power stations installed to buffer against periods of decreased river flows. Norway is extremely well placed to face the next few decades and will become one of a small number of oil and gas producers through a period of exorbitant oil prices. Norway is fantastically beautiful. Take the road over the mountains from Oslo, through Lom, and down into Aurlandfjord. Check out the breathtaking Flåmsbana (mountain railroad) to Myrdahl . . . and then don't leave.

Outside the hallowed halls of western Europe and the eco-friendly beauty of Scandinavia is the troubled and volatile part of Europe that we can crudely lump as eastern Europe. This is the region that links the wealthy West with Russia, the Middle East, and North Africa and serves as a zone of transition from the wealthy part of Eurasia to the impoverished. All the poorest European countries are found in this region, with Albania and Moldova close to developing-nation standards. The maps in this part of the world have been rewritten many times over the last century, thanks to two world wars, the rise and fall of the Soviet Union, and the disintegration of Yugoslavia, to name a few events.

Eastern Europe is an important transit region for Russian and Middle Eastern oil and natural gas en route to western Europe. Big problems have arisen in recent years as the former Soviet states of Ukraine, Georgia, and Belarus have attempted to exert some level of control over the pipelines traversing their countries. Vladimir Putin has handled them with an iron fist.

Eastern Europe is heavily dependent on fossil fuels, although the former Soviet states have varying levels of nuclear capacity. There is little oil in the region, except in the Caucasus. Large reserves of coal are found in Ukraine, Poland, the Czech Republic, Hungary, and Slovakia, and coal is a mainstay for electricity generation throughout eastern Europe. Where oil has been imported for electricity generation, this is gradually being replaced by natural gas.

Eastern Europe is significantly less wealthy than western Europe and has made rather poor progress in developing alternatives to fossil fuels for energy. Declines in the availability of oil and natural gas in eastern Europe will result in economic decline and an increased reliance on coal, but the coal industry in this part of the world may not outlast oil by long.

Europe will play a pivotal role in the next three decades. Of the three cornerstones of the global economy (the United States and east Asia being the other two), Europe has the most diverse economy and geopolitical structure. Europe has a more or less stable population and good supplies of most resources, except oil and natural gas. Europe is in desperate need of alternative sources of energy and is making some progress toward an alternative energy future. It has an abundance of technological and innovative capacity. We look to Europe for leadership in the coming decades and hope that it will come.

The biggest question in Europe, as the great recession wears on, will be the coherence of the response. The geographic and political fragmentation of Europe presents more localized and diverse markets but also enduring risks. A well-managed, cooperative Europe should ride out the coming depression relatively well and emerge as the dominant center of power by midcentury. With significant conflict, however, such as we saw in the equivalent period of the previous century, all bets are off.

THE NEW CONSUMERS

> **You can do whatever you want around a sleeping elephant, but when he wakes up, he tramples everything.**
> Actor Malik Bowens, commenting on Muhammad Ali's emergence from his rope-a-dope to defeat George Foreman in the Rumble in the Jungle (from the movie documentary *When We Were Kings*)

Han China was a center of world power rivaling the Roman Empire around the time of Jesus. It was brought to the brink of global domination through the fifteenth century until isolationism, among other things, opened the door to Europe. A later resurgence in the twentieth century was then thwarted by the disastrous policies of Mao Zedong. It seems to Westerners that China has always been a poor country, but this is not the case. China has always been knocking on the door as a major global power, and as the era of Chairman Mao finally gave way to the leadership of Deng Xiaoping, the Chinese elephant has awakened again, and the world's most populous nation is booming.

It was a bad time to wake up.

The world is already full, struggling for resources, damaging its environment, filling its atmosphere with greenhouse gases, and becoming increasingly economically interdependent. The last thing the world needed was another superpower to compete on the global commons, and China may be the straw that breaks the camel's back.

Everyone is investing in China because of its immense growth, but the growth is built on a shaky ecological foundation and the investments are not sound.

While India has become the services hub of the world, China has become its manufacturing hub. It has become more efficient to ship goods manufactured using cheap labor and resources from China, at the other end of the world, than to manufacture them at home. China manufactures huge volumes of goods but has poor quality control. Contaminated pet food, toys with lead paint, and fake heparin are just the tip of the iceberg. The real problems with China's economic miracle are that the resources it appears to have in abundance are actually sorely lacking, and China's rapid growth is destroying its environment. The so-called Chinese economic miracle could unravel in a hurry.

First and foremost is the problem that will soon be faced by everyone—oil depletion. This will be an especially big problem for the Chinese because they not only lack oil on their own territory but also have rather weak access to foreign oil. Europe and the United States are well established in all the major oil-producing regions, and China is forced to pick up the scraps. It is doing just that with investments in Sudan and Angola, among other places, and has developed better relationships than most with Hugo Chavez in Venezuela, Ahmadinejad in Iran, and Qaddafi in Libya, but there is not enough oil to feed the Chinese economic giant. China has a long way to go to secure its needed Middle Eastern oil supply, and you can only begin to imagine how upset China was when the United States moved into Iraq in 2003. China is now the world's second-largest consumer of oil and its third-largest importer, and it will be the first of the heavyweights to suffer for the lack of oil. Oil is where the big problems for China begin and end, but there is a world of trouble in the middle.

One of the remarkable things about the Chinese has been the way they have been able to live on the same piece of land for thousands of years without screwing it up. Agriculture emerged in the Yellow River and Yangtze River valleys at least eight thousand years ago and remains there still. Considering the ecological debacles of the short-lived civilizations of central and west Asia, this is quite an astounding achievement. It's a shame, then, that this last burst of civilization, intent on supplying Wal-Mart stores an ocean away, seems bent on ending the world's best track record.

Soil erosion and desert encroachment are robbing China of productive land. The grazing lands of its north and northwest are being swallowed by the Gobi Desert, while the rich soils of the wheat-producing Loess Plateau are being washed into the Yellow River. Overirrigation is rapidly depleting the aquifer beneath the North China Plain, China's biggest agricultural region. These agricultural failures are coupled with the continued expansion of urban sprawl onto some of the country's most productive soils. China has lost as much as a fifth of its croplands in the last half century and, for the first time in eight thousand years, the twenty-first century has seen China become a net importer of grains. China may be in the middle of an economic miracle, but it is barely able to feed itself.

Water is a major limitation to Chinese agriculture and is also lacking in many population centers. Ironically, excessive rain causes frequent floods in the south, while drought is a pervasive problem in the north, and so a dramatic solution to China's water problems has been to begin the construction of immense canals. China plans to reengineer the hydrology of the country, draining water from the Yangtze River into the Yellow River. The first of three canals is well advanced, but I doubt the Chinese will ever get the project completed. Their economic collapse will come during construction.

Adding to China's environmental problems is global warming, which, particularly in western China, is not some vague, theoretical future problem. It is a here-and-now problem that is accelerating desertification. The land has been overexploited, and the additional impacts of global warming may be more than it can handle in the northwest. In typical fashion—on a massive scale—the Chinese have been building the Green Wall of China. Millions of trees are being planted to arrest the encroachment of the Gobi Desert, although it is as yet unclear how effective this particular megaproject will be.

China's economic boom and demand for energy has been fed largely by coal, and fully three-quarters of China's colossal energy needs are met by highly polluting, pulverized coal-fired power plants. It will remain this way despite the Three Gorges hydroelectricity megaproject and the biggest new investmenst in nuclear power in the world. A shocking five

Beijing pollution. On this day in May 2008, the Weather Channel insisted that we should be witnessing sunshine and clear skies. No such luck. Photograph courtesy of Steve Hallett.

thousand Chinese coal miners lose their lives underground each year. In November 2006, a Chinese court sentenced Liu Shuangming and Wang Youjun of the state-owned Chenjiashan coal mine to five years in prison for "extremely outrageous" action that led to an explosion at the mine that killed 166 miners.[24] Extremely outrageous, maybe—but not extremely unusual.

I was not surprised to encounter air pollution in Beijing when I visited for the first time in 2007, but it was much worse than I had expected. What was surprising, however, was that the pollution seemed to be just as bad in other Chinese cities. During two weeks in China, while the weather forecast was telling me "clear, blue skies," I saw the sun twice. I guess it was out there, somewhere, beyond the haze. Pollution from sulfur dioxide, particulate inhalation, and mercury are major problems. Many factories were shut down in advance of and during the Olympics to make the air breathable. China is now the world's biggest emitter of carbon dioxide, and this dubious distinction is largely due to a booming economy powered by coal.

The land, water, and air pollution and the mining hazards are a horrific legacy of China's economic explosion, but China's biggest problem might simply be running out of coal altogether. If this happens abruptly, the Chinese economic boom will end. China does have large reserves of coal, but the volumes being mined are so prodigious that supplies may well be in jeopardy. The Chinese coal industry is made up of thousands of small town and village mines that cause enormous land degradation and health impacts. Chinese coal is becoming harder to extract, and China might hit "peak coal" with a bump in the years to come. It is virtually impossible for anyone to predict when that might happen, but China has less than half the reserves of the United States and is depleting them twice as fast. China is growing apace in a shrinking world, but it has major water, food, and energy problems and is outgrowing and degrading its resource base.

The beginning of China's collapse will start with trade. China has become the master manufacturer for the West. That will soon end. The model of importing goods from across the oceans is economically viable only when the cost of shipping can be overridden by the savings in production. It will become increasingly difficult to produce and ship Chinese products efficiently as fuel prices climb. As the great recession begins to bite, demand will fall and China will be stuck, for the first time, with a struggling urban middle class. This decrease in demand will constrict the Chinese manufacturing sector, and its export economy will shrink. Chinese cities will become increasingly overpopulated, and unemployment will climb. Inflation will spiral out of control, and China will likely suffer one of the first really big stock market crashes of the coming recession. As businesses fail, the entire economy will stagger, and as China attempts to fall back on its millennia-long rural industries, it will find them overstretched on degraded land. Much of its best land, it will then realize, is now under concrete.

The failure of the Chinese experiment in communism caused enormous hardship across this beautiful country, but those historical blots may seem minor following the impending failure of its experiment with capitalism. China will be shut out from its lofty dreams of achieving first-world living standards, and, as it sees its dreams dashed and its economy contracting, China will also realize the damage it has done to its land base.

China faces huge political problems in a country that is now essentially communist and capitalist at the same time. Calls to increase welfare and services are increasingly drowned out by calls for faster economic reform. In the new Chinese free market, the need to support the investments of the new yuppie class is often proving to be more important than former communist ideals of preserving rural communities and peasant farmlands. But China's deputy environment minister Pan Yue fears a major political crisis if the country's environmental problems cannot be solved. He expects upward of one hundred and fifty million refugees escaping the collapsing West into the cities of the East. The fear

Chongqing construction. The rapid growth and development of China is borne on the back of thousands of displaced, temporary workers, such as this rice farmer from Sichuan Province earning extra money as a construction worker in Chongqing. Photograph courtesy of Steve Hallett.

of democracy is a minor issue in a country with millions of internally displaced people; the fear becomes chaos and anarchy.

The calls for democratization in China are likely to grow, but such change will be difficult, and it is impossible to predict how prodemocracy movements will play out. Much of the world expected major change following the stunning protests in Tiananmen Square in June 1989. But that's two decades ago now, and political progress has been only modest since that time. I am generally surprised, in conversations with my Chinese colleagues, that there is not more restlessness for change. I think the Chinese people have seen enough of the devastation that regime change in their huge country can cause. China is not champing at the bit for a change in government, at least not while the economy is booming. Things will be different, of course, when the boom ends.

> **God forbid that India should ever take to industrialism after the manner of the West. If our nation took to similar economic exploitation, it would strip the world bare like locusts.**
>
> Mohandas K. Gandhi[25]

In the seventeenth century, when the British East India Company was setting out on its trading mission that would create an empire, India was dominant over Britain by almost any measure you could care to mention. Over the next two centuries India became a possession of Britain, and much of its wealth was exported. It has been a long, hard road, but India is once again becoming a global economic power and a serious trading partner. Its recent growth has been breathtaking, and from an industrial and economic backwater in the 1970s, India has become a global hub for high-tech manufacturing and services. India has taken half a century to regroup and reorganize since independence and partition in 1947, but the recovery is now well under way, and India is one of the great economic success stories of the twenty-first century.

Following its years of colonial domination, India was initially hesitant to engage in international trade. Where trade was permitted, it was bound in a miasma of red tape—to a degree to which only India can aspire—and operated under tight state control. As a result, economic growth was initially slow. This partial and gradual trade liberalization was frustrating to many investors and was criticized by most economists, but India's slow development probably prevented it from being caught in debt traps. India remains particularly protective of its retail sector and determined to maintain its system of mom 'n' pop stores. Wal-Mart, among others, has been barred from India to date.

The first key breakthrough in the development of India came with the green revolution. India had a relatively solid agricultural base in the 1960s, and when the green revolution offered mechanization, fertilizer, pesticides, and improved rice varieties, India took advantage. Yields doubled in a few short years. Indian agriculture remains much less productive than agriculture in the most developed countries, and its earnings from agricultural exports are modest, but Indian agriculture is relatively productive and diverse—for now.

The second success of India was its investment in education, which created a cadre of skilled professionals in centers such as Bangalore. The secondary and university education system in India, through the latter part of the twentieth century, was outstanding. India's now-booming Internet technology hubs are its former education hubs, demonstrating the huge return on that investment.

The last big ace in the hole for India (especially over China, for example) has been the fact that most of its education system uses English. Thanks to a high level of English fluency and writing skills in India (a few "thrices" and "bamboozles" notwithstanding), thousands of companies have been created in India to perform tasks such as transcribing medical records and telling people like me, very politely, to pay my American Express bill, kindly, anytime in the next few hours, at my convenience.

So, with increased agricultural production and a skilled workforce, the wheels of industry eventually began to turn. Once they were turning, the rest of the world recognized the opportunities for trading with India, and the economic recovery began. One of India's major breakthroughs into the world economy seems to have come with Y2K. With an impending computer disaster looming as computers were expected to freak out attempting to shift from 12/31/99 to 01/01/00, thousands of Indian computer geeks were called upon to save the world. Searching through computer code requires a high, but not excessive, degree of skill, and Indian technicians waded diligently through terabytes of code for very low pay. After Y2K, many companies retained their Indian colleagues, and computer outsourcing blossomed into a major service industry. India's GDP has grown by close to 10 percent per annum for most of the last two decades.

India's model of economic development has been extremely unusual. It has not followed the traditional model in which agricultural reform and modernization lead to the development of a labor-intensive manufacturing base with improved efficiencies, creating wealth, and then the eventual emergence of a financial and services industry. India has, well, cheated. It has basically skipped all the irritating middle ground. It still has cumbersome agricultural and manufacturing sectors, but it has jumped straight in as a major provider of high-tech services.

This strange rise of India[26] creates some significant problems. It may sound like things are going well in India, but for most people they are not. The dazzling growth is very badly distributed, and hundreds of millions of Indians still live in crushing poverty. The explosion of the Indian economy has made the wealthy and middle class much better off, and it has grown the middle class significantly, bringing many people out of poverty, but the poorest are still poor and are vulnerable in new ways. The Indian economic boom has simply passed most of its population by, as if a new India has been created in a bubble above the old India.

Indians live a collection of distressingly separate lives, but the new, modern India of IBM, Microsoft, and Infosys still lives on the same land base as the slums of Dharavi (Mumbai), Yamuna Pushta (Delhi), and Moti Jheel (Kolkata). What's more, all these urban dwellers, both rich and poor, live on the same land base as hundreds of millions of farmers scattered across a diverse countryside. While Indians might exist in separate economic worlds, they still share the same ecological one.

India's soaring population adds more than twenty million people each year. Even worse is the rate of urbanization, and India already has some of the world's biggest and nastiest cities. Mumbai and Delhi each have populations well in excess of twenty million. Population pressure increases the risk of disease, and the lack of fresh, clean water, electricity, and sanitation services confounds the risk. Millions of Indians suffer from food-borne and water-borne illnesses and, as a measure of the scale of the difficulties of urban living in India, millions suffer from respiratory disorders from cooking on inefficient wood stoves in poorly ventilated shacks.

The biggest health threat for India, however, is HIV/AIDS, and there is great concern that a major epidemic could be just around the corner. India has been spared an epidemic to date, but this has not been thanks to good management. Consider these two facts: Although less than 1 percent of its population is infected, India has the largest number of HIV-infected people in the world. South Africa's HIV infection rate was less than 1 percent in 1990 and then ballooned to over 15 percent in little more than a decade. [27]

At the time of Gandhi and Nehru, the focus of agricultural policy was for self-sufficiency—*swadeshi*—and even after the green revolution, agriculture has remained primarily small scale. This will serve as a mixed blessing for India. While increased agricultural productivity is needed, and many are calling for modernization, mechanization, and intensification, there is an even more urgent need for sustainability. Low-intensity farming practices, unproductive though they are, may limit the amount of pressure that can be put on the land and may reduce the negative impacts on soils and water resources in the long term. But agricultural pressure has already caused serious depletion of some of India's most important underground aquifers, particularly in the Punjab region. As the great recession deepens, the cost of food will climb and many Indians may be unable to afford expensive, imported food. More food must be grown at home, but how, if India's breadbasket becomes India's ecological basket case?

Paul Ehrlich's *The Population Bomb* was roundly criticized for its predictions of an Indian population crash in the 1970s.[28] India went from strength to strength at that time, and its population was fed on the dramatically increased yields delivered by the green revolution. But Ehrlich's Malthusian dilemma has returned, as it always must. The green revolution did, indeed, feed a dangerously high population—but that population has since doubled.

The great recession will hit India very hard. India has only recently become a major importer of oil, but its access to increasing volumes of cheap oil has been vital to its economic growth. India will stagger under the weight of increasing oil prices. The news will worsen as recession strikes Europe and the United States. As the global economy stalls, the Indian economy will be precariously balanced on the fortunes of the companies it serves in the West. If too many of these companies go under, India's recently rich will be returned to the ranks of the millions of forever poor. The economic news will be troubling, but the ecological news will be disastrous. All this will happen in a depleted, degraded country supporting one of the most populous nations on earth. India's short sojourn into the first world will barely last a quarter century, and it will soon be returned, dejectedly, to the third.

LEFT BEHIND

The economic gulf between north and south was torn open in the colonial era when the rapidly developing nations of Europe extracted the resources they needed from the rest of the world. Many of the countries they dominated have struggled ever since. The Europeans were able to do this because they possessed energy resources and developed the first advanced technologies. They were also the first to develop capitalist economies demanding imports. The gulf has widened ever since, and the rules of so-called free trade have legalized the processes in the last half century.

Many countries in Central and South America, the Caribbean, Central and Southeast Asia, and the Pacific region are achingly poor by Western standards, but few of them experience the poverty of sub-Saharan Africa. It's hard to overstate the differences between the poorest African countries and the richest Western ones, and you could use almost any measure to compare them, from healthcare and welfare sys-

The lake city of Ganvie, Benin. Clean freshwater is hard to come by here, but apparently you can refresh your life with Coke. . . . Photograph courtesy of Steve Hallett.

tems, life expectancy, nutrition, environmental protection, and infrastructure, to economic activity. I suppose you could compare the average numbers of hours of television viewing per teenager, if you wanted.

The most important comparisons, however, should be made in energy use, land use, and population growth, because most of the problems related to poverty stem from these factors. Agriculture is primitive, and most sub-Saharan Africans are subsistence farmers, and yet the land is overworked and degraded by sheer weight of numbers. Populations are large despite the lack of land and the energy resources needed to support them, and so the poorest countries of the world are trapped in a series of vicious poverty cycles.

Access to energy is generally very poor. The distribution of electricity, for example, is often limited to just a few urban centers. Even when oil has been found in poor countries, it has done them little good. Significant oil wealth has been available in many countries, and signifi-

Benin gas station. Gasoline, likely procured on the black market from neighboring Nigeria, is sold by the bottle on the outskirts of Cotonou, Benin. Photograph courtesy of Steve Hallett.

cant development should have been possible, but, stuck with inadequate resources for exploration and the lack of a trained, skilled workforce, poor nations have had to rely on multinational corporations to harvest their oil "for them." The lion's share of the oil wealth has been taken by the importers.

The nation of Chad became the world's newest oil exporter in 2000, and its people held out great hope that they would see significant development from a large new revenue stream. By 2003, they remembered their history and realized that they should have known better: oil income has rarely benefited poor nations. With backing from the World Bank to the tune of nearly three hundred million dollars and the subsequent investment of more than four billion more from companies— primarily ExxonMobil, ChevronTexaco, and Petronas—a pipeline was constructed from Chad's oil fields, through Cameroon, to the Gulf of Guinea.[29] Chad's oil revenues went quickly to weapons, which were used by the government to fight rebels. The US government also put money into the country for "antiterrorist training." After four years of the oil pipeline, Chad has become significantly less stable, and the bulk of the population has become even poorer. The conflict in Chad has also exacerbated the humanitarian disaster in Sudan's Darfur region.

So has anybody gained from the opening up of Chad's oil to foreign investment? Sure: the investors, the oil companies, and the countries to whom the oil is exported. Another job well done by the World Bank.

Nigeria has had similar problems, and its huge oil reserves around the Niger Delta have completely failed to bring about any development. Thousands of impoverished local communities have been dispossessed of their now-polluted land by the oil infrastructure. A terrorist group— MEND (Movement for the Emancipation of the Niger Delta)— targeting the oil companies has added its own brand of anarchy and destabilization to the situation but reminds us that one man's terrorist is another man's freedom fighter.

It is relatively easy to understand the scale of the problems faced by the poorest countries of the world and many of their causes, but what will happen in these countries through the coming decades? What will be the consequences of peak oil and global warming? Will essential natural resources continue to decline in poor countries as the global economy stagnates, or will they recover? Will population pressures continue to climb or will they abate?

I think we should expect very different outcomes in different countries, but the short-term prognosis looks bad. Whatever resources are demanded by the global economy will surely be snatched up by the rich countries first. We have already seen the fishing fleets of Europe moving into the waters of West Africa as fish stocks in their own waters collapse. Biofuel interests have already begun to move into poor countries, and I think we can expect them to commandeer increasing acreages in the south for the production of liquid fuels for the north. Meanwhile, the shipment of emergency food aid to poor countries will be jeopardized in a world in which American grains are used for bioethanol and any surplus becomes too expensive to ship for famine relief. Many poor countries, especially in Africa, import huge volumes of grains, and increases in the price of food will cause greater hardship.

Global climate change is caused predominantly by the rich, but it will have some of its most severe impacts upon the poor. Crop production is already pushed to the limits in many parts of the semiarid tropics, and the combination of more heat and less water would result in increasing crop failures and land abandonment.

The contraction of the global economy will be formally documented with economic measures such as GDP, exchange rates, and balances of trade among the mature economies. The biggest impacts, however, will be felt by the poor, whose conditions will worsen.

CHAPTER 10

END OF EMPIRE

A MULTIPOLAR WORLD

> **[A superpower is] a country that has the capacity to project dominating power and influence anywhere in the world, and, sometimes, in more than one region of the globe at a time, and so may plausibly attain the status of global hegemon.**
>
> Alice Lyman Miller,
> "China as an Emerging Superpower?"
> from *Stanford Journal of International Relations*[1]

Marxist philosophers Antonio Negri and Michael Hardt set out a new schematic of imperialism in their landmark book *Empire*, in which they argued that a new postmodern empire formed of national and supernational entities had risen to power.[2] Their notion was not of an empire centered in any particular nation-state, such as the former colonial empires of Europe that projected their dominion openly, but of an economic empire of corporations and institutions dispersed throughout the industrialized nations that controls the global economy covertly.

The vision of the global economy as an empire has been a rough framework for antiglobalization activism and philosophy, although "antiglobalist" is a weak descriptor for the hundreds of groups that object to various aspects of globalization. The clash of ideals between globalists and antiglobalists is, to some degree, an extension of the tension between socialism and capitalism that served as the backdrop for the Cold War. Antiglobalist activists have relatively little in common, ranging from anarchists to concerned capitalists, but they all recognize that although the global economy has grown, the gulf between the rich and the poor has widened. They also share the belief that the economic power centers of the world are causing a drawdown of resources, for their own gain, that is imperiling the poor and powerless. But their enemy is complex and abstract, and its point of control is found in different places by different commentators. Many place the center of empire in the United States or, more generally, in the West, while others view globalization as a construct of giant corporations that certainly appear to be its major beneficiaries. Many who have sought to define a control center for empire highlight the disastrous policies of the International Monetary Fund (IMF), the World Bank, and the World Trade Organization (WTO), which, contrary to their avowed goals, have served to widen the gap between the rich and the poor.

The ideology of globalization appears benevolent to most people, and it is based on the simple and seductive theories of Adam Smith: equality is best served by the invisible hand of the market. Proponents of free trade believe that it is the best mechanism for promoting the wealth of nations, both rich and poor. And, if trade were truly free, it might perform much better than it has. But free trade is a myth. Trade among nations operates on an uneven playing field under a system of rules drawn up by a handful of its players. With an imbalanced system in place, the market then sets the price, and so the patterns of trade that operate today serve to weaken the poor and strengthen the rich.

There is certainly good support for the notion of a controlling empire when we consider the many ways that Western corporations have manipulated the terms of trade, but the imagery of empire is too strong.

Its captains and generals, for example, operate with relatively little coordination, and although they have helped to create significant global wealth disparity, they have done so largely inadvertently.

The world is not directed by a controlling empire but is rather running on capitalist autopilot. There are certainly troubling relationships among powerful corporations, Western governments, and international agencies that shape the global economy in favor of the rich, but the much more powerful force is one not of control but of a lack of it.

The globalization of trade has consolidated economic and political power in the hands of the wealthy, it has disenfranchised the poor, and it has threatened the environment, but this is inevitable where goods and services are highly mobile and an umbrella of free-market economics is provided. A corporation is required to serve its shareholders as efficiently as possible, so it must secure the best resources as cheaply as possible and find the most efficient ways of discharging its wastes. A corporation is required to follow the law, and most do so, but it also has the power to influence lawmakers. We should not be surprised to find, after a few decades of free trade, that the rich and powerful have consolidated their positions and the poor and powerless have fallen further behind.

Nobody is to blame because everybody is to blame. Nobody is directing this monstrous global empire to ruin the world; it is directing itself. And here lies the crux of the looming global crisis. Globalization has been running on autopilot, enriching the wealthy at the expense of the poor. It has been burning through its energy supplies and other resources and destroying the environment in the process, and we are finally approaching the point at which the consequences will affect us all.

The global economy and the notion of a sinister empire that controls it—partly real, partly perceived—are predictable by-products of the petroleum interval. Without the transformation of the world by oil, the global economy as we know it could never have arisen. It is free-market economics at the peak of the petroleum interval, and so the real architect of the modern world has been the abundance of cheap energy offered by oil. The economic systems of the modern world are simply a part of this two-hundred-year glitch in the history of civilization. These systems were built on the vast and ever-growing supplies of oil through the first, glorious half of the petroleum interval. Through its second, perilous half, as the oil supply declines and we struggle with its multiple, disastrous legacies, these economic systems will fail.

As the energy crisis deepens and the links in the global economic chain are broken, one by one, the world will change in many ways. Those with the political, technological, and military capacity will likely do what they can to manipulate the terms of international trade. But as the impacts of the energy crisis tighten their grip, the balance of geostrategic power will shift; indeed, the shift has already begun. To claim any particular nation as the center of a postmodern empire is to miss the point. The United States and western Europe enjoyed the lion's share of the world's economic wealth over the last half century. Now, however, India, China, and Russia, among others, are in resurgence. Europe remains strong. The United States is slowly losing its stranglehold. The financial crisis, beginning at the end of 2008, has raised pervasive questions about value of the US dollar, the reliability of American investments, and the superiority of unrestricted free-market capitalism. The Iraq debacle and the long, difficult struggle in Afghanistan, meanwhile, have demonstrated the limitations of America's military reach. If it cannot control even a single country in the Middle East or central Asia, how can America be considered a superpower?

I see a continued degradation of America's economic and military dominance through the coming decades, as the decline of oil uncouples the economic control that American corporations exert over the globalized world. There will certainly be great powers in the world, but not a superpower. The relative strength of these different powers and the relationships among them are impossible to determine because each faces a unique set of problems and opportunities. Those that are able to maintain the most effective systems (particularly energy supplies) and transition out of fossil fuels into efficient alternatives will see their power, relative to other nations, enhanced. Those that transition less effectively will fall behind.

I predict two overarching trends over the next half century. First, corporations will gain less from international trade, and the global economy will regionalize and localize once more. Second, the military reach of the United States will decrease, and Europe, Russia, India, and China—and, to a lesser extent, Brazil—will be able to hold sway over their respective regions. The world will become increasingly multipolar with a number of nations vying for global strategic influence. It will be a dangerous half century.

SHORTENING THE INTERREGNUM

At the trial of Hari Seldon on Trantor, the administrative center of the Galactic Empire, around 12,000 GE ...

> Prosecutor: Is it not obvious to anyone that the Empire is as strong as it ever was?
>
> Seldon: The appearance of strength is all about you. It would seem to last forever. However, the rotten tree trunk, until the very moment the storm blast breaks it in two, has all the appearance of strength it ever had. The storm blast whistles through the branches of the Empire even now. Listen, and you will hear the creaking. We can predict the fall. A second Empire will rise, but between it and our civilization will be generations of suffering humanity. We must fight that.
>
> Prosecutor: You contradict yourself. You said that you could not prevent the so-called fall of the Empire.
>
> Seldon: We cannot prevent the fall, but it is not too late to shorten the interregnum which will follow. We are at a delicate moment in history. The huge, onrushing mass of events must be deflected

just a little. It cannot be much, but it may be enough to remove years of misery from human history.

Isaac Asimov, *Foundation*[3]

On the whole, I see these last few decades as the most disastrous in the history of humankind. Our immense technological innovation, powered by the petroleum interval, has stripped the world of resources, robbed it of untold numbers of species, and altered the climate. People seem to think that there are technological fixes that will drag us out of our dilemmas or, that even if the technologies are not already available, they will arrive in time. Most of these fixes are either inadequate, insufficiently developed, or will be slow to be adopted, and I do not think faith in technology is warranted.

A serious energy crisis can no longer be averted by a switch to alternative energy. Population reduction without great suffering is impossible, and sudden improvements in resource conservation do not seem likely. The climate is changing and will continue to change no matter what we try to do. Economic and environmental disaster is in the cards, and the reshuffling of the dominance of nations will occur to a greater or lesser degree. It is time that we face up to the fact that we are entering an era of hardship over which we have little control. The next half century will be marked by increasing resource demands and decreasing resource supplies. The largest problem will be increasing demands for energy coupled with declining supplies of oil, but superimposed on this will be a still-growing population on a degrading land base incapable of producing sufficient food. All these problems are coming to a head on the backdrop of a changing climate. We need to accept that the time has finally come. Our glittering model of civilization has passed its peak, its reign is ending, and we are entering an interregnum—a period between reigns—a dark age of one kind or another.

This moment has come before, and other civilizations have faced this test—Easter Islanders, Maya, Greeks, Romans, Hisatsinom—but all failed. Faced with a declining resource base, they pushed back against nature and steepened their collapse. We are at this impasse once more. Our resource base is inadequate for the colossal empire we have built, and it cannot be saved in its current form. We can no longer afford to focus our energies on trying to save the world as it is. It is time to switch our focus to prepare for a more distant future.

I know this message is rather pessimistic and it sounds like an admission of defeat. I also recognize that it sounds as though I am suggesting that we should simply give up and let the collapse occur, but this is not my message at all. Rather, it is a call to reexamine the fight. If we are fighting to save our current way of life—to save the world as it is—then we cannot win, and we are wasting our energy and resources. But if we are fighting for the future, we can contribute in a thousand valuable ways. We need to recalibrate our sights and reorient our strategy away from this vain and costly battle and focus in a new direction. We can work to soften the landing and put in place systems that will catalyze a recovery: we need to focus on shortening the interregnum and seeding the rebirth.

Investments in the development of alternative energy technologies and the protection of land are essential. Almost anything that can be done to replace fossil fuels with renewable energy technologies will be valuable, as long as it does not compromise the land base. Anything that can be done to maintain the integrity of wilderness areas, productive farmland, and clean water and air will be valuable. There is much to be getting on with even though it may seem to be having little impact.

The two biggest problems that face us are both related to the combustion of fossil fuels: the looming specter of peak oil and global climate change. As a result, some strange bedfellows have appeared, as both environmentalists and industrialists recognize the need to replace fossil fuels to save their businesses or mitigate global warming. Some environmental groups are even debating the advantages of nuclear energy, lauding its ability to reduce carbon dioxide emissions. A few short years ago, environmentalists were almost unanimously the sharpest critics of nuclear power. Meanwhile, energy-hungry industrialists are seriously considering renewable energy where they make sound financial sense. You can be sure that oilman T. Boone Pickens is not pushing wind energy just for the good of the environment.

In my mind, 2006 was the year the world woke up and the mood began to change. Perhaps we can thank oil prices, Al Gore, or the loss of Alpine skiing time, but there is a feeling that the winds of change are beginning to blow. The great recession is upon us, and it will put immense stress on our economies. We must bend without breaking. The size of the retooling effort that we need is staggering, and our economies will indeed stagger in the interregnum. Even as we approach the edge of the abyss, however, the seeds of recovery are beginning to be sown.

PART IV

A GENERAL THEORY

The last century has been an era of remarkable human achievement characterized by groundbreaking developments in science and technology, the burgeoning of political freedoms, an explosion in material wealth, and the emergence of a global economy. We congratulate ourselves for making such progress, thanking our own ingenuity and force of will for our transformation from primitive to advanced. But our ascendance has been linked much more closely to our stumbling upon an abundance of energy in the form of black gold. So if the arrival of black gold, not our force of will, brought us to this pinnacle, will its departure, against our will, sweep us away?

If our recent history is this simple, then our future is clear: the decline of oil heralds collapse, no planning is required, no further conversation is necessary, no action, however well meaning, will be of significant value, and we are manifestly doomed. There are many consequences of our current predicament that are now beyond our control, especially those that will be visited by global warming, but there are many other threats that are not yet *faits accomplis*.

Some people look at the suite of problems we face and conclude that we are essentially defenseless. They have little hope that any response can be mustered, perhaps seeing humans as incurably greedy. Others, armed with the same information, conclude the opposite. They have great hope and trust in human ingenuity. Humans are essentially good, this second group believes, and everything will work out.

Humans clearly have the intellectual capacity to create a better future, even in the face of the current challenges, but do they have the will? Yet it's much more than having the will because humans operate in complex groups, and group behaviors can counter those of their individual members. So we must also ask if communities have the capacity to solve our current problems and build a better future.

I'm a very big believer in human goodness, and I think most people do the right thing when they can. So how can good people sit around a flat-screen television in a four-bedroom house in America, Japan, France, or Britain, eat three square meals a day, and not share their house with the local homeless or their income with the third-world poor? Surely this makes them bad people. And yet I know lots of these people. These same people might rush into a burning building, risking their life to save a stranger; climb into a tree to rescue a stranded cat; or go out of their way to help someone's grandma across the street with a kind word and a friendly smile. If there is a car crash, these people will stop and help. They are good people. They will do the right thing when they can, even something as apparently pointless as building a better world. Perhaps the most important thing we can do is to figure out how to prevent ourselves from getting in the way of our own desire to do the right thing. The political systems we forge influence the communities we can build and have a great influence on the citizens we can be.

There is an enormous need for people to reconnect. We first need to reconnect with each other, and this is best enabled by functional communities, but even more urgent is our need to reconnect with the natural world. This does not mean that people have to go live in a forest like Thoreau at Walden or gather wild berries and acorns and trap rabbits and squirrels to sustain themselves (I hope). It is important, however, that people understand how they are connected to the land. No matter how distant the connection may seem, our support systems, at base, are natural systems. Natural systems are not only the wild places absent of humans. We are living things, too, and we have a legitimate place in nature. We can be an integral part of functioning natural systems, and beyond simply setting aside small areas to be preserved as natural and allowing the rest to be trashed, we should also see ourselves as a part of nature and recognize that the stability of our societies is directly linked to the stability of the environment in which we live.

We design political systems to allocate natural resources among people. People on the left side of the political equation believe that the common good is best served by distributing more of the common wealth from rich to poor. People on the right believe the common good is best served by preserving wealth in the hands of those who are best placed to invest it for everybody—but this political discussion is becoming increasingly irrelevant. Neither ideology has the capability of countering the new problems that have emerged. We need a general theory of economics that has as its first priority the protection of natural resources, ahead of their distribution. It is impossible to distribute resources that have been overexploited. (The distribution of global climate change will take care of itself.)

Choosing political systems from the ones we have available is to rearrange the deck chairs on the *Titanic*. We need political systems that enable people to function within communities that can protect their resource bases, and we need governments that protect the resources of their nations and the world as a whole, above all other concerns. We also need international agencies that prevent nations from exploiting the resources of others and degrading natural systems outside their borders.

Is it possible to create such systems in the modern world? No: it is quite impossible. The political systems that we have will hold on until collapse. What we can do, however, is put whatever small pieces we can into place. We can work to save whatever remnants of the natural world we can; we can do many simple but important things that will enrich and diversify our communities; and we can plan for a future when new, ecologically aware economic and political systems become not just the strange ideas of the fringe but the undeniable necessities of the mainstream.

CHAPTER 11

ECOLOGY IS THE FOUNDATION OF ECONOMICS

Our political leaders are mostly lawyers, and our economists are mostly businesspeople. "Well, of course, they are," you say. We want the leaders of our governments and the managers of our assets to understand how legal and financial systems work. Politicians are responsible for directing the collection and investment of public monies into infrastructure and social programs. Economics is the realm of financial investments. Political and economic systems have become so complex that we also want people who are highly trained and specialized in these fields to guard our interests. Does this sound strange to you?

Yet these are not the people we want in charge at all. If the system works, it's fair enough to put its specialists in charge, but now that the system needs to be changed, these are the last people we need. They are the least likely to detect problems outside their field of expertise and the least likely to initiate change.

If there is a type of specialist that would be best suited to manage our affairs right now, it would not be a classically trained economist but an ecologist. Economists know how financial systems work, but ecologists know how natural systems work. A government full of ecologists would be a disaster, too, of course, although White House press conferences would be a hoot. What we really need are generalists, or, as Robert Heinlein put it: "A human being should be able to change a diaper, plan an invasion, butcher a hog, conn a ship, design a building, write a sonnet, balance accounts, build a wall, set a bone, comfort the dying, take orders, give orders, cooperate, act alone, solve equations, analyze a new problem, pitch manure, program a computer, cook a tasty meal, fight efficiently, die gallantly. Specialization is for insects."[1]

Ecology is the foundation of economics because all economic activity is ultimately dependent on the environment. At the very least, we need to bring economics into line with the four laws of ecology that I introduced in the first chapter.

The first law of ecology: *Energy can neither be created nor destroyed.* We are at the peak of the petroleum interval and are about to embark on a great energy transition. The decline of oil is the decline of the most easily obtained, most energy-dense, and most versatile source of energy civilization has ever seen. Oil cannot be created. All other sources of energy, with the exception of nuclear power, are much harder to squeeze from the environment, and their efficiency will be much lower than that of oil. Maintaining the flow of energy through systems is essential, whether they be ecological or social systems. We must recognize the importance of peak oil and respond with investments in new energy systems, but we must, at the same time, recognize the other laws of ecology.

The second law of ecology: *You can never do one thing.* Harvesting the environment for food, energy, and other resources will have unintended consequences. These unintended consequences may remain limited in scope or they may cause ripple effects into other parts of our environmental and economic systems. An important characteristic of systems is their ability to absorb shocks. Systems that are tightly interdependent may transmit these shocks like tumbling dominoes. Systems that are comprised of robust, independent units may absorb shocks more easily. One effect of globalization has been to increase our interdependence, increasing the risk that regional problems will spread into global ones. Political and economic decisions can have far-reaching ecological consequences. Ecological problems can have serious political and economic consequences.

The third law of ecology: *Diverse systems are more stable than simplified systems.* Ecological systems gain stability from diversity and become vulnerable when they are simplified. Social systems appear to have similar characteristics. One economic size does not fit all, and it is time we quit trying to fit all cultures into the same simplified—and vulnerable—model.

The fourth law of ecology: *All organisms, including humans and their societies, are subject to the laws of ecology.* Many of the activities of humans, especially over the last century, have looked rather like a war on nature—but why wage a war on something you are a part of? It makes no sense. I think part of the problem is that we tend to think of ourselves as separate from nature. We are not. Where nature goes, so, ultimately, do we.

PHOENIX

> Harry: Your bird; there was nothing I could do. He just caught fire!
> Dumbledore: Oh, and about time too. He's been looking dreadful for days. Pity you had to see him on a burning day.
>
> J. K. Rowling,
> *Harry Potter and the Chamber of Secrets*[2]

The mythological phoenix, a beautiful peacocklike bird with red and gold plumage, was supposed to have lived for five hundred years. At the end of its life it would build a nest of cinnamon twigs, and then both the bird and its nest would be consumed by a fierce fire. Out of the ashes would emerge a new phoenix that would live for five hundred years in its turn.

Cycles are common in ecological systems; the end of one life-cycle event marks the beginning of the next. Even the simple high school demonstration of boom-and-bust in a conical flask ultimately shows this response. If we inoculate yeast into a flask of nutrient broth, its population grows exponentially but then exhausts its nutrients and crashes. This is where the experiment usually ends. Left on the lab bench longer, however, the goopy mass of dead yeast cells will become colonized by other microbes and (smelly) life will flourish again. An Indiana cornfield left uncultivated will eventually become a forest. A forest, consumed by even the hottest wildfire, will regrow. Even the most degraded land, left long enough, will eventually recover.

We could use Easter Island for the analogy. The story of the civilization that flourished and then collapsed on the remotest habitable island of the Pacific Ocean would seem to be complete, but it is not. Easter Island is now a territory of Chile, with a decidedly pleasant society and a solid income base from tourism. Its population lives quite comfortably. Restoration work has even brought tree plantations to the island, thereby repairing some small (minuscule) measure of the island's former forested glory. The story of Easter Island did not end with the battle on Poike in 1680, and it is still not over. As Easter Island has gone though a cycle of growth, collapse, and regrowth, so might global Easter Island.

The next half century or so is going to be a period of great uncertainty, great difficulty, and significant hardship. With climbing prices and declining supplies of oil, our societies will suffer in many ways. They will certainly attempt to maintain the current fossil fuel model as long as they can. Some regions and nations will retain supplies of oil and natural gas longer than others and their geopolitical power will be enhanced. The burning of coal for electricity and its conversion to liquid fuels is certain to increase, as is the installation of nuclear power plants and the erection of solar arrays, wind turbines, and the like. Again, the nations that are well positioned to quickly put these systems in place will suffer less than others in the global marketplace. Across the world, however, the gradual passing of the petroleum interval will create massive problems, and all nations will suffer. In the medium term, these difficulties are largely unavoidable.

The combustion of fossil fuels has wrought massive damage on the land, in the seas, and in the skies, and the coming years will see little abatement. We are on a collision course to the great recession, and there is nothing we can do to prevent the hardships of the coming decades. Is there any hope that a bright new future lies beyond?

Even now, the seeds of a renaissance are being sown. Some seeds have even begun to germinate, and others are being sown each year. It is possible that the seeds of recovery may grow into surprising new technologies that will change the world very suddenly, but that is unlikely. We know what is needed. The technologies, systems, and communities we need have already been discovered. The challenge is not to hope for miracles but to put known solutions methodically in place.

As we career down our path into recession over the next few decades, many of the right ideas are gaining traction, albeit often only on a pilot scale. As we approach and hit the nadir, it will be with familiar techniques and technologies that the recovery will be launched. We will emerge from the great recession with a suite of new energy sources and food production systems, and humanity's experiment in cultural evolution will take on a new shape. We cannot know, beyond certain generalizations, what this will look like, but (barring a disastrous descent into nuclear war, I suppose) our civilization will go on. What is important, then, is to put good systems in place rather than to allow bad ones to fill the void on their own.

THE FUNDAMENTAL NEED FOR GROWTH

Economists make a set of assumptions that are mutely accepted as normal and then use them to set a range of priorities. But some of their assumptions are patently absurd from an ecological perspective, and, as a result, the wrong priorities are set.

The first assumption is that our continued well-being requires a constant increase in the rate of acquisition of resources, production of energy, and accumulation of material wealth: that there is a fundamental need for economic growth. The second assumption is that the marketplace will continue to provide all the necessary resources and energy that are needed for this growth, and that competition will ensure that they remain affordable. The third assumption is that the resources required for these activities are unlimited and that we cannot cause irreparable damage to life-supporting processes by acquiring them. This assumption inserts the disclaimer that even if a resource should become depleted the marketplace will stimulate innovation and deliver a substitute.

It is taken as heresy to challenge this growth model since decreasing consumption leads to economic instability and contraction and is tantamount to (eek!) socialism or (double-eek!) communism. But the mutely accepted models of growth-insistent, ecology-blind economists need to be discarded. They are all false.

These assumptions all made perfect sense in a world in which resources seemed to be unlimited, so they have worked well over the last century and a half. Glitches occurred, of course, when the finite nature of the world became apparent in some limited way, but with resources always at least adequate and energy sources ever increasing, the overall model has worked perfectly. Nor have our impacts on the environment, although heartbreaking in many ways, yet been large enough to challenge the overall growth model either.

Economists seem to think that the economy is fundamentally driven by supply and demand (shrieks from the audience: *"It is, it is!!"*). It's complete heresy, I know, but supply and demand does not work when limits of a resource are reached, substitutes are inadequate, and the damage caused by acquiring it is too great. It always has—I know, I know—but that's because there have always been reserves that could be drawn on in times of high demand or replacements that could be found for failing resources. But sometimes essential resources actually run out and cannot be replaced. The Hisatsinom could not replace their soils, the Romans could not replace their forests, and we cannot replace our oil. When there is no more oil in the ground there will be no amount of demand that can make more appear. Replacements will come, but the options presented to date are inadequate, and there will be a serious disruption in supply.

Some of the essential resources that we are depleting will not recover for a long time; some will never recover. The changes in the global climate that we have set in motion will present pervasive difficulties for centuries. These are ecological problems far outside the scope of supply and demand. The financial systems of the capitalist may be highly evolved and complex, but they cannot function through a sustained downturn of an essential resource. The modern economy is like a shark that needs to keep swimming forward to move oxygen over its gills. If the shark stops moving, it suffocates. The capitalist shark breathes oil, but the ocean in which it swims is drying up.

So we find ourselves at an impasse, needing two things that appear to be in irresolvable conflict: we need continued economic growth, but we must arrest economic growth. The current growth model will continue to damage our support systems and will run headlong into the coming energy crisis. It should not be maintained as it is. On the other hand, any claim that the current model can be halted and replaced would be forlornly naive. The coming decades are going to be extremely difficult because the scale of changes needed is beyond our capacity.

The solution, I believe, lies in the establishment of a mixture of social and economic models that can support innovation without stressing the environment. We need to accept that different solutions are required in different places. Each community should be considered as a part of its natural environment and so its needs will be unique to the needs and constraints of its specific location.

We need political and economic systems that are able to support innovation and, yes, many types of growth. We need to promote personal growth and technological growth. Without this we fall into the socialist utopia traps of Soviet socialism and Maoism, in which a lack of opportunity leads to an abundance of misery. At the same time, however, we need political and economic systems that prevent and curtail unsustainable resource extraction and limit damage to the environment. We need stability—economic, political, and environmental—innovation, and democracy. Getting to this point in our history, if, indeed, it is possible at all, will take generations.

THERE IS NO SUCH THING AS A FREE LUNCH[3]

Despite the dangers of competitive markets, competition is essential: without it comes misery of the communist form. There is also need for growth and innovation, but there are types of growth we need and types we can do without. The biggest ecological flaw of free-market economics is that it generates externalities. The economy can boom in the short term at the expense of the environment, but it cannot boom forever if its ecological debts accumulate.

The invisible hand naturally finds the lowest financial price for goods, but it does not find the lowest ecological price. Markets must spur innovation without generating damaging externalities, and, if externalities must be generated—and externalities are always generated as per the second law of ecology—then their cost should be added to the economic balance sheet.

Take, for example, the problem of disposing of the mountains of trash generated by the borough of Manhattan, New York. Economically speaking, this trash incurs only the cost of collecting, shipping, and dumping. It is a big transport-logistics problem, but a relatively clear-cut one. But what is the real cost of all that trash?

The Fresh Kills landfill on Staten Island was the longtime repository for New York's trash, supplied by a virtual conveyor belt of barges crossing New York Harbor every day. It was declared full after fifty-three years of use and closed in March 2001 amid a huge controversy about the pollution it had caused to the surrounding area.

Manhattan's trash now leaves the island by land and water to land-fills all over the east, from upstate New York to Ohio and the Carolinas. One of the many sites—and not the biggest—is an island in the Delaware River near Tullytown, Pennsylvania, that has become a six-thousand-acre dump receiving roughly a million tons of New York City garbage per year. The landowners of Tullytown are paid $5,000 per year for having this monstrosity in their backyard, so now we know the cost of trashing someone else's backyard—literally. Whether or not this is a payment or a buyout is a matter of opinion, but $5,000 hardly covers the wide range of ecological costs to the Tullytown area.

A community that understands the value of its environmental resources would not, given the choice, accept this price. The longer-term consequence of setting such a low ecological price on trash is that it is too easy to keep wasting resources. New York City recycles very ineffi-ciently and might be encouraged to put better recycling programs in place if waste and recycling were appropriately costed. It has not been economically viable to do this in a nonrecycling, nonconserving society that does not include ecological costs in its calculus. Adding the ecolog-ical costs incurred by garbage disposal would provide a direct incentive to conserve resources, reduce the amount of trash generated, and improve the methods of its management. Disposal is cheaper in short economic terms, but waste reduction and recycling are much cheaper in the long term.

Consider an Indonesian community that allows a Chinese timber company to conduct logging on its land. The trees will be sold for peanuts and carted away. The community is paid an amount in cash (or not) that might seem considerable in the short term. But the community has not sold only wood; it has sold a forest and all the resources and ecological ser-vices that came with it. When the cash from the timber sales is spent, the true value of the forest may become abundantly clear. Forests are not just stands of timber yearning to become two-by-fours. A community that understands the true value of a forest would only sell it at a price that would seem exorbitant to economists—but not to ecologists.

Forcing industries to pay both the economic price and the ecological price for the materials they use and the goods they produce and distribute is an effective way to reduce their impacts. There are four main mechanisms that can promote fair, competitive markets and innovation while paying for environmental impacts: effectively enforced regulations, the removal of subsidies from polluting industries, increased taxation of polluting industries, and tradable emissions permits (cap-and-trade, explained below). Each of these approaches has pros and cons, and none is suited to all situations.

The global economy, and each national economy within it, is desperately lacking in regulation. That this is pervasive across all sectors was demonstrated by the recent so-called financial meltdown beginning with the popping of the US housing bubble in 2008. The lack of regulation of the financial industry caused serious economic contraction but is trivial compared to the lack of regulations protecting the natural environment. Regulations need to fully account for the ecological impacts of economic activities, and they must be properly monitored and enforced. Here also is where the realignment of subsidies and taxation is important.

First of all, subsidies should not be needed in an economy with genuinely free markets. Governments subsidize selected industries in order to give them an additional advantage in the marketplace and because they perceive the strength of those industries to be in the national interest. They might also be influenced just a tad by dominant industries that can invest in powerful lobbyists. The allocation of subsidies is driven almost exclusively by economic interests rather than environmental interests, and this must change. Subsidies are a tool used to drive economic growth but not sustainability. Immense subsidies flow to some of the most polluting industries: coal, oil, natural gas, automobiles. Subsidizing these industries is tantamount to subsidizing pollution and global warming.

Subsidies should be stripped from these industries and applied to activities that promote sustainability and community building.

The levying of taxes is calculated using similar logic. Polluting industries that should be taxed heavily enjoy tax abatement. Taxes can be used as a powerful tool for reducing pollution or other forms of exploitation by taxing the emission of pollution and the use of natural resources directly. The more you pollute, the more you pay; the more resources you use, the more you pay. This would make perfect sense to any economy that accounted for ecology in its models.

One of the problems with direct regulation through taxation, however, is that it does not take into account the differing opportunities companies may have to reduce the volume of resources they extract or the amount of pollution they cause. Intuitively, it seems logical to simply put the greatest restrictions on the worst polluters, but it can be much more practical to enable those companies with the best opportunities to reduce pollution to do so.

Imagine you want to halve the amount of sulfur dioxide emitted by two coal-fired power stations. One power station is poorly designed, and it is very difficult for this one to make the reduction. The other power station is well designed; it can reduce its emissions not only by half but by three-quarters. If we impose a tax on any sulfur dioxide emissions higher than the target rate, the poorly designed power station will struggle and may not achieve those reductions. The well-designed power station, meanwhile, will meet the goal but may not bother reducing its emissions as much as it can. It may be much more beneficial to let the two power stations trade emissions. If the well-designed power station can reduce its emissions by three-quarters, it can then trade credit for these extra reductions to the poorly designed power station. The result is that our emissions targets are met and the clean industry is paid directly by dirty industry, creating a strong financial incentive.

This system is known as cap-and-trade. A desired total amount of emissions for a given industry is set—capped—and then the companies within that industry set about deciding how to allocate their finances into reducing their emissions or paying their competitors—trading—to make up the difference. Cap-and-trade has been used or attempted in a number of industries and has had successes and failures.

One of the most successful cap-and-trade systems was the one used in the United States for sulfur dioxide emissions from coal-fired power plants during George H. W. Bush's administration. The driving force was to reduce the problem of acid rain. What was particularly revealing about this program was how much easier it turned out to be to reduce sulfur dioxide emissions than the coal industries had claimed it would be. The power companies kicked up the usual wailing protests that the cap-and-trade system would be too much of a financial burden and would cause electricity prices to spike. No such thing happened. When given the appropriate incentives under cap-and-trade, the power companies quickly incorporated scrubbers to remove a large proportion of their emissions, and sulfur dioxide emissions fell nationwide.

The beauty of the sulfur dioxide program was its simplicity. The problem was clear, the culprits were relatively few, the pollutant was easily monitored, and remediation was technically straightforward. Other cap-and-trade systems are much more challenging.

Considerable success has been achieved with some inshore fisheries. Cap-and-trade has been instituted for fish in Iceland and New Zealand, where people can purchase permits on the free market. The number of permits is capped to ensure that fish are removed in sustainable numbers. Since the market is open, the cost of permits is dependent on how many people want them. If the demand is high, the price goes up, and so the permit trade regulates the size of the fishing fleet. There have been very positive results here, also. Overfishing has been curtailed in both cases, and fisheries are in recovery. One of the drawbacks with this system, especially in Iceland, is that the permit system has enabled the larger operators to dominate the market. Many small businesses, and even villages, have been squeezed out of the fishing business.

The big goals for cap-and-traders are greenhouse gases, especially carbon dioxide, and finding a way to set up a cap-and-trade system that could curtail emissions of our worst greenhouse gas has been the business of the United Nations at the Kyoto and Copenhagen climate meetings. Here, the situation is much more complicated. The idea for carbon is the same as for sulfur: cap the amount of carbon dioxide that can be emitted and then let the players trade. But this system is too difficult to manage and risks making things worse. I think the push for cap-and-trade for carbon should be abandoned.

First, the cap is virtually impossible to set. What level of carbon dioxide emissions can we agree on? Second, carbon dioxide emissions are virtually impossible to monitor fairly. Whereas nearly all sulfur dioxide emissions come from a small number of power-station towers, carbon dioxide emissions come from billions of dispersed sources. Many of these sources, such as those from millions of individual households and vehicles, from the use of fertilizers on farms, or from burning leaves in your backyard, are virtually impossible to measure. Third, credit for reduced emissions and carbon capture are very difficult to assess. There are simply too many potential dodges out there. How much credit does one get for producing biofuels rather than gasoline? Well, that would depend on whose math you used. There is a green haze around biofuels at the moment, but I think they save virtually no carbon at all. How much credit should you get for paying for trees to be planted somewhere in the tropics? Well, that might depend on whether or not they actually survived and grew.

The biggest problem that I see with cap-and-trade for carbon, however, is that it gives a green light to consumption but is still blind to ecology. It now considers two parts of an economic equation rather than one—cash and carbon rather than just cash—but it still disregards all the other impacts that industry can have, such as resource depletion or land degradation. I fear that many secondary problems would be worsened. I think a much more effective approach to carbon reductions is through subsidies and taxes, unsubtle as they may be. Quit subsidizing carbon emitters and tax them. Cheap gasoline and electricity promote short-term economic growth but cause ecological drawdown and risk long-term economic collapse. While unappealing, expensive gasoline and electricity is a good thing. The higher prices make consumers confront the real cost of their supply and the real cost of the ecological damage caused by their use.

THE JEVONS PARADOX[4]

William Stanley Jevons was ahead of his time. He had figured out something very important during the early days of the Industrial Revolution. Jevons noticed that Britain's consumption of coal increased dramatically after James Watt's brilliant redesign of Thomas Newcomen's steam engine. Watt's steam engine could now do more work while consuming less coal: it was much more efficient. To most people, it probably seemed that Watt's engine would reduce coal consumption because each machine used less coal, but Jevons realized the deeper truth. He knew that more mines would be dug—and deeper, that more steam engines would be needed, and that, as a direct result of the new, more efficient engine, coal consumption would increase. He also knew that other coal-powered machines would be designed. Sure enough, coal-powered trains and ships soon appeared.

The first machines powered by fossil fuels had arrived. This was a turning point, and Jevons recognized it. These were sure to be improved and added to, and they were about to change the world. And the most important point was this: the more efficient they became, the faster this process would be. We have not yet looked back—but the time is coming.

It seems like a no-brainer that a more efficient car causes less pollution than a nasty clunker, right? Well, it does, of course, but that's not the end of it. There is a counterintuitive problem known as the Jevons paradox that warns us about the dangers of improved efficiency. The paradox is that improved efficiency, while it may reduce the consumption and pollution caused by an individual item, leads to greater adoption and increased use, eventually resulting in more consumption and pollution overall. So does that mean that you should trade in your environmentally disastrous Prius[5] for a gas-guzzling Hummer? Probably not, but we might live to regret the invention of the Nano, by Tata Motors.

For every mile you drive a more efficient car you generate fewer emissions and you spend less money. Great: it's a win-win for you, but you are likely to drive more.[6] You may not drive much more, and so your overall expenses and emissions will probably still be lower than they were before, but you are likely to drive a little more rather than a little less. First then, the emissions savings is not as great as you would calculate from the direct trade of old car for new. Second, since you are driving more, there are further consequences. If everybody is driving a little more—which they will, on average, whether or not you actually do—there is more traffic. More roads are needed. More roads enable more cars . . . and the increased efficiency of these cars actually increases overall consumption and emissions.

A better example than the Prius is the Nano. This is a tiny, cheap, superefficient[7] vehicle. It is so cheap to purchase and run that it may have the capacity of ringing in a new era of car use in India. If the Nano can do this, despite its efficiency, it is likely to also ring in a new era of environmental damage.

The overall effect of efficiency, then, is not to decrease the impacts of a technology but to increase them. It may well decrease the impact per use, but not the total impact. This has been the historical trend. Coal-powered steam trains produce copious emissions per trip, but, because they are inefficient, the trip is taken less often. Modern cars are much more efficient than steam trains, and the combustion of gasoline is much cleaner than that of coal, but gasoline-burning cars, overall, generate far more emissions than steam trains did or ever could have. Steam trains ran on thousands of miles of track. Cars run on millions of miles of road.

Engineers seem to think that there is an engineering solution to every environmental problem, but, as the second rule of ecology states: you can never do one thing.[8] Build a dam across the Yangtze River, and you get clean energy, but you also modify an ecosystem. Figure out a way of fixing atmospheric nitrogen, and you get fertilizer, but you also set in motion a massive overhaul of agricultural systems—and landscapes. Design and market the environmentally conscious Prius, and you have another powerful machine that consumes energy. Technology, at its core, has been a means of extracting the resources of the environment with ever-increasing efficiency. Efficiency, then, is not a panacea but a part of the overall model. We must be very wary of technological fixes, especially those that purport to mitigate environmental problems.

This is not to say that technology is all bad, and I am not an anti-technologist. There have been many technologies that have had enormous benefits and limited Jevons paradox ramifications. Many examples exist in the field of medicine, such as antibiotics and vaccines: powerful technologies that manage disease with few environmental problems.[9] Advanced communications systems have also contributed much to the last few decades of growth while having only modest environmental impacts.[10] Technologies such as these will be central to our recovery because, as we bump up against the end of oil, we will at least do so with our eyes open, and as the global climate changes, we will have daily updates and constant access to analyses. Previous civilizations threatened by collapse lacked such knowledge. The coming decades will see us struggle with disastrous legacies of the petroleum interval, but the legacy of advanced communications will be extremely valuable. There is no longer any excuse for becoming the unwitting victims of the environment; the information necessary to make the right decisions is available.

CHAPTER 12

A NEW FOUNDATION

Only a crisis—actual or perceived—produces real change. When that crisis occurs, the actions that we take depend on the ideas lying around. That, I believe is our basic function: to develop alternatives to existing policies, to keep them alive and available until the politically impossible becomes the politically inevitable.

Milton Friedman, Nobel Prize–winning economist,
Capitalism and Freedom[1]

The prevailing political and economic system is one of free-market economics dominated and manipulated by the economic interests of a group of wealthy, democratic sovereign nations. It has grown to encompass the entire world and is largely unregulated with respect to its impacts on the resources and environment of the planet. It has become a global economy, it has enormous momentum, and there is no obvious way it can be substantially changed. The global economy continues to grow, consume, and pollute. Meanwhile, the danger mounts rapidly. Oil declines are upon us. Forests, fish, soils, water sources, and species are disappearing rapidly, and the destruction of ecosystems is accelerating. The world is already warming, and the climate is already changing. The proverbial irresistible force cannot be stopped before it meets the proverbial immovable obstruction. It would be great to be able to prescribe changes that could prevent disaster, but that it not possible. These prescriptions, then, are changes suggested for those who will follow after the crash.

Let's decide what systems we would like to put in place for a recovery beyond the petroleum interval. What work can we be doing now that will help future generations? In any case, we will improve some things right now as we start to build a new foundation.

THE LOW-HANGING FRUIT

Even now, as we begin to struggle through the first years of the great recession, there are lots of adjustments that can be made relatively easily. Since the biggest challenge of the coming years will be energy availability, the most obvious adjustments can be made by saving energy. This can be done both by adopting currently available technologies and processes and by developing improved technologies. Both these approaches are alive and well already, and supporting them is vital.

The recent push to increase the scope of the fours Rs—reduce, reuse, repair, recycle—has already created a number of excellent government and community programs, and these programs must be promoted and expanded. While most people currently recycle out of a sense of morals, they will become increasingly dependent on recycling when materials become more expensive and scarcer. Having the best possible systems in place as early as possible will enable us to respond more quickly to preserve materials such as specialized plastics and metals like copper and zinc.

I also expect an increasing niche for the neighborhood mechanic who can fix your washing machine, television set, or bike. We have become increasingly inclined to build unfixable products with cheap materials, accepting that we will simply use them until they break and then replace them. The products are cheap, of course, only if you ignore their costs to the environment. This trend is one that we must reverse, and products should be increasingly built to last rather than to perish.

There are massive energy savings that can be made in almost all sectors, and many of these can be made without having to endure any great hardship or jumping any great technological hurdles. We overheat and overcool our houses and businesses, which leak heat like sieves. Our cars are much bigger than they need to be, and we drive them more often than we need to. We travel much farther on vacation than we need to in energy-guzzling planes. The economic incentives for us to improve our efficiency will undoubtedly increase as energy becomes increasingly expensive. The easy fixes will be to trade Paradise Island for Punxsutawney and to get there in the new Prius you traded for the Pontiac (as long as you don't drive more in the Prius than you used to in the Pontiac). Using less energy in the home is easy if you can accept a few minor changes in seasonal temperature. Wear a sweater in winter, and, hey, in summertime, strip down. Large amounts of energy can be saved in homes with a little insulation. More insulation is better, but significant improvements can be made with the simplest methods, like sealing up plug sockets, windows, and doors.

Beyond the simplest methods, there are a number of programs that can be put in place easily to promote efficiency. One model is the program enabled by the William J. Clinton Foundation in which bank loans are made to companies that wish to improve the energy efficiency of their buildings. The banks are repaid, with interest, entirely from the energy savings.

One of the biggest failures of the US government over the last few decades has been its reluctance to challenge the automakers. Allowing themselves to be swayed by auto industry lobbyists, the fuel efficiency standards required of vehicles in the United States (which are called the CAFE[2] standards) have remained virtually unchanged since the 1980s. This has, of course, cost both the automakers and the government dearly in the last few years. As the great American car was systematically replaced by the better, more efficient Asian one, the American auto industry crumpled. And it has cost dearly in carbon emissions. Increases in CAFE standards need to be robust and ongoing. This not only will reduce the emissions from the gasoline-powered cars that we have but also will stimulate the development of their necessary replacements.

More complicated means of saving energy will take longer to put in place but are still feasible and can be initiated immediately. One important goal should be the redesigning of communities for the end of the petroleum interval. They might have more bike paths—we can build those now. Tell your local government that you don't want any more roads. The ones you have, however, could probably carry more buses. New developments might leave space for farmers' markets and set land aside for community gardens. We have learned a good deal about the kind of mixed-purpose and mixed-income communities that foster neighborliness rather than hostility.

There are a thousand things every individual can do. Plant a veggie patch in your front yard instead of trying to keep up with the Jones's pristine golf-green lawn. Ride your bike or walk to work. Build a composter. You know the drill.

A NUCLEAR-HYDROGEN ECONOMY?

The great energy transition begins now. Oil will go into decline within a few years, and our economies will be craving energy over the next half century. Renewable sources cannot possibly fill the oil void, and if we want to maintain our economies we have only one choice: nuclear power. Taking a historical view, the eventual ascendance of nuclear power is probably inevitable. It completes our energy trend from wood to coal to oil. The extrapolation of this trend of increasing energy efficiency does not backtrack from oil to wind, solar and biomass, but continues through to nuclear—and when we finally crack the problem of controlling nuclear fusion, we will be propelled yet another step. I'm not sure this is the best option because if we do manage to replace oil with nuclear power, it will enable us to continue destroying the planet in hundreds of ways. Our carbon emissions would decline significantly, which would be great, but our consumption of most other resources would resume. Nonetheless, if you want to reduce the size of the coming collapse, here is your one choice for energy. Take it or leave it.

The challenges are enormous because our nuclear capacity is grossly insufficient to replace oil. There are serious political, economic, and technological hurdles to overcome in order to bring nuclear power up to a scale that can deliver the energy we need, but it does have the potential to become the world's dominant energy source. As markets demand energy despite high prices, it will become clear, even to the most stubborn observers, that nuclear power is the only source with sufficient capacity.

The nuclear debate has already begun to shift. It was strongly influenced by the inevitable—and justified—fears following Hiroshima, Nagasaki, Three Mile Island, and Chernobyl. The fervor of the antinuclear movement, given focus by the Campaign for Nuclear Disarmament, has balanced the debate decisively against nuclear power since the 1970s. But the tide is turning. Even many environmentalists are now promoting nuclear power, thanks to its relatively small carbon footprint. And the tide will continue to turn as investment is diverted increasingly toward the nuclear industry. The Obama administration, in March 2010, announced secured loans for the construction of two new nuclear power plants in Georgia, the first such proposals in three decades.

The first important question related to the nuclear industry is not whether or not we should invest in nuclear power but whether or not we will be able to limit the environmental disaster of uranium mining and find suitable ways of managing nuclear waste. Part of the solution to both these problems could come from new generation reactors that require less ore and generate less waste, but when energy is scarce, the markets will demand we construct whatever reactor designs we have.

There is an urgent need for research and development to improve the safety of this technology in advance. Governments must, in advance of the inevitable adoption of increasing volumes of nuclear power, support the infrastructure that is needed to make it as safe as possible.

The second important question is how long it will take to revive the nuclear industry. I expect a significant time lag and do not think nuclear power can be brought on line in step with the decline of oil.

Generating sufficient volumes of energy is not the only problem our economies face, because not all sources of energy are easily directed to all applications. We will also require effective solutions to the problem of transportation. Trains, planes, and automobiles all run on liquid fuels, which are refined directly from oil, and it is extremely difficult to develop versatile transportation systems that use alternative systems. If our new energy model is based on the generation of electricity, the problem remains of putting this into vehicles. Electric vehicles will play a role, but I believe that the only viable, long-term solution to this problem is hydrogen.

Hydrogen has the distinct disadvantage that it cannot be simply pumped out of the ground or sucked out of the atmosphere. There is no source of free hydrogen, so, first, it has to be made. Hydrogen, then, is not a source of energy at all but merely a carrier of energy. Consequently, the future of energy generation does not rest with hydrogen, but the future of energy delivery might.

Hydrogen can be made from natural gas, and this technology is in place, although natural gas will continue to be devoured by other industries as long as it lasts. Hydrogen can also be made from coal, and this is likely to be the first major source. Hydrogen will not flow in great volumes from coal and gas, but it will encourage technology to improve and infrastructure to be developed. Lastly, hydrogen can be made from water, using electricity generated from any source, including nuclear, and when we can generate and handle large volumes of hydrogen from water, the recovery will be under way in earnest.

Hydrogen is actually a much more efficient fuel than either gasoline or natural gas, so an economy based on hydrogen has the potential to be much more productive than an economy based on oil—eventually. In *The Hydrogen Economy*, Jeremy Rifkin describes the eventual transition into a hydrogen economy as a process of *decarbonization*.[3] Again, our historical model of wood-to-coal-to-oil has delivered a much more efficient and productive energy source at each turn. These fuels have come with progressively more hydrogen and less carbon. Natural gas contains only a quarter the amount of carbon contained in coal. Hydrogen, of course, contains none.

The most promising mechanism for putting hydrogen to work in vehicles is through fuel cells, although there remain some significant technological barriers to fuel-cell design and production. The cost of a fuel cell that is sufficiently lightweight and powerful remains prohibitive for production-run vehicles. This is a classic catch-22 situation in which adoption cannot occur until infrastructure is in place, and infrastructure cannot be put in place until a critical mass of adoption has occurred. I expect this problem to be resolved, however, when sufficient research and development, driven by economic demand, is brought to bear, although this is not certain.

Hydrogen planes have flown, and hydrogen cars and buses have run. The space shuttle burns hydrogen fuel. Iceland has announced its plan to become the first hydrogen economy in the world and runs a small fleet of hydrogen buses.[4] The technology is available and simply needs to be perfected and adopted. It will take a long time to make this transition, but as we finally emerge from the great recession, I foresee a much more productive form of power driving the world's economies.

Each previous energy transition, despite the fact that it eventually delivered massive gains in efficiency and productivity, was problematic at the time. Coal, for example, was initially considered far inferior to wood, and it was only when wood fell into short supply that the "wonders" of coal were revealed. Oil took some time to make it from the lab bench to the gas tank, and even the transition into the petroleum interval was slow at first. The transition to a nuclear-hydrogen economy faces obstacles, and only time will tell how well we solved them when the pressure was on. Our energy future will eventually see the passing of the petroleum interval and the birth of the nuclear-hydrogen economy.

A RENEWABLE ENERGY ECONOMY?

> **At the edge of the abyss the only progressive move you can make is to step back.**
> Alwyn Rees, Welsh anthropologist (1911–1974)[5]

The only alternative to a nuclear-hydrogen economy is a renewable energy economy, but we are not even close to being able to replace oil with sufficient renewable energy to support a diverse, thriving society of seven billion over the next century. This route takes civilization through a massive economic collapse and probably also through a significant population decline. So here's an ethical conundrum for you: which is preferable? Do we maintain our way of life by adopting nuclear energy on a large scale, or do we restrict nuclear power, stick to a renewable-only policy, and accept that the intervening period will be distressing?

The downside seems too horrific to even consider, but is there an upside? Well, yes, there is a significant upside. Imagine a world with a human population small enough to thrive without damaging the environment, using nonpolluting sources of energy, employing soil-building agricultural practices, and harvesting fisheries sustainably. This little utopian vision does not have to be backward thinking—no image of thatched-roofed huts required—it could also have high-tech communications, advanced medical systems, functional democracies, and the like.

At the same time, however, we cannot assume that a world powered by renewable energy would be environmentally benign. Fossil fuels cause the greatest environmental impacts, but all sources of energy have impacts.

I remember attending a seminar at Lancaster University when I was an undergrad in the 1980s. A scientist from Nova Scotia came to give a talk on the environmental impacts of the Bay of Fundy hydroelectric plant. His biggest concern was that altered tide levels in the mudflats of the bay were impeding the feeding of migrating birds. I asked what the alternative to the hydro project was. The answer: Nova Scotia's abundant high-sulfur coal. It seemed like a no-brainer to me: build the hydro project and take the lesser of two evils. I still feel that way, but it's a reminder that no energy project, especially a large-scale one, is impact-free. Hydro projects in the Pacific Northwest are a frequent focus of environmental activism because they destroy salmon runs.[6]

The environmental impacts of an energy project are related not only to the energy source but also to the scale. Hydro projects disrupt the rivers or estuaries in which they are placed, wind turbines can cause bird kills, and solar projects utilize large quantities of plastics and precious metals. Biofuels are by far the worst: they replace croplands and wildlands. Developed on a scale that would be able to support our current population at its current levels of consumption, the impacts of renewables would increase by orders of magnitude. It is not, then, our sources of energy that are causing our greatest impacts but our demand for it.

This new utopian world that we are struggling to imagine will have enormous challenges, and the greatest of them will be energy. Can a society thrive and enjoy the benefits of the technology we now have at our fingertips—each of which requires energy—while at the same time reducing its consumption and impacts to levels that are sustainable?

FOOD THAT DOESN'T COST THE EARTH

> **Live each day is if it were your last, but farm as if you will live forever.**[7]

Agriculture has been revolutionized over the last century on the back of petroleum products, but its future reveals pervasive vulnerabilities. Although yields have increased steadily over the last century, it is not at all clear that they will continue to increase into the next. Even more frightening in this overpopulated world is the danger that yields may go into decline. Two tensions exist that are extremely difficult to reconcile. On the one hand, an overpopulated world suffers from malnutrition and food shortages, and many people believe that anything that can increase agricultural productivity, so that more people can be fed, is justified. On the other hand, land is overexploited and degraded, agricultural systems are in decline, all the while amid calls for agriculture to become more sustainable. In short, we are unlikely to be able to increase food production without using more inputs, especially fertilizer and energy, and we are unlikely to be able to preserve the land base without using less. So do you choose the land over people? It seems like an easy question, but it is not.

The agricultural problems of the world are set to change dramatically as oil and gas supplies dwindle. Lacking in natural gas–derived fertilizer, and suffering from the inefficiencies of smaller, less-powerful farm machinery, agriculture will need a makeover. New agricultural models will be needed that can produce a healthy diet for a huge population without abundant, cheap inputs on a land base in need of rehabilitation. In a crowded world, we need agricultural systems that are sustainable at all levels. They must be able to sustain large populations and the natural resources upon which they depend so that they can sustain themselves in the long term. These issues are not easily resolved and call for a range of different solutions in different places.

Damage to farmland is manifested in three fundamental ways: the loss of productive land to urbanization, the loss of quality soils to degradation and erosion, and the depletion of freshwater resources. The sand dunes are now only a hundred miles outside Beijing, and when they are lifted by the wind, they blow in to compound the already-desperate

Christophene plantation. This is no way to treat a rain forest. The sudden arrival of men carrying sticks and cutlasses encouraged me to move on after I took this photo. Hundreds of acres of trees have been felled to make way for the production of christophene, a cucumber relative, on the steep slopes of Trinidad's glorious Northern Range. Photograph courtesy of Steve Hallett.

This is how erosion begins: as small rills, into which water flows. As the water gathers volume and speed, rills become channels, and channels become gullies. The steeper the land, the faster the water, the bigger the problem. Photograph courtesy of Steve Hallett.

pollution situation in that city.[8] The Gobi Desert has been creeping south, swallowing farmland in its path, as the demand for food encourages farmers to overgraze marginal grasslands. The so-called Green Wall of China is an eight-billion-dollar antidesertification campaign that aims to construct a three-thousand-mile shelterbelt of trees. It would have been simpler to have managed the land more carefully in the first place, but China, having found itself in this drastic position, has decided that it needs a drastic solution. Twenty-five million hectares of trees have already been planted. This project recognizes, at least, that economic sustainability is fundamentally linked with the environment. There is concern, however, that the shelterbelt is establishing poorly in many places, and my expectation is that a mere eight billion dollars will not be enough to right the wrongs of decades of overgrazing.

Reforestation has been carried out in other areas with remarkable success. Large tree-planting efforts in Kenya earned Wangari Maathai the Nobel Peace prize in 2006, a great recognition that environmental protection, leading to agricultural sustainability, is the first essential step on the road to economic sustainability. Reforestation projects in Niger have also been able to delay the encroachment of desert (in this instance the mighty Sahara), stabilizing soil and maintaining agricultural land that would otherwise have been consumed by sand. The contrast between rehabilitated and overgrazed land in the region could not be starker. One area has trees and pasture, the next has nothing but shifting sands.

In much of Southeast Asia, population pressure forces people into the forests and hills to grow upland rice. They cut the forest to grow rice and then watch as the soil washes away into the valley below. In areas where the land base has been degraded, agriculture is in serious decline, and action needs to be taken immediately to prevent further vulnerability. On sloping terrain in the Philippines, farmers are encouraged to pursue a system of cultivation known as alley cropping. At first sight, alley cropping seems like a losing proposition because it requires part of the field to be planted with small trees or shrubs, leaving less total acreage for the cultivation of rice. Farmers who have tried alley cropping, however, have had much success. Soil moved on the sloping land by rainfall is trapped in lines of shrubs. Land needs to be reclaimed and maintained. Soil fertility needs to be improved or, at least, its decline arrested. Long-term solutions are to be found not in inorganic fertilizers and pesticides but rather in sustainable land management.

A return to sustainable farming seems impossible in many parts of the world, but, as harsh as it may seem, the protection of the land needs to be the first priority, even above the production of food. If the land cannot first be protected, then food production cannot be sustained.

In Western countries, where farming is highly productive, agriculture has become an industrial enterprise that is dependent on petroleum products. Farming, of all human endeavors, should generate energy; it

What seems like a quaint rural scene of coffee plantations masks the underlying degradation of the land. Throughout these slopes, among the coffee plants, large, exposed rocks can be seen. These rocks were covered by rich, productive soil just two decades ago. Soil-sapping and erosion-promoting crops like coffee generate much-needed income but threaten the long-term sustainability of land across Central America. Photograph courtesy of Kevin Gibson.

converts sunlight, water, and air into food, after all. But industrial agriculture does not produce energy; it consumes energy. Agriculture should produce calories in a closed system that returns nutrients to the land by cover crops, carefully planned rotations of crops, and the mixed production of crops with livestock, but it has become an input-output system in which energy is poured onto the land as oil to be removed as crops. By the time your food makes it to the supermarket shelf, many times more energy has gone into making it—from fertilizers, farm machinery, and packaging and distribution systems—than is gained, in calories, when you consume it. We are, quite literally, eating oil and natural gas. As we near the end of the petroleum interval and our cheap agricultural inputs become more expensive, and then scarcer, our food production systems, sophisticated as they are, are in danger.

The hidden costs of food run deep into the fabric of society, and it is difficult to unravel them all. The modernization—petrolization—of agriculture has contributed to pervasive changes across the landscape.

The soils of China's Loess Plateau were formed over hundreds of thousands of years from dust blown off the Tibetan Plateau. These soils supported China's first agricultural societies at least eight thousand years ago and have served as one of the country's breadbaskets ever since. It is no small matter that overexploitation over the last half century has seen deep gullies form across the landscape and terraced fields slump down mountainsides. Photograph courtesy of Steve Hallett.

Diesel power made the first inroads by rendering horses obsolete. As horses were pushed out of their pastures, more acres of grains were planted. Diesel then made it unnecessary to keep livestock on the farm, so the cattle were packed off to specialized facilities of their own, their pastures to be planted with still more grains. Farms have become specialized operations and have steadily grown and consolidated.

Farming communities have suffered as a consequence since fewer people were needed to raise crops. Many farms have even stopped growing their own vegetable gardens, and the great American farm hardly resembles the quaint rural image that most people still picture. A modern farmer might be almost as divorced from his food supply as a banker or a stockbroker. He no longer really produces food. Rather, he

No-till corn. One of the most valuable changes in American agriculture over the last quarter century has been the retention of crop stubble in the field through the winter achieved by reducing the amount of tillage performed on large acreages. This has significantly reduced rates of soil degradation and erosion. Photograph courtesy of Steve Hallett.

grows immense lawns of grains and sends them off for processing. They are transformed into a vast array of products at some distant industrial plant or converted into animal protein at industrial scale feedlots. Once he has finished driving his industrial-sized machinery over his land for the day, he drives off to the local Wal-Mart to buy his pizza pockets and cupcakes. It is a great irony that steady increases in agricultural productivity over the last half century have steadily destroyed the family farm, steadfastly eroded rural communities, and inexorably redesigned the landscape into an industrial production system.

Without the availability of cheap oil, farming operations will shrink and distribution chains will shorten. Industrial agriculture is ensnared in a system of supersized operations that have little flexibility and small profit margins. Farming is experiencing diminishing marginal returns, and it will be extremely difficult to move out of this system into a more localized pattern of farming. That, however, is exactly what is required. More people will be required to work on farms to make them run. If we want to continue eating oil, what will we do when the oil is gone? Without inorganic fertilizer, soils will need to be maintained by good management rather than cheap inputs. Farmers will need to incorporate more complex rotations into their production to combat pests and diseases and maintain soil fertility.

From the perspective of the agricultural economist, then, the end of the petroleum interval is daunting. But what about from the perspective of the land? Here we can be much more optimistic. Decreased farm inputs may enable the rebuilding of soils and the rediversification of the rural landscape. The folks who will suffer the most will be the large agribusinesses, monstrous food processors, and retailers, but it's hard to feel bad for them. These industries have most of the political and financial clout and will fight the transition, but their demise, despite what they will tell us, will not spell the end of agriculture. Eventually, but only after a long and painful period of restructuring, it can mark the rebirth of agriculture as a true support system for human societies.

The knowledge for this transition still exists, but it is not necessarily in the hands of the farmers who currently run the big operations. Nor is it in the hands of agribusiness giants like Archer Daniels Midland or Monsanto. Even more alarming is the fact that this knowledge is being lost from the agricultural universities, which are becoming increasingly diverted into biotechnology and compromised by short-term research demands that detract from long-term, visionary studies. They sometimes look more like the research arms of agribusiness than institutions of independent inquiry. Rather, much of the knowledge we will need in the future might rest with the hippies and small, organic farmers. Shocking, but true: the much-maligned organic growers and sustainable agriculture "ecofreaks" remain capable of producing crops outside the industrial farming model. Smaller-scale operations with fewer inputs are what we have to look forward to in the future, and so these guys may be the guardians of some of the skills we will need.

Michael Pollan, in his wonderful book *The Omnivore's Dilemma*, describes a week he spent at a sustainable farm in Virginia.[9] While there, Joel Salatin, the owner of Polyface Farm, explained to him the detailed management practices that go into incorporation of a range of different crops and animals on his highly productive farm. Polyface Farm uses virtually no inputs—the exception being supplemental feed for chickens. The chickens, he explains, clean the land and add nitrogen, while the cattle graze in an intensive rotation that promotes the growth of grass. Salatin and Pollan remind us that farming is an energy-intensive proposition, but at Polyface Farm, the energy comes primarily in the form of hard work and deep thinking rather than fossil fuels.

Another sustainable farming system incorporates chickens and fish into Japanese rice production, known as the Aigamo method. The fish provide fertilizer, the chickens help with the weeding, and all components of the system make good eating. Inputs can be minimal to nil, but, again, a significant investment in physical and mental human energy is required.

Farming's most valuable renewable resources—hard work and creative thinking—have largely been replaced by oil and natural gas on most modern farms, but the transition back can be made. Sustainable agriculture is not only a question of agriculture itself but also a broader question of sustainable land use. The effective management of agriculture at the landscape level can have huge impacts on the management of watersheds, aquifers, and wilderness areas, and there is an array of intangible benefits, as well as measurable ones, to be gained from effective management of agricultural regions.

So, once again, we link the economy to the land. In agriculture, it is abundantly clear that short-term gains can be made by pushing the land to its limits. Push it too far, however, and it will make you pay. Well-managed, diverse ecological systems, on the other hand—and agricultural systems are ecological at their heart—are extremely resilient. As long as too much is not taken from the land, or the land is given sufficient time to recover, it can grow food indefinitely.

A LAND ETHIC

A thing is right when it tends to preserve the integrity, stability, and beauty of the biotic community. It is wrong when it tends otherwise.
Aldo Leopold, American environmental writer[10]

The promotion and support of sustainable agriculture and the preservation of fertile farmland is probably the most important way we can advance a land ethic, but the concept can be broadened much further. There is immense pressure on ecosystems all over the world, and I think we can simply condemn nearly all these pressures as bad. Something that tends to prevent people from logging the forests of the Amazon basin is right because expanding the acreage of soybean and sugarcane production in Brazil is wrong. Something that tends to prevent the logging of Indonesian forests is right because the asinine planting of palm trees for environment-destroying biodiesel is wrong. The setting aside of land for protection by systems such as national parks is right. The destruction of natural habitats for the creation of new highways in a world that has more than enough cars already is just plain wrong.

The Great Law of Peace of the Haudenosaunee[11] mandates that chiefs consider the impacts of their decisions on the "seventh generation yet to come." The Haudenosaunee had already occupied the eastern Great Lakes region for thousands of years when Europeans arrived. The region was a landscape of pristine forests, rivers, and lakes, with scattered villages and small-scale cultivation. The Europeans gradually displaced the Haudenosaunee and converted the forests into farmland and the lakeshores into cities, a process that took about seven generations.

For the Haudenosaunee, it had been comparatively easy to think of the seventh generation forward. Possessing relatively little technology, they had a limited capacity to degrade their environment.[12] Most resources recovered as rapidly as they were harvested, and the human population remained within the carrying capacity of their environment. This equilibrium persisted not just for seven generations but for nearly seven hundred. Looking to the seventh generation yet to come might not have seemed so hard when relatively little change had occurred from the seven generations that had gone before.

But the world is no longer stable, and we have been flung onto a violent roller coaster ride. There has been so much change in the last seven generations—and this is true for the Haudenosaunee more than anyone—that looking seven generations ahead seems like looking into a desperately distant and unknowable future. Our population is huge, our levels of consumption are prodigious, and our technological capacity is transformational. The land that the Haudenosaunee occupy today bears no resemblance to the land occupied by the seventh generation that came before, and, as a result, neither do their communities.

It might seem like the changes we need to make to recover functioning communities on a stable land base could never be made, but never is a very long time. Few of the changes we need can be made quickly, and it is now perhaps better to relinquish our short-term visions and accept that we can no longer "save the world" as it is. With foresight and planning, major changes are possible, but only if we look to the seventh generation yet to come.

BREAKING THE FERTILITY TRAP

> **As you improve health in a society, population growth goes down. You know, I thought it was . . . before I learned about it, I thought it was paradoxical.**
>
> Bill Gates, founder of Microsoft[13]

To discuss solutions to the problem of overpopulation is to embark upon a journey over tempestuous ethical waters. Two problems combine to strip the world of resources: there are too many of us on the planet, and too many of us consume large volumes of resources. Here we tackle the first problem, that of overpopulation, and the mathematics are simple. There are more people living on the planet than it can sustain, and the force of those numbers is wreaking havoc. There is only one way to decrease population: ensure that more die than are born. The ethical dilemmas are manifestly obvious, and finding solutions is a dangerous thicket.

This is undoubtedly the most difficult question facing a world of seven billion people (projected to reach nine billion in another two generations), and it is also the most obvious barrier to enabling a healthy and vibrant society on a still-beautiful world in another seven generations. The issue has been tackled by numerous science fiction writers, such as Aldous Huxley in *Brave New World* and Lois Lowry in *The Giver*.[14] Huxley introduces a society in which childbirth is replaced by cloning so that new individuals can be made only when required. Lowry's society maintains the vigor of its population with euthanasia. Both societies maintain a stable population with abundant resources and are introduced as utopias. They are quite the opposite, of course, and by their close, both societies are revealed as dystopias of the worst kind. Is there any way to maintain a sustainable global population without a descent into the realm of science fiction? Actually, I find the fears of science fiction compelling, and I'm not sure there is.

Other science fiction writers, however, depict devastated future worlds that are no less disastrous.[15] Their worlds suffer various calamities wrought by an exploding population, and I'm not sure we can avoid these calamities either. That population control appears so frequently in the science fiction literature indicates that it is a problem of massive proportions. That realistic solutions so rarely appear in the nonfiction literature demonstrates its intransigence. The problem of overpopulation can, apparently, even in our imaginations, only be solved in a bizarre and uncomfortable way.

A stable population could form the bedrock of a sustainable global society. Looking to the seventh generation, this might be the single most important opportunity to create a socially and environmentally stable civilization. It would be lovely if we could limit the global population to, say, four billion by the time that generation is born. Is there any way to get there without yielding our humanity?

Science fiction is fun, but history is for real, and we have seen what can happen when a society becomes overpopulated. The population problem may be "solved" by genocide. Other factors operate, of course, but the dominant ethnic groups occupying Armenia (1915–1923), Germany (1931–1945), Bangladesh (1971), Cambodia (1975–1979), Rwanda (1994), Bosnia (1995), and Sudan (2003 to present)—and there are many other examples—all attempted to make space for their preferred race: themselves. If population pressure is one of the fundamental triggers for genocide—and I believe it is the most fundamental of all—then our projected increase toward a population of nine billion is a major cause for concern.

The solutions at the end of the population equation—death—are euthanasia and murder, and these are not solutions at all. So are there any realistic solutions at the beginning of the equation? Can we reduce birthrates? Here we also meet some great difficulties. There have been a surprising number of government-sanctioned eugenics (compulsory sterilization) programs that have targeted minority populations. These programs have not been aimed at population control per se, and the numbers of people sterilized in these programs have been much lower than those murdered in genocides, but the list of countries that have carried out eugenics programs is startling. It includes the compulsory sterilization of various groups by the German Nazis and the Roma (Gypsies) by Czechoslovakia under Soviet communism, but it also includes government-sanctioned sterilization programs against the American Indians by both the United States and Canada as recently as the 1960s.[16]

The biggest experiment in population control has been China's one-child policy that encompasses many of the issues of population control, both the obvious and the subtle. The one-child policy was initiated in 1979 at the beginning of Deng Xiaoping's economic reforms, after passing of the Mao Zedong era. Since then, China has been transformed from a communist politic with a closed economy to a communist politic with one of the most open, free-market economies in the world. The one-child policy determined to restrict families to a single child.[17] China has come close to doing this, and its population growth has been reduced dramatically. Much of China's recent economic explosion may have been impossible without this policy. Estimates vary, but a reasonable estimate would indicate that without the one-child policy the population of China would now be 1.6 billion rather than 1.3 billion. This represents a reduction roughly equivalent to the current population of the United States. The benefits of the one-child policy, in economic terms, are quite clear.

But the one-child policy has caused enormous social fallout. First, the right to raise a family without interference is widely viewed as a basic human right. Second, the desire of many families for a son rather than a daughter has led to the widespread abandonment and murder of newborn girls. Third, the young school- and college-age population is now disproportionately male. As these little princes grow older, they may find that they won't be handed everything, as was the case when they were younger. Fourth, the population is aging. The secondary impacts of the one-child policy are many and varied, such as reports that Chinese women are using fertility-enhancing drugs to increase their chance of a multiple birth, and the suggestion that single-child-brat syndrome[18] has now made it from America to China. One of the most upsetting consequences of the Sichuan earthquake in 2008 that trapped and killed large numbers of children beneath collapsing school buildings, on top of the immense scale of the tragedy in the first instance, was the dawning realization that whole towns, whose families had lost their only child, had suddenly lost an entire generation.

The one-child policy places us face-to-face with the ethical dilemma of population control. Inaction is disastrous. Action is riddled with social contradictions. Perhaps the one-child policy can only be assessed dispassionately: how much suffering is caused by the policy and how much suffering is saved? There is no mathematical formula into which we can plug the subjective data we have, but I see the policy, on measure, as a success.

Compare the populations of China and India over the last three decades. India's population was a quarter-billion less than that of China's in 1980, but it will surpass it in the next few years. In little more than a quarter century, the population of India will have doubled, and poverty is increasing rapidly among India's poor. Which government has caused more suffering with its population policy? China, with its socially repressive one-child policy, or India, with its policy of laissez-faire? I think time will tell that the answer is India.

For the next part of this discussion, we must depart China and India for a while and consider those countries that are both desperately poor and overpopulated. They include some countries in Asia, notably Bangladesh, but the vast majority is in sub-Saharan Africa. This is where the fertility trap has reached its most devastating nadir, and where breaking that trap seems most hopeless.

Infant mortality climbs in places that lack adequate resources and health services. The problem is confounded by a lack of welfare and pension support, and children are required to support people in their old age. Losing children in childbirth and infancy raises the stakes, resulting in more pregnancies. More children are born and more children die as both the fertility rate and the mortality rate climb in a disastrous spiral. This is the paradox Bill Gates commented on in the quotation at the beginning of this section, and most people—myself included—might, at first, expect the opposite. Surely people who are better off would be more likely to have children since they would be better able to support them. The actual trend, alas, is the opposite. The fertility trap, at its base, is a terrible iteration of the tragedy of the commons. Rates of pregnancy and infant mortality increase as security declines. Insecurity not only causes misery but also accelerates it and propels it into the next generation.

The fertility trap appears intractable, and this problem, above all others, is one that requires the long view. This is not a problem that can be solved overnight but only over generations. Where do we begin? Since the fundamental problems of the fertility trap are food insecurity and health insecurity, we must begin there.

The story of malaria appears to be just another impossible problem of the impoverished third world, but it is also the story of the first-world countries that conquered it. Malaria was prevalent in much of Europe in the nineteenth century. It was a major problem in the swampy Netherlands and common in the English Fen country,[19] and it was a tactical consideration during the Napoleonic wars. The Roman Campagna, a swampy area at the mouth of the Tiber River, was rife with malaria until it was drained by Benito Mussolini in the 1930s. It is mostly forgotten that malaria was common in the United States at the time of the Civil War.

French engineer Ferdinand de Lesseps dreamed up the idea of building a canal across the Isthmus of Darien[20] to connect the Atlantic and Pacific Oceans, and his grand project began in 1886. It was abandoned only three years later after more than twenty thousand workers had died of yellow fever and malaria, and work on the canal had ground to a halt. Such is the power of disease to suppress economic development, and it prompted Ronald Ross to declare in 1902: "Malarial fever is important not only because of the misery it inflicts upon mankind, but also because of the serious opposition it has always given to the march of civilization."[21]

A decade later Theodore Roosevelt resumed the challenge, but he did two things quite differently. First, he engineered the civil uprising in Colombia that would form the breakaway nation of Panama, with which he could "work." Second, he took malaria seriously and listened to his biologists. All workers on the Panama Canal project were required to take quinine; its bitter taste was disguised in pink lemonade.[22] They were also ordered to sleep under bed nets, all standing water was coated with oil, and water containers were screened. Malaria was rapidly brought under control and work on the canal was not delayed.

It would sound like all should be well. Malaria had succumbed to the will of humankind, who had proven that malaria was both preventable and manageable. So why do millions of people still die of malaria every year? They clearly don't need to.

Quinine was expensive, coming from plantations of the Andean cinchona tree, and was soon replaced by the cheaper analog, chloroquine, which became the sole drug used to combat malaria. Efforts to control malaria by other means fell by the wayside, but then malaria began to evolve resistance to chloroquine. By the 1970s chloroquine was ineffective in much of the world. Replacement drugs were developed, but they were much more expensive and out of reach of the poor.[23] Multinational corporations and organizations can operate under the protection of antimalarial drugs while working in malaria-infested areas, but the local people have been abandoned. Bed nets and other mosquito avoidance techniques can be deployed to deliver significant improvements for only a few dollars. Some of this happens, but not enough. Kudos to those such as Bill and Melinda Gates, who, through their foundation, have begun to tackle this issue. They have had some regional successes, but malaria is still winning the battle. The story of malaria, of course, echoes and reverberates in the stories of HIV/AIDS, cholera, measles, yellow fever, guinea worm, and many other diseases. Each one is preventable or manageable. Cholera, for instance, is endemic in nature all over the world, and all that is needed to prevent it from causing dreadful epidemics is clean water. Yet we seem unable to make this happen.

Malaria provides a powerful insight into the real economic enemies of developing nations. Failing to prevent the preventable, millions endure unnecessary suffering, and their societies continue to stagnate. If there is one key to economic development in these countries, it is basic healthcare. We can't expect poor countries to drag themselves out of poverty until their citizens can drag themselves out of their sickbed.

Coupled with health security must be food security, and, here again, we run up against massive systemic problems, vicious cycles, and seemingly intractable commons dilemmas. Unsustainable populations lead to unsustainable resource use, land degradation, and declining agriculture—cycling back into further population pressure and instability. There is no single place to break this vicious cycle, and it needs to be tackled at multiple points.

First, populations should not be propped up by the provision of food from other continents—and here again another ethical dilemma stares back at us blankly. How can we refuse to provide food to malnourished, starving people? We have to do our best to provide food to alleviate short-term, acute famines. To stand aside and watch people die in the name of "attaining a more sustainable population" would be callous and evil in the extreme. But we don't only export grains to alleviate suffering.

Large volumes of grains are imported into Africa on an ongoing basis, and this has two effects. First, it simply enables the support of a population that is too large for its land base. Second, it suppresses the development of local agriculture because we also dump cheap grains onto poor countries to make money. Corporate interests gain significantly from cheap grain dumping. These include agricultural commodity groups that view food aid as a good write-off for surplus grains and shipping companies that make good profits from delivering them. But although the dumping of cheap grains might seem like a kindness, it actually creates a pervasive trap. African farmers cannot rely on prices in their own marketplaces remaining stable, and in addition, they have to compete with cheap grains produced with the aid of first-world farming subsidies. Agricultural markets are suppressed, and farming is permanently held back at subsistence levels. Instead of sending food to Africa, we should send the means, financial and material, to support local production—we should subsidize it, like everywhere else.

Most countries in sub-Saharan Africa do not even come close to feeding themselves, and so the rival dilemmas are clear. The removal of food aid would exacerbate the crisis of malnutrition in the short term and would risk famine and a humanitarian crisis. Continuing to send food would further support an overlarge population that is having devastating impacts on its environment. A long-term plan is required, then, in which food aid is scaled back gradually and replaced with development projects that support the land base. The long view is essential.

I conclude that the fertility trap, which plays out in its most remorseless way in sub-Saharan Africa, is fundamentally a problem of overpopulation, food insecurity, and health insecurity. With smaller, more sustainable populations within the limits of their environmental carrying capacity, there is a much better chance that developing countries can be effectively governed. None of this seems possible at the moment but may become possible within the long term, and so the solution to the fertility trap has, at its base, not population management at all but land management. Without sustainable ecology, there can be no sustainable economy and only limited development. Only with a stable ecology and a stable economy will the conditions prevail under which health security, food security, and stable populations are possible.

LIFEBOAT ETHICS

> **We are all the descendants of thieves, and the world's resources are inequitably distributed. But we must begin the journey to tomorrow from the point where we are today. We cannot remake the past. We cannot safely divide the wealth equitably among all peoples so long as people reproduce at different rates. To do so would guarantee that our grandchildren and everyone else's grandchildren, would have only a ruined world to inhabit.**
>
> Garret Hardin, "Lifeboat Ethics: The Case against Helping the Poor"[24]

Garrett Hardin was a very interesting character and a very important thinker. His exposition of the tragedy of the commons revolutionized thinking about how to manage common-pool resources, and his lifeboat ethics essay is similarly challenging. Both concepts have stimulated considerable discussion, but, thankfully, we can answer both contentions with a strong rebuttal. The tragedy of the commons appears to teach us that commons should be abandoned because people are incapable of managing them, and much policy has focused on transferring common-pool resources to either government control or privatization as a result. But the contention is false. Commons can be and have been effectively managed by functional communities, as we shall see in the next chapter. Lifeboat ethics also makes a seductive but false contention. It is unfair to blame poor countries for overpopulation.

Lifeboat ethics contends that the rich countries that have developed to the point that their stable economies can maintain sustainable populations should protect themselves from the exploding populations of poor countries. We simply cannot allow populations to flow from overpopulated poor countries into rich countries, it is claimed, because the rich countries would also then become overpopulated. The philosophy is seductive because it is partly true, but the ways in which it is false are extremely important.

That stable populations are possible has been demonstrated by most Western nations, particularly in Europe. The fertility trap is not unbreakable. Europe as a whole has a population growth rate near zero, and its population is expected to remain more or less static over the coming decades. Japan's population is declining. This situation is actually considered by many economists to be a population problem. Birthrates are too low, they tell us, the population is aging, and the workforce is shrinking. Nonsense. Allow immigration. Problem solved.

So how has the Western world managed to stabilize its populations? First, population stabilization is a natural consequence of economic stability, good healthcare, and retirement security. These circumstances are all in place in most Western countries, but this is only part of the explanation. The second reason is that Western countries import large volumes of resources and support their populations with resources not only from their own territories but also from other parts of the world. Such is the power of free-market economics. One country can support itself on the back of another. This is fine because resources are free to flow under the rules of free trade. People, of course, are not. And then we refuse to let them into our lifeboat—the same lifeboat stocked with their rations.

CHAPTER 13

RECONNECTING

My fate is to live among varied and confusing
storms but for you, perhaps, there will follow a
better age. When the darkness has been dispersed,
our descendants can come again in the former
pure radiance.

Petrarch, Italian scholar and humanist[1]

W e are so horribly disconnected. So many of our communities
function badly, from impoverished neighborhoods that
breed insecurity and criminality to wealthy bedroom communities that
allow commuters little more than a nightly resting place to gated communities in which an antiseptic suburban lifestyle can shut out the rest
of the world. We are disconnected as nations also. Wasn't globalization
supposed to bring us together and break down walls? It has done the
opposite, building real and virtual walls that separate the haves from the
have-nots.[2] The walls are porous to resources but impervious to people.

As the world fills, the planet warms, resources disappear, oil and gas
go into decline, and the global economy slumps under its own weight,
we are careening down a path that will confront us with social challenges
on a grand scale. Conditions will be ripe for dysfunctional communities
to steer us down perilous paths. As we rebuild, we must do so with a long
view—a view toward future generations that can suppress our destruc-

Sichuan village. Not everywhere is suited to mechanization, and perhaps that will serve the people of the Sichuan basin well. Contoured valleys support multiple crops with corn, beans, and a wide array of other vegetables grown on the higher slopes, and rice paddies maintained at the lower levels where the abundant summer rains can be channeled. The bottom of the valley is often converted to a modest fish farm. Coupled with the chickens roaming backyards along the slope, each valley produces a diverse, healthy diet. Photograph courtesy of Steve Hallett.

tive tendencies toward greed, racism, and violence, and can support the better sides of our natures.

We are disastrously disconnected from the natural world. We feel as though we have to drive off to go see it every now and then, and perhaps camp in it for a long weekend, but we rarely consider ourselves a part of the natural world. We act as if we are its controllers and managers but not one of its community members.

If human societies are ever to survive in the long term instead of going through repeated cycles of boom and bust, we need to redefine ourselves as a social, small-group mammal, and we need to design communities that can live within the limits of their environments. We also need our individual nations to coexist within the limits of the global environment.

IS SOCIALISM DEAD, AND IS CAPITALISM DOOMED?

> **Socialism collapsed because it did not allow the market to tell the economic truth. Capitalism may collapse because it does not allow the market to tell the ecological truth.**
> Øystein Dahle, former vice president of Exxon Norway

Karl Marx's landmark *The Communist Manifesto* was published in 1858, more than a century and a half ago. I don't think we should be too surprised to find that it is imperfectly attuned to the needs of the third millennium. Marx's theory was designed for a particular group of people in a particular place at a particular time. For those people, there and then, it contained a good deal of wisdom. His audience, as it happens, was not Russia, a country with a very large agrarian population, but the industrial workers of western Europe. He actually formed many of his ideas in my hometown of Manchester, England, where he and his colleague Frederick Engels observed the plight of exploited mill workers during the Industrial Revolution. The working class was growing rapidly to serve the expanding needs of industry, and Marx thought that this new capitalism was vulnerable to overthrow by an increasingly numerous and disenchanted populace. Capitalism would burn out, Marx believed, and it could be pushed to that point by a popular communist revolt from which a new egalitarian society could emerge.

It did not happen that way. The communist revolution came in Russia rather than in Germany or in Britain, and then two world wars broke out. By the end of the Second World War, the socioeconomic calculus had shifted dramatically. Germany had been defeated by the combined efforts of the Soviet Union, the British, the Americans, and their allies, and the world sidled directly into the Cold War. The two remaining great powers—by no coincidence, the two great oil producers—faced off against each other. The Soviet Union slid increasingly from a grand social experiment to a brutal dictatorship and was eventually crushed by the power of American capitalism. The artificial depression of oil prices through the 1980s that pushed the Soviet Union into bankruptcy also played a large role.

The end of the Soviet Union sealed the deal on the great political question of the twentieth century. There had been, it seemed, only two possible ways of governing. Capitalism won the Cold War, and now there was only one possible way. Karl Marx had been quite wrong. Capitalism did not bring about its own demise but only grew stronger.

There remain few bastions of communism, and each is very interesting in its own right. China is allegedly communist, but, in the words of one professor I met in Beijing, "It is nonsense to think of China as communist. We have some of the old politics, but our economics is now more Western than the West." Communism has yielded to capitalism peacefully in China and has done so completely. At the opposite end of the spectrum, North Korea is one of the last remaining demonstrations of failed command-and-control economics. It has become an economic failure, a political pariah, and an ecological disaster zone. The only remaining communist nation of any credibility is Cuba, which has proven remarkably resilient.

Cuba's economy was crushed at the fall of the Soviet Union and has been constantly squeezed by the US embargo ever since, and yet it has survived. Cuba is not without its problems, and there are significant human rights abuses, but its government's management of the economic crises it faced in the last thirty years has been remarkable. One major success in Cuba has been an effective reorganization of agriculture based on effective land management, an emphasis on sustainability, and a solid system of land ownership.

Cuba became an instant test case for what might happen at the end of the petroleum interval. With its big brother no longer providing cheap oil and grains and no longer buying its sugar at elevated prices, Cuba plummeted immediately into a deep depression and suffered sudden and serious food shortages. It took Cuba barely a decade to reorganize its agriculture. Plantation lands were rehabilitated as thousands of new farmers put the land back into the production of staple crops in the countryside—and many vegetable gardens in the city, arranged in effective cooperatives. Cuba has not become a major exporter and does not have a highly productive agricultural sector, but it does have a strong, self-sufficient agricultural base, and one that is built on a solid, sustainable foundation. Its post–Cold War survival has been truly remarkable.

Cuba was held together (or repressed, depending how you see it) by Fidel Castro for forty-nine years. It's difficult to know what will become of Cuba in the next few decades. Fidel has been replaced by his brother, Raúl, and the political dynamic may be shifting somewhat. Changes in the relationship between Cuba and the United States could have far-reaching consequences if the relationship between two nations that should be cooperating with each other can break their churlish political deadlock.

The governments of the rich countries have all operated on the same basic model for the last half century in which democratically elected governments have distributed the wealth of free-market economies. The philosophies of how to distribute wealth and whether or not there are certain industries and services that should be managed by the government or the markets has been the major political question, and many countries have reduced their political offerings to two parties, a more conservative party and a more liberal party, such as the Conservatives versus Labour in the United Kingdom, and the US division of Republicans and Democrats. Another sign that socialism is truly dead is the way that these parties have generally drifted toward conservatism in recent years.

Tony Blair's New Labour movement was successfully elected in Britain following the broad adoption of more centrist and conservative policies. "Best conservative prime minister in years," declares my mum. In America, Arlen Specter, senator for Pennsylvania, was able to defect from Republican to Democrat with nary a change in policy stance. Sweden has probably been one of the most liberally governed democratic countries since the war, but even there the Social Democratic Party has been gradually pushed rightward.

The question of socialism versus capitalism has consumed our political thinking in recent history, but it is increasingly irrelevant. The problem now is that the rhetoric is becoming a distraction. With socialism discarded as a failure and capitalism elevated to the status of successful ideology, there appear to be few options for a new politics. But both socialism and capitalism suffer the fatal flaw of being growth-oriented and nature-blind. They differ on how to divvy up the spoils, but each is capable of parceling out environmental destruction in good measure. Somehow, we need to find a new way of managing nations with political systems that can incorporate ecological considerations into their calculus.

The biggest need in politics is to design systems that can protect the environment. This demands an enormous shift *away* from our orientation on growth and *toward* sustainability. This seems impossible from our current vantage point. Our current systems are deeply entrenched and have enormous momentum. It is unlikely that any substantial systemic change can be made until the current system has broken down of its own accord. Only then will a redesign be possible, but there are certainly things that can be done to tweak the system, and while these may not do much, they are better than nothing. Among these tweaks are the appropriate realignment of subsidies and taxes and the institution of appropriate cap-and-trade systems. Another thing we might be able to do is reduce the destructive power of corporations.

Most people distrust corporations, so they are a politically juicy target for populists and so possibly some progress might be made here. Corporations are the quintessential externalizing machines and the primary vehicles of capitalism and globalization, and part of this is due to their special status as entities. We must confirm that corporations are not people by stripping them of such rights. In the United States this means repealing their First and Fourth Amendment rights, which were expanded by the Supreme Court in early 2010. We need to get the corporations out of politics by reducing their capacity to lobby.

Second, we should ensure that by making the people who run corporations more accountable by rolling back limited liability laws. If the CEO and directors of a corporation cause it to do harm to society, they should be held liable and should not be allowed to pass the buck. We should also mandate environmental disclosures from corporations in the same way that we mandate financial disclosures. We should then ensure that corporations are made more responsible for the costs of any environmental harm that their activities might cause. Some environmental costs may be deemed necessary and may be supported by the government, but this should be done transparently. Take the example of the 2010 BP oil spill in the Gulf of Mexico. The risks of deepwater drilling were obscured and the economic benefits overblown by both BP and the government. And the aftermath? Enormous damage to coastal ecosystems, communities, and businesses against a BP first-quarter profit for 2010 of $5.6 billion.[3] If our economy causes environmental damage, we should know why it is necessary, how much of the damage is being remediated, who is paying for it, and what will be the impacts and long-term costs of the damage that cannot be remediated. We need to dilute the ethos of shareholder primacy so that corporations pay a broader mind to the impacts of the activities beyond just the short-term wealth of their shareholders.

Capitalism will be the dominant political and economic force into the foreseeable future, and it cannot be substantially challenged until it brings about its own collapse. I believe that it will cause its own collapse, which will be disastrous. When this happens, it will be imperative to rein in capitalism and expose the ways it has encouraged creeping environmental damage so the same problems may be avoided in the future.

We have finally found a political system within which democracy can be maintained rather stably and that can promote individualism and innovation. Capitalism has provided us with a wonderful half century of prosperity and stability, but it has the fatal flaw that it sells the environment at a discount price. We have bought the environment cheaply and greedily, but the ecological warehouses are running out of supplies and are filling with wastes. Capitalism is not doomed and cannot be removed by our political will. But capitalism dooms us and may well be removed by the invisible hand of nature.

Redressing the fundamental flaws of socialism and capitalism requires us to reconnect to natural systems, and the place at the crossroads of human societies and natural systems is the commons. The commons are dangerously threatened by exploitation by communities, as explained by Hardin's tragedy of the commons, and this sits at the heart of sustainability questions. Socialism and capitalism are both so deeply flawed because, by excluding commons systems, they remove communities from the natural systems with which they should be intimately associated, and they divorce us all from nature. Socialism attempts to control the commons with government bureaucracies, and capitalism sells the commons into private ownership. Only a government that can support the commons can ensure both functional communities and natural systems and support a stable society in the long term.

THE TRIUMPH OF THE COMMONS

Every new enclosure of the commons involves the infringement of somebody's personal liberty. Infringements made in the distant past are accepted because no contemporary complains of a loss. It is the newly imposed infringements that we vigorously oppose; cries of "rights" and "freedom"

fill the air. But what does freedom mean? Individuals locked into the logic of the commons are free only to bring universal ruin; once they see the necessity of mutual coercion, they become free to pursue other goals.

Garrett Hardin[4]

The tragedy of the commons is one of the most devastating consequences of poorly structured communities, and it occurs when each individual in a group competes for a limited common-pool resource. Each person takes a part of the resource for his or her own and causes a depletion that is shared by all.[5] Each person does this quite rationally, even if he or she understands that destruction of the resource may be the inevitable result. Any individual reducing his or her extraction of the resource would lose benefits directly, would conserve the resource very little, and might be rapidly outcompeted by his or her neighbors. The tragedy of the commons becomes an unrelenting vicious cycle; the resource depletes and collapses, and everybody fails.

Mastering the commons has become one of the imperatives of both socialists and capitalists, and of both environmentalists and industrialists. The two most commonly employed mechanisms for avoiding the tragedy of the commons are outside management and privatization. Both these approaches aim to exclude communities from commons. Either one is far better than the tragedy, but they both have their problems. There is a third way. This third way is much more difficult to operate, and is therefore riskier, but it maintains communities on their land and trusts the land to the community that lives on it rather than to some distant government bureaucracy or indifferent corporation. Intact commons, if they can be managed effectively, are the most desirable land-use strategy.

The classic image of the tragedy of the commons, and the image that Garrett Hardin may have had in mind when he wrote his classic paper,[6] is of the medieval English commons. The resource users in this image are herders, and the common-pool resource is an area of pasture upon which they are all free to let loose their herd. This image has the herders repeatedly increasing their herds even as the pasture degrades. The pasture is eventually trashed and useless for herding. But this is not what happened on the medieval English commons at all.[7]

The commons system in medieval England persisted for hundreds of years and did not end as a result of land degradation. Furthermore, the English commons were not areas of public land with free, open access: they were quite the opposite. They were areas of land to which rights of access were clearly defined and for which an extensive system of laws was in place. Commoners had rights to use a particular piece of land only in a clearly prescribed way. The numbers of animals of each species that a commoner could turn out onto the land and the times of year when they could do so were predetermined. Many of the rules regarding access to the commons appear to be very ancient, and many were probably in place before the preparation of the Magna Carta (1215) when they were formalized anew.

One important practice on the commons was stinting, which limited the number of grazing animals. Stinting laws restricted commoners to graze in summer only the number of animals that they could support through the winter. Overstocking would reduce the availability of winter feed and naturally reduce the number of animals on the commons. In many ways such as this, the commons were managed with an inherent understanding of their finite carrying capacity: advanced ecological concepts for medieval England, one might think.

Application of the law was an important factor in the prevention of the overexploitation of the commons, and there are plentiful records of such laws being enforced. More important, however, seems to have been the influence of cohesive communities and the adherence to well-accepted norms that such communities encourage. "What will the neighbors think?" is not a new concept. Nor is the idea that the Joneses will hide their lawn mower from you if you refuse to let them hack down their rogue tree with your chainsaw.

The common lands of medieval England persisted as community-managed lands for centuries, and they should be held up not as a tragedy or a failure in land management, as they have been, but as a triumph. There have been thousands of examples of the tragedy of the commons, and we are living many of them right now, but the medieval English commons was not one of them. The medieval English commons eventually went into decline at the onset of the Industrial Revolution as people flocked to the cities, land-use patterns changed, and enclosure movements walled off the English countryside. Sheep were needed to produce wool for the new factories, and so they were put on the land. People were needed to labor in the factories, so they were shipped off to the cities. Or as Sir Thomas More put it: "Sheep eat men."

This may be viewed as tragic, of course, but not as a tragedy of the commons. We have much to learn from successful commons-management systems, and it is imperative to recognize that common-pool resources are not automatically doomed. They can be managed in the long term by cohesive communities that understand the land on which they live.

Manageable as the commons may be in theory, however, and despite some glorious examples of the well-managed commons of yesteryear, our failures grossly outweigh our successes. The tragedy of the commons is being played out to its fullest, remorseless, devastating extent in all corners of the modern world today. Cohesive communities that understand the land on which they live are now a rare thing. Even rarer are communities that have been able to resist the onrushing tide of seven billion competing on the global commons. Is there any hope that commons systems can ever work again?

There is significant hope. We know that agriculture can be sustainable in the long term, and that land can be managed by communities. We have seen it done before, and we know how they did it. We also know that the commons often end in tragedy, but we know how the many failures came about. This is a big pillar upon which we can build.

Elinor Ostrom, the 2009 Nobel laureate for economic science, has defined some general principles for the management of commons.[8] The boundaries of the commons, and the resources accessible to those with access, should be clearly defined. It is also important that higher levels of government should acknowledge and support the community that lives on and governs the commons in question. The governance of a commons demands particular care. It should involve the community broadly, inviting all those using the commons and those affected by its use to participate. Rules should be comprehensive, with effective resource monitoring, efficient mechanisms of conflict resolution, and scales of sanctions against freeloaders. Most important, the rules should be adapted to each set of local conditions rather than adhering to some generally adopted norm. For larger, more complex commons, multiple layers of management will be needed that can support actions at the local level.

Our land is overfull and the demands on it are overlarge, but we should consider the world we would like the seventh generation of our descendants to enjoy. Do we want our legacy to be a degraded, overworked landscape in which every scrap of dirt is owned by someone, and all others are barred? Or would we prefer to build communities that share and manage the land following sound ecological principles?

COMMUNITY OF NATIONS, NATIONS OF COMMUNITIES

We tend to reserve the term *community* for small, closely interacting groups that are relatively easy to manipulate and manage. Communities operate at multiple scales, however, and towns, counties, states, or nations can be considered as communities also. Nations are grouped into regions and, ultimately, comprise a "community of nations."

Communities can degrade or prosper relatively quickly. Poor neighborhoods are susceptible to crime and distrust, while it is easier to promote security and goodwill in wealthy neighborhoods. This is not always the case, of course. Poor neighborhoods are often highly functional and supportive, while wealthy neighborhoods can be sterile and disconnected in their own way. Poor neighborhoods are generally clearly separated from rich neighborhoods, often with fences, and poor nations are separated from rich nations.

Communities can be shaped by a wide range of public policies that can be either effective or disastrous. One example is through zoning laws that are used to allocate municipal land to different uses, such as parks, businesses, and housing developments. A lack of green space and the consolidation of low-income housing into high-density enclaves can contribute to insecurity. At its worst, ghettos can result. Adequate green space and mixed-income residential areas, and, even better, mixed communities with interlaced residences and small businesses, promote security and functional, diverse communities. This is relatively easily achieved (although frequently neglected) on a small scale because the interrelationships among different sectors of the community are readily grasped. Local government can also be particularly effective because it is embedded in the community it serves. A small community is also much more likely to be well connected to its land base if it is partly rural, and it can be self-supporting if it is well integrated.

Larger communities are much more difficult to manage because government becomes increasingly separated from its community and its land base. Larger communities also tend to be managed by more complex hierarchies of bureaucracy and interact with a more complex array of resource issues. The government of large communities is particularly prone to being disconnected from the natural world. Politicians tend to be trained in disciplines like law and finance rather than ecology, and they interact most frequently and effectively with other like-minded individuals and groups and have a tendency to manage communities without grasping the ecological ramifications of their decisions. Since they are located in the town or city, and usually in or near its business district, they come face-to-face with urban issues much more frequently than with rural issues. Landscapes are managed from a city-centric point of view.

If we place the environment at the core of economics rather than at its margin, we can more fully understand the true value of economic decisions, much more easily understand their likely long-term impacts, and more readily design economic systems that build genuinely sustainable communities.

The freight train of globalization has streamlined our economies to feed off the choicest pastures of the global commons. Nations have specialized into service centers, manufacturing centers, or tourism destinations, and the like. Only poor countries retain economies that are based predominantly on their own local resources, and these countries tend to suffer from the loss of those resources through export and degradation from overpopulation, among other things. This specialization has created pervasive vulnerabilities as the drawdown of resources occurring in a source country may be invisible or of limited immediate concern to the country that is importing them.

The specialization of nations makes them unnecessarily vulnerable to the depletion of any imported resource upon which they rely, such as Middle Eastern oil for the United States, gadget consumers for China, Indian steel for the Middle East, or Australian beef for Japan. The specialization of Western nations away from agrarian economies into service and technology centers has gradually increased their need to import raw materials from other countries, and the trend away from self-sufficiency has been a key component of globalization.

Economic self-sufficiency requires a country to have a high level of diversity in its activities and a strong base of primary production, but self-sufficiency is anathema to globalization. The invisible hand of the global free-market economy directs countries to source materials from wherever they are cheapest and to specialize—the invisible hand of the global environment be damned.

The overall trend of globalization is to specialize us into globally sourcing, economically efficient consumers. It accelerates our destruction and deepens our vulnerability. This trend is one that is in desperate need of reversal. That it cannot be reversed, however, is clear. We are deeply locked into the current economic model, and it will only change substantially when it drags us to its, and our, inevitable failure.

There are, however, a thousand things we can be getting on with. All activities that will make communities and nations more self-sufficient will make them both more resilient to the coming collapse and more able to recover thereafter. We need to be doing whatever we can to redesign communities to be as diverse and self-supporting as possible.

A CALL TO ARMS

> **The era of procrastination, of half-measures, of soothing and baffling expedients, of delays, is coming to its close. In its place we are entering a period of consequences.**
> Winston Churchill, speech to the House of Commons,
> November 12, 1936

There's always a tendency to think, or at least to hope, even in the most desperate of times, that things will turn out for the best. There's good reason for this: sometimes they do. Mostly, however, we come back from the brink only when we make a change of plan.

I am reminded of the classic Muhammad Ali moment at the end of the first round of the Rumble in the Jungle, when Ali came up against the mighty George Foreman. Ali knew he was outmatched by Foreman, but he had spent months preparing, even going so far as using the media to make Foreman think he was going to "float like a butterfly" and use his speed to keep out of Foreman's way. Instead, he came out in the first round swinging, hoping to catch Foreman by surprise and hurt him early in the fight. It didn't work. Foreman was unhurt. Worse, he was enraged. Ali knew that his plan had failed and that he was in big trouble. He was going to get pummeled. In the movie documentary *When We Were Kings*, Norman Mailer gives his ringside recollections as we watch the troubled Ali in his corner, waiting for round two:

> The nightmare had finally come to visit him. He was in the ring with a man he could not dominate, who was stronger than him, who was not afraid of him, who was going to try to knock him out, who could punch harder than he could and who was determined and unstoppable. It's the only time I saw fear in Ali's eyes.
>
> Ali looked as if he looked deep into himself and said: "OK, this is the moment . . . this is the hour. . . ."[9]

Ali picked himself up from his stool, the steely determination returning to his face, and emerged from his corner for round two.

After months of planning and preparing, Ali had discovered that his plan was no good. He had to change course right then or get knocked down. He went to his famous rope-a-dope on the spongy ropes of the Kinshasa ring and teased and taunted Foreman "C'mon George, I can't feel it—is that all you've got?" Ali let Foreman throw all his fury against him until Foreman wore himself out.

Seven rounds later, Foreman was on the canvas.

That's how it is. When things are spinning out of control, you either have an "Ali moment" or you fold.

The Ali-Foreman fight serves as a particularly strong analogy because of what Ali realized in his "moment." He could not win quickly, as he had hoped, and so he settled on a longer-term strategy. The seven rounds through which he rolled and dodged on the ropes, battered by Hurricane George, are the seven generations through which we must bend, without breaking, through the great recession. When the storm has blown itself out, however, perhaps we can bounce off the ropes and fight back.

I remember my mum once getting a fit of the giggles after my siblings and I had stayed over at Grandma's house for a weekend[10] when we were small children. Grandma had given us a lukewarm bath in three inches of water. What's the deal with that? When she wasn't looking, I added another luxuriant foot and a half of piping hot water and poured in the required half bottle of bubble bath. When poor old Grandma returned to the bathroom she was aghast. She had raised two children through the war. I was a product of the postwar boom. We had a rather different view of bath time.

During the war the whole of Britain pulled together in an immense, communal effort to defeat Nazi Germany. Desperate times led to desperate measures, and it became a moral obligation to contribute to the war effort in any way possible, but this was not, despite what people might prefer to believe, entirely the result of a million acts of altruism. The British government pulled out all the stops and used a combination of fierce persuasion and potent legislation to bring the country onto a wartime footing.

One pervasive measure was rationing, especially restricting the use of gasoline and other things considered to be luxuries (like bath water[11]). By 1942, even essential goods, including food and clothing, were heavily rationed, and the government controlled the smallest activities of people's lives and coerced them into participation with an onslaught of propaganda—with great success.

My grandparents ran a corner store during the war.[12] They also kept chickens, grew vegetables on the back lot, and participated in the raising of the community pig, among other things. The government scrutinized every transaction carried out in their shop to ensure that rations were distributed properly, and my grandparents were required to keep minutely detailed books. On one occasion, a few ounces of butter went unaccounted for, and the inspector apparently brought Grandma to tears, exhorting her that "there can be no mistakes in wartime. Mistakes are nothing less than criminal negligence."

Huge savings were made in food and raw materials. Enormous recycling campaigns for bottle tops and just about everything else were organized. Food consumption fell by more than 10 percent from 1940 to 1944, household electricity consumption fell by more than three-quarters, and motor vehicle use fell by 95 percent.[13]

A sacrifice of that size would seem impossible in the fight against anything other than a foreign oppressor. Furthermore, the sacrifice would seem to be one that would cause much suffering and hardship. Bear in mind, however, that the health of the British remained good during the war, and the nation had a sense of purpose. In such times, much can be achieved. Doesn't it strike you as odd, the way many folks look back on the war? They speak of horror and hardship but nonetheless seem to remember a time of cooperation and a sense of community. They seem to miss that.

So then, I guess the questions are simple: Can we brand global warming as Adolf Hitler? Can we brand peak oil as Emperor Hirohito? Apparently not. The rallying cries for these new wars are made from a few dissenting voices rather than from a unified government directing a unified populace. Nonetheless, the wartime effort does teach us that much is possible.

The world is filled with hope for a brighter future. Most people seem to think that technology will continue to drive this civilization to ever-greater heights of achievement. But if my assessments are correct, over the next few decades, the opposite will happen.

Increasing numbers of people are coming to the realization that the world has dug itself into a serious hole. The recognition of global climate change is high, and there is a desire, at least, to avoid the worst of its impacts. On the other hand, the recognition of peak oil is low. Most people still think we can dig (drill?) our way out of trouble and avoid a major calamity. I think they underestimate the size and nature of the challenge.

I hope for a sustainable future in which people can live in all regions of the planet in a way that does not damage their land base and does not require one group of people to be downtrodden to support the wealth of others. This also may be a vain hope but perhaps a target for which to aim. We are heading into a time of great upheaval, but this will at least give us the chance for a do-over as the world reorganizes itself and recovers.

The end of the petroleum interval will create such a set of upheavals that it will be as if all the cards we have on the table were suddenly thrown into the air. The confusion will be great, and it will be made worse if we grasp, desperately, for whatever cards we can reach and attempt to claim them as our own. Rather, while the cards are in the air we have the opportunity to collect and rearrange them in a new and better way. The great energy transition upon which we are embarking is not a time for trying to save the world as it is but a time for reshaping the world as we would prefer it to be. The end of the petroleum interval will be a time of great hardship and confusion but also a time of opportunity.

There are some important facts that people and their governments need to absorb as they attempt to shorten the pain of the energy transition and design a new future. First, we must accept that the petroleum interval is at its zenith and the days of abundant oil and natural gas are numbered. Alternatives must be found. Second, we must adopt the mindset of a full world with limited resources. The improvement of our lot in life no longer rests upon growing economies by attempting to increase our efficiencies of resource extraction and economic growth. We must act on the universal truths, which should be self-evident, that quality of life is more important than quantity and that sustaining the environment is infinitely more important than exploiting it for short-term economic growth.

For the world to emerge into a brighter and better future, we will need to unite not in competition but in the organization of sustainable communities in which population explosions are averted, where energy generation is nonpolluting, and where agriculture does not come at a cost to the environment. Fish might even be harvested from the sea with one eye on today's catch and the other on the maintenance of the fishery.

The essential characteristic of such a society would be sustainability rather than growth. Alas, much of our human nature is contradictory to this vain utopian dream.

Our latest model of human society is just about played out, and we are entering a period of great uncertainty. We are in the middle of a phenomenal two-hundred-year hiatus in the history of civilization brought about by the discovery of oil. The first hundred years, as we put ever-increasing volumes of black gold to work, has been an era of astounding growth. The next hundred years, as the petroleum interval winds down and comes crashing around our heads, will be tough. There is no longer anything we can do about this; the roller coaster has already passed its tipping point.

Hoping for the best helps one sleep at night, but now is the time to plan for the worst, for, whatever society might emerge in the unforeseeable future, our fate over the next few decades is grim. We need to plan to mitigate the suffering, but, even more important, we need to put in place systems that will pave the way for an eventual recovery.

The coming years will bring much confusion, and it will be extremely difficult for individuals and governments to figure out what can be done to make matters better. In this, I can offer only a limited number of specific prescriptions, but two things are certain. Recovery from the coming depression and the building of a better world will be successful where an ethos of sustainability replaces an ethos of growth, and where people share and conserve, rather than compete for and consume the precious resources of the planet.

ACKNOWLEDGMENTS

Thanks are due to many people who helped with the writing of *Life without Oil* with critical discussions, editorial suggestions, ideas, and moral support. I am very fortunate to have a wonderful family that is not only loving and supportive but also really, really smart. Friends and colleagues provided a number of useful critiques and insights, as did many of my students, especially those in my honors class at Purdue University. My boss has been especially patient while I have had my head buried in this book when I should, perhaps, have been doing other things. Working with my coauthor, agent, and the people at Prometheus Books has been a joy. My father, David Hallett, passed away before I began writing this book, but he is present, nonetheless, on every page. Heartfelt thanks go to many people, but here is the cast of characters whom I would like to acknowledge by name: Hannah Bergeman, Stephanie Del Paine, Kevin Gibson, Peter Goldsbrough, Christine Hallett, John Hallett, Judy Hallett, Margaret Hallett, Lynn Johal, Melissa Kruger, Baldwin Mootoo, Alison Picard, Deryck Wilde, and John Wright.

NOTES

Prologue: The Invisible Hand

1. Interview with Anne Katosh in C. Sagan and T. Head, *Conversations with Carl Sagan* (Jackson: University of Mississippi, 2006).

2. Odd fella, that Prince Phillip. What do you suppose he did when he heard of the cult? Explain to them that he was not a god? No, he sent them photos of himself. Now they can worship him all the better.

3. Britain: the western edge of the "known world" at that time.

4. S. Milgram, *Obedience to Authority: An Experimental View* (New York: Harper Collins, 1974). T. Blass, *The Man Who Shocked the World: The Life and Legacy of Stanley Milgram* (Cambridge, MA: Basic Books, 2004). P. Zimbardo, *The Lucifer Effect: Understanding How Good People Turn Evil* (New York: Random House, 2008).

5. G. Hardin, "The Tragedy of the Commons," *Science* 162 (1968): 1243–48.

6. And some other residents of Palo Alto, California, of a similar age.

7. A. Smith, *An Inquiry into the Nature and the Causes of the Wealth of Nations* (London: J. M. Dent & Sons, 1910).

8. In fairness to Adam Smith, he knew this, and his writings contain numerous caveats to the power of the invisible hand.

9. Some energy also comes from geothermal sources and from the spinning of the earth that contributes weather patterns (and therefore wind), and some energy comes from the moon: tides. The only exception is nuclear power, which comes from the splitting or fusing of atoms.

10. Best known as the Serenity Prayer. Two things: First, I have omitted

the word *God*, with which the prayer (it is most often said as a prayer, after all) usually opens—the message is just as good for atheists and polytheists. Second, although this prayer has been widely adopted by, and associated with, Alcoholics Anonymous, it has much older origins, although its original author is not known.

11. R. Allen, *How to Save the World: Strategy for Conservation* (London: Kogan Page, 2006). A. Bourseiller, *365 Ways to Save the Earth* (New York: Abrams, 2008). B. Taylor, *How to Save the Planet* (Oxford: Oxford University Press, 2006). J. Yarrow, *1,001 Ways to Save the Earth* (San Francisco: Chronicle Books, 2007). J. M. Sleeth, *Serve God, Save the Planet: A Christian Call to Action* (Peabody, MA: Zondervan, 2007).

Chapter 1. Seeds of Civilization

1. M. Angelou and J. M. Elliot, *Conversations with Maya Angelou* (Jackson: University of Mississippi, 1989).

2. R. Dawkins, *The Selfish Gene* (New York: Oxford University Press, 1976).

3. With the exception of some viruses that use only RNA.

4. See http://www.nasa.gov/. Oddly enough, that's just before my British driver's license expires, so it should save me some annoying bureaucratic hassle.

5. The Sichuan earthquake of May 2008 was the result of the slippage of tectonic plates as the Indian subcontinent continues to push deeper into Asia, raising the Himalayas and the Tibetan Plateau.

6. Prehumans likely used wood more than stone and probably much earlier, but wood tools would be less likely to be preserved at archaeological sites. The Stone Age was actually more likely just a subset of the Wood Age.

7. I. Tattersall, *The Last Neanderthal: The Rise, Success, and Mysterious Extinction of Our Closest Human Relatives* (New York: Westview Press, 1999).

8. G. Blainey, *Triumph of the Nomads: A History of Ancient Australia* (Melbourne: Macmillan, 1975).

9. There is nothing natural about many of our "natural systems." The hand of humankind has shaped our environment for hundreds of thousands of years. Nowhere is this more obvious than in the grasslands, which have been managed—even maintained—by fire and grazing for millennia.

10. A brilliant description and analysis of the defeat of the Inca at Cajamarca by Pizarro is to be found in J. M. Diamond, *Guns, Germs, and Steel: The Fates of Human Societies* (New York: Houghton Mifflin, 1997).

11. J. Swift, *Gulliver's Travels* (London: Jones, 1826; London: Benjamin Motte, 1726).

12. So humans and plants coevolved, or, more precisely, plants and human cultures coevolved.

13. As an example, the wild progenitor of corn appears to be a grass called teosinte that still grows in the uplands of central Mexico. It has a small, terminal spike with a handful of plumpish seeds. The modern corn plant has monster cobs halfway down the plant packed with huge numbers of much larger seeds. The yield of modern corn is orders of magnitude greater than teosinte.

14. (Gary Larsen's cartoon "Wild Poodles of the Serengeti" is a *Far Side* favorite.) Some parts of the world missed out on domesticated animals. Few animals were domesticated in Africa, especially not large ones. The zebra looks like a good alternative for the horse but turns out to be very difficult to raise and ride. The elephant looks like a good option as a food animal but reproduces too slowly to be of real value. Other parts of the world destroyed their chance at having large, farmable herd animals. The first Americans caused the rapid extinction of the giant sloth, and the first Australians caused the extinction of the giant wombat; the New Zealanders, the extinction of the moa; and the Mauritians, the extinction of the dodo. The list is huge. Perhaps history would have played out differently if these animals had been domesticated, because the evolution of agriculture was the first and most important influence on the evolution of human societies.

Chapter 2. The Ghosts of Empires Passed

1. The current (Polynesian) name for Easter Island is Rapa Nui.

2. T. L. Hunt and C. P. Lipo, "Late Colonization of Easter Island," *Science* 311 (2006): 1603–1606.

3. E. von Däniken, *Chariots of the Gods? Unsolved Mysteries of the Past* (New York: Putnam, 1969).

4. J. Van Tilburg, *Easter Island: Archaeology, Ecology, and Culture* (Washington, DC: Smithsonian Institution Press, 1994).

5. The Easter Islanders may have had the worst tooth decay problem in the history of the world, perhaps because a scarcity of freshwater forced them to rely on sugarcane juice for fluids. The teeth of folks found in burial mounds are riddled with cavities.

6. J. M. Diamond, *Collapse: How Societies Choose to Fail or Succeed* (New York: Penguin, 2005).

7. C. P. Lipo and T. L. Hunt, "Mapping Prehistoric Statue Roads on Easter Island," *Antiquity* 79 (2005): 158–68.

8. J. Van Tilburg, *Easter Island: Archaeology, Ecology, and Culture* (Washington, DC: Smithsonian Institution Press, 1994).

9. Diamond, *Collapse*.

10. D. Steadman, "Extinctions of Birds in Eastern Polynesia: A Review of the Record, and Comparisons with other Pacific Island Groups," *Journal of Archaeological Science* 16 (1989): 177–205.

11. C. J. Stevenson, J. Wozniak, and S. Haoa, "Prehistoric Agriculture Production on Easter Island (Rapa Nui), Chile," *Antiquity* 73 (1999): 801–12.

12. Diamond, *Collapse*.

13. W. Mulloy, "Contemplate the Navel of the World," *Americas* 26 (1974): 25–33. The battle site on Poike dated from lovely human remains and signs of fighting, such as smashed skeletons, and the like.

14. In the early days of colonization it was significantly less arid. . . .

15. There were a number of groups in the ancient southwest with the Hisatsinom, notably the Hohokam and the Mogollon, and a number of subgroups including the Salado and Sinagua. I use the term *Hisatsinom* rather than *Anasazi* because this is the name used by the Hopi, who are among their direct descendants. The Diné are descendants of Athabascans, who migrated to the area much later. For a brief and simple overview, see S. L. Walker, *Indian Cultures of the American Southwest* (Bellemont, AZ: Camelback/Canyonlands Venture, 1994).

16. T. Kohler and M. Matthews, "Long-Term Anasazi Land Use and Forest Production: A Case Study in Southwest Colorado," *American Antiquity* 53 (1988): 537–64. You can still see the original timber in many of the ruins,

such as those at Wupatki National Monument (northern Arizona) or Mesa Verde National Park (southwest Colorado), often with small cores that were removed by scientists and that have since been plugged.

17. J. Betancourt, T. Van Devender, and P. Martin, *Everything That You Might Want to Know about Packrat Middens* (Tucson: University of Arizona Press, 1990).

18. The most common game seems to have involved two teams trying to send a ball through rock hoops high on the walls of a ball court without using their hands. A different game may have been played on an elaborate stadium court at Copán where carved animal heads on a long, smooth rock slope probably bore nets into which a ball was projected. Historians speculate that the winners might have been chosen to pass into a glorious afterlife by being sacrificed at a ceremony following the game. . . . Not so many dominant franchises, then.

19. The Mayan Long Count calendar has become famous because it comes to its end on December 21, 2012. It ends on this date because the calendar "began" on August 11, 3114 BCE, and simply runs out of numbers, ending one era—*Baktun*—and perhaps beginning another.

20. My kids will tell you just how tall that thing is, but the view is certainly worth the climb, even if you have to drag your five-year-old up there. And, if you're going to Chichen Itza, the main attraction of the region, you *must* go to less well-known Ek Balaam. It's just down the road, but as my kids will attest: it's way cooler.

21. G. R. Willey, "Maya Archaeology," *Science* 215:260–67.

22. D. A. Friedel and V. Scarborough, "Subsistence, Trade, and Development of the Coastal Maya," in *Maya Subsistence: Studies in Memory of Dennis E. Pileson*, edited by K. V. Flannery (New York: Academic Press, 1982).

23. The Mayan eras are generally broken down into a number of different stages: the Early Preclassic, before 1000 BCE; the Middle Preclassic, 1000–400 BCE; Late Preclassic, 400–50 BCE; Protoclassic, 50 BCE to 250 CE; Early Classic, 250–500 CE; the Hiatus, 550–600 CE; Late Classic, 600–800 CE; Terminal Classic, 800–1000 CE; and Postclassic from 1000 CE.

24. T. P. Culbert, "The Mayan Downfall at Tikal," in *The Classic Maya Collapse*, edited by T. P. Culbert (Albuquerque: University of New Mexico Press, 1973). D. Webster, *The Fall of the Ancient Maya: Solving the Mystery of*

the Maya Collapse (London: Thames and Hudson, 2002). W. A. Haviland, "A New Population Estimate for Tikal, Guatemala," *American Antiquity* 34 (1969): 316–25.

25. The Mayans were not averse to torturing their enemies using many techniques, such as thumb screws and the like. One of their more brutal methods was to tie the victim into a ball and roll him down the steep steps of a pyramid. Lovely.

26. M. W. Binford, et al., "Ecosystems, Palaeoecology, and Human Disturbance in Tropical and Subtropical America," *Quaternary Science Review* 6 (1987): 115–28.

27. D. A. Hodell, J. H. Curtis, and M. Brenner, "Possible Role of Climate in the Collapse of Classic Maya Civilization," *Nature* 375 (1995): 391–94.

28. Also known, less romantically, as "Ruler B."

29. François-René de Chateaubriand (1768–1848). French writer, politician, and diplomat. His final and definitive work was *Memoires d'Outre Tombe* (*Memories from beyond My Grave*).

30. Yeah, well, as a botanist, I might give a slightly different definition of "living thing." There *are* a few plants scattered around. . . .

31. R. J. Dubos, *The Wooing of Earth* (New York: Scribner, 1980).

32. A rhizome is a horizontal underground stem from which new sprouts can shoot. Often called a "runner."

33. R. M. Adams, *Heartland of Cities* (Chicago: Aldine, 1981).

34. M. H. Hansen, *The Shotgun Method: The Demography of the Ancient Greek City-State Culture* (Columbia: University of Missouri Press, 2006).

35. J. D. Hughes, *Pan's Travail: Environmental Problems of the Ancient Greeks and Romans* (Baltimore, MD: Johns Hopkins University Press, 1994). This is a really impressive text that comes from the extensive reading of ancient texts, generally written for other purposes, from which Hughes has gleaned enormous amounts of information about the state of these ancient environments, the human impacts upon them, and human attitudes toward them. It cites from a wide array of ancient sources, including Aristotle, Cicero, Hippocrates, Homer, Plato, Plutarch, Seneca, Sophocles, Theophrastus, Varro, and Virgil.

36. Herodotus, *Histories.* Various editions are available, including one

with an introduction by J. M. Marincola and translation by A. de Selincourt, 2nd ed. (New York: Penguin, 2003). The passages used are as cited by Hughes, *Pan's Travail*.

37. Plato, *Critias*. Various editions are available, including one with a translation by B. Jowett (New York: Dodo Press, 2007). The passage is used as cited by R. Meiggs, *Trees and Timber in the Ancient Greek World* (Oxford, UK: Clarendon Press, 1982).

38. Hughes, *Pan's Travail*.

39. E. Gibbon, *The History of the Decline and Fall of the Roman Empire* (New York: Modern Library, 1932). First date of publication not known; Gibbon died in 1794.

40. Check back on your literary classics to read about his trials and tribulations with Remus. . . .

41. The western part of the empire declined and fell rapidly, but the eastern part remained the main regional power for considerably longer, until the Ottoman Empire finally captured Constantinople in 1453.

42. Gibbon, *History of the Decline and Fall of the Roman Empire*.

43. Ibid.

44. Stone construction was, of course, widespread; the great aqueducts, etcetera, etcetera, but wood was preferred for most buildings and may have been gradually replaced by stone as much due to the lack of wood as to the preference for stone.

45. T. A. Wertime, "The Furnace versus the Goat: The Pyrotechnologic Industries and Mediterranean Deforestation in Antiquity," *Journal of Field Archaeology* 10 (1983): 445–52.

46. Hughes, *Pan's Travail*. M. Williams, *Deforesting the Earth: From Prehistory to Global Crisis* (Chicago: University of Chicago Press, 2006).

47. Lucius Junius Moderatus Columella (4 BCE–ca. 70 CE).

48. Much of Britain was deforested during the Stone Age. Flint axes are inefficient, but, if used often enough and for long enough, they can denude vast areas. Many British landscapes, such as Dartmoor in southwestern England, bear the legacy of ancient deforestation to this day.

49. Hughes, *Pan's Travail*. Williams, *Deforesting the Earth*. S. C. Chew, *World Ecological Degradation* (Lanham, MD: Altamira, 2001). W. F. Rud-

diman, *Plows, Plagues, and Petroleum: How Humans Took Control of Climate* (Princeton, NJ: Princeton University Press, 2005).

50. J. Rifkin, *The Hydrogen Economy: The Creation of the Worldwide Energy Web and the Redistribution of Power on Earth* (New York: Jeremy Tarcher/Penguin, 2003).

51. Seneca's full name is not known; he is referred to as Seneca the Elder (ca. 54 BCE–39 CE).

52. Attila the Hun, sometimes referred to as the Scourge of God, was one of the biggest problems for the Romans, as he was constantly hassling the northeastern boundaries of the empire.

53. Alaric the Visigoth sacked Rome in 410. This event is often used to mark the end of the Western Roman Empire.

54. W. G. Van Waateringe, "The Disastrous Effects of the Roman Occupation," in *Roman and Native in the Low Countries: Spheres of Interaction*, edited by R. Brandt and J. Slofstra, *British Archaeological Reports International Series* 184, 1983, pp. 147–57.

55. E. Forster, "Columella and His Latin Treatise on Agriculture," *Greece and Rome* 19 (1950): 123–28.

56. Ibid.

57. T. Homer-Dixon, *The Upside of Down: Catastrophe, Creativity, and the Renewal of Civilization* (Washington, DC: Island Press, 2006).

58. Ibid.

59. Middle Ages, medieval era.

60. J. A. Tainter, *The Collapse of Complex Societies* (Cambridge: Cambridge University Press, 1988).

61. B. J. Meggers, "Environmental Limitation to the Development of Culture," *American Anthropologist* 56 (1954): 801–24. Diamond, *Collapse*.

62. Tainter, *Collapse of Complex Societies*.

63. K. V. Flannery, "The Cultural Evolution of Civilizations," *Annual Review of Ecology and Systematics* 3 (1972): 399–26. G. Ferrero, *Ancient Rome and Modern America: A Comparative Study of Morals and Manners* (New York: Putnam & Sons, 1914).

Chapter 3. The Fossil Fuels Savings Bank

1. As an oversimplification: dead plant material tended to form coal, whereas dead animal/microbial material tended to form oil.

2. L. Mumford, *Technics and Civilization* (New York: Harcourt Brace, 1934).

3. It has been argued that the construction of stone buildings by the Greeks, Romans, and other civilizations, magnificent though they are, might be better viewed as a sign of wood supply problems.

4. It's a lovely irony that iron was needed to cut the trees that were needed to make charcoal so that better iron could be smelted to more efficiently cut trees. This theme is repeated: steam engines invented to drain mines to get coal to drive steam engines to get coal. . . .

5. Peak wood is the point at which wood supply flattens and begins to decline, irrespective of increased efforts at production. This is an important concept that we shall see later with "peak dam" and, most important, peak oil.

6. M. Williams, *Deforesting the Earth: From Prehistory to Global Crisis* (Chicago: University of Chicago Press, 2003).

7. W. R. Catton, *Overshoot: The Ecological Basis of Revolutionary Change* (Champaign: University of Illinois Press, 1980).

8. E. Williams, *Capitalism and Slavery* (Chapel Hill: University of North Carolina Press, 1944). Eric Williams would go on to form the People's National Movement in Trinidad and Tobago and then become that country's longtime prime minister, leading his country from 1956 through independence from the British and until his death in 1981. It is not without reason that he is often referred to, in Trinidad, as the "father of the nation."

9. Coal had also been used in China, possibly for much longer, so why did the Chinese not become the first industrial nation? There are many possible explanations, but one may be that the Chinese had not yet deforested the land to the point at which coal became a necessity.

10. Pronounced *k'nnen*.

11. A form of "smokeless fuel."

12. *Sorbus aucuparia*. An Australian tree, *Eucalyptus regnans*, also carries the common name Mountain Ash.

13. Richardson is currently governor of New Mexico.

14. ... and therefore with much to answer for, in my opinion. His comment "It is not coming up with new ideas that is difficult; it is getting rid of the old ones" has renewed prescience.

15. Rockefeller guaranteed the volume of oil by putting it in **blue barrels**: bbl = barrel = forty-two gallons.

16. D. Yergin, *The Prize: The Epic Quest for Oil, Money, and Power* (New York: Simon & Schuster, 1992).

17. It's hard to imagine a commercial steam plane running on coal....

18. Named for New York (*ny*) and London (*lon*).

19. Pardon the pun?

20. Also known as the *Millennium Bug*.

21. T. L. Friedman, *The World Is Flat: A Brief History of the Twenty-First Century* (New York: Farrar, Strauss & Giroux, 2008).

Chapter 4. Divorced from Nature

1. As modified from the similar, earlier comment made by Winston Churchill.

2. W. F. Ruddiman, *Plows, Plagues, and Petroleum: How Humans Took Control of Climate* (Princeton, NJ: Princeton University Press, 2005).

3. The Australopithecines.

4. I speak in the past tense because this is just about done with, although not entirely.

5. In the case of Oldham, mostly from southern Pakistan.

6. S. Milgram, *Obedience to Authority: An Experimental View* (New York: Harper Collins, 1974).

7. T. Blass, *The Man Who Shocked the World: The Life and Legacy of Stanley Milgram* (Cambridge, MA: Basic Books, 2004).

8. P. Zimbardo, *The Lucifer Effect: Understanding How Good People Turn Evil* (New York: Random House, 2008).

9. Three examples not intended to be of similar magnitude. Adolf Eichmann was considered by many as the "architect of the Holocaust" and responsible for the brutality and murder of millions. He was captured by Mossad in Argentina years after the Second World War, tried, convicted, and executed in

Israel. William Calley was convicted for his role in the My Lai massacre in Vietnam. Lynddie England was the most "memorable" of the US military accused of torture at the Abu Ghraib prison in Iraq. She was photographed smiling as inmates suffered at her feet. The testaments flooded in that Lynddie was "just a regular girl," "a nice girl," and so on and so forth, and nobody could understand what was going on. In the light of the Zimbardo experiments, we can see that her niceness in one environment and cruelty in another may not be unusual at all.

10. G. Hardin, "The Tragedy of the Commons," *Science* 162 (1968): 1243–48.

11. A better example, I think, is Shakespeare. Some of his finest plays— *Romeo and Juliet*, for example—are "tragedy," rather than simply "tragic" because of that same "remorseless working of things." Or, as Dr. Frank (Michael Caine) and Rita/Susan (Julie Walters) explain it, quite wonderfully, in *Educating Rita* (Acorn Pictures): Frank: "We must not confuse tragedy with the merely tragic. Macbeth for instance . . . the flaw in his character . . . leads to his inevitable doom. Whereas . . . in the newspaper . . . 'Man Killed by Falling Tree' is not tragedy." Susan: "It is for the poor sod under the tree!"

12. W. G. Sumner, "The Banquet of Life," in *Earth-Hunger and Other Essays*, edited by A. G. Keller (New Haven, CT: Yale University Press, 1987).

13. Interestingly, this was all happening at about the same time as the Easter Island fiasco. J. M. Diamond, *Collapse: How Societies Choose to Fail or Succeed* (New York: Penguin, 2005).

14. An impolite term applied to native people of Liverpool, meaning "wretches."

15. An impolite term applied to native people of Greenland and North America, meaning "wretches."

16. P. Mellars, *The Neanderthal Legacy: An Archaeological Perspective from Western Europe* (Princeton, NJ: Princeton University Press, 1996). P. G. Bahn, "Triple Czech Burial," *Nature* 332 (1988): 302–303.

17. The date of publication of Darwin's *On the Origin of Species*.

18. J. Perkins, *Confessions of an Economic Hit Man* (San Francisco: Berrett-Koehler, 2005).

19. All in all a pretty solid career—Butler was one of the US Marines'

most distinguished officers and was twice awarded the Medal of Honor; he also alerted Congress to what he described as a coup plot against President Franklin Delano Roosevelt.

20. Robert Heibroner, "The Worst Is Yet to Come," *New York Times*, February 14, 1993.

21. In March 2010, the US Supreme Court ruled to lift restrictions on corporate political campaign spending. Most problematic is the fact that it grounded its decision in First Amendment rights protecting free speech. It seems to me that the ability of a wealthy corporation to speak freely might be somewhat greater than yours or mine. . . .

22. H. Cleaver, *The Contradictions of the Green Revolution* (University of Texas, 1972). Online at https://webspace.utexas.edu/hcleaver/www/cleaver contradictions.pdf (accessed December 28, 2010).

23. J. W. Loewen, *Lies My Teacher Told Me: Everything Your American History Textbook Got Wrong* (New York: Touchstone, 1995). K. Reilly, *The West and the World* (New York: Harper & Row, 1989). S. Kumar, *The CIA and the Third World* (New Delhi: Vikas, 1981).

24. N. Klein, *The Shock Doctrine: The Rise of Disaster Capitalism* (New York: Metropolitan Books, 2007). N. Klein, *Fences and Windows: Dispatches from the Front Lines of the Globalization Debate* (New York: Picador, 2005).

25. V. Shiva, *Earth Democracy: Justice, Sustainability, and Peace* (London: Zed Books, 2005). V. Shiva, *Manifestos on the Future of Food and Seed* (Cambridge, UK: South End Press, 2007). V. Shiva, *Soil Not Oil: Environmental Justice in a Time of Climate Crisis* (Cambridge, UK: South End Press, 2008).

26. Shiva, *Earth Democracy*.

27. J. Stiglitz, *Globalization and Its Discontents* (New York: W. W. Norton, 2002).

PART II: THE PETROLEUM INTERVAL

1. J. W. Loewen, *Lies My Teacher Told Me: Everything Your American History Textbook Got Wrong* (New York: Touchstone, 1995). H. Zinn, *A People's History of the United States: 1492–Present* (New York: HarperCollins, 2003).

2. M. J. Economides, R. Oligney, and A. Izquierdo, *The Color of Oil: The History, the Money, and the Politics of the World's Biggest Business* (Katy, TX: Round Oak Publishing, 2000).

Chapter 5. The Great Energy Transition

1. K. S. Deffeyes, *Beyond Oil: The View from Hubbert's Peak* (New York: Hill and Wang, 2005).

2. M. K. Hubbert, "Nuclear Energy and the Fossil Fuels," Spring Meeting of the American Petroleum Institute, San Antonio, Texas, March 7–9, 1956. Later published in *Drilling and Production Practice* by the American Petroleum Institute, 1969, and then in *Energy Bulletin*, March 8, 2006.

3. Thomas Ahlbrandt, World Energy project chief for the United States Geological Service, quoted in R. Williams, "Future Energy Supply #2: Natural Gas Potential," *Oil & Gas Journal*, July 21, 2003, pp. 20–28.

4. Energy Information Agency of the US Department of Energy.

5. Great Kevin Bacon moment from the 1992 film *A Few Good Men*.

6. H. Groppe, "Peak Oil: Myth vs. Reality," Denver World Oil Conference, November 10–11, 2005. Proceedings available online at http://www.energybulletin.net/gpm (accessed February 12, 2007).

7. The oil embargo of 1973 and the Iran-Iraq war of 1979 are the most obvious ones.

8. C. J. Campbell and J. H. Laherrère, "The End of Cheap Oil," *Scientific American*, March 1998, pp. 78–83. R. Heinberg, *The Party's Over: Oil, War, and the Fate of Industrial Societies* (Gabriola Island, BC, Canada: New Society Publishers, 2003). Deffeyes, *Beyond Oil*. J. K. Leggett, *The Empty Tank: Oil, Gas, Hot Air, and the Coming Global Financial Catastrophe* (New York: Random House, 2005).

9. Deffeyes, *Beyond Oil*.

10. The Kashagan field is not quite the bargain it might have been, however, because its oil has a high sulfur concentration and is harder to refine.

11. M. R. Simmons, *Twilight in the Desert: The Coming Saudi Oil Shock and the World Economy* (New York: John Wiley & Sons, 2006).

12. J. W. Loewen, *Lies My Teacher Told Me: Everything Your American History Textbook Got Wrong* (New York: Touchstone, 1995).

13. Campbell and Laherrère, "The End of Cheap Oil?" Heinberg, *The Party's Over*. Deffeyes, *Beyond Oil*. Leggett, *The Empty Tank*.

14. Simmons, *Twilight in the Desert*. Heinberg, *The Party's Over*.

15. Cited by Leggett in *The Empty Tank*.

16. R. Sandrea, "Hubbert Revisited #1: Imbalances among Oil Demand, Reserves, Alternatives Define Energy Dilemma Today," *Oil & Gas Journal* (July 12, 2004): 34–37.

17. http://www.bp.com/.

18. Ibid.

19. L. Carroll, *Through the Looking Glass, and What Alice Found There* (London: Dent, 1954).

20. L. Aalund and K. Rappold, "Horizontal Drilling Taps More Oil in the Middle-East," *Oil and Gas Journal* 91 (1993): 47–51. G. C. Thakur, "Horizontal Well Technology—A Key to Improving Resources," *Journal of Canadian Petroleum Technology* 38 (1999): 55–60.

21. G. F. Gause, "The International Politics of the Gulf," in *International Relations of the Middle East*, edited by L. Fawcett (Oxford: Oxford University Press, 2005).

22. J. R. Christensen, E. H. Stenby, and A. Skauge, "Review of WAG Field Experience," *SPE Reservoir Evaluation and Engineering* 4 (2001): 97–106. M. S. H. Bader, "Sulfate Removal Technologies for Oil Fields Seawater Injection Operations," *Journal of Petroleum Science and Engineering* 55 (2007): 93–110.

23. C. H. Chapman, *Fundamentals of Seismic Wave Propagation* (Cambridge: Cambridge University Press, 2004).

24. R. Sandea, "Hubbert Revisited #3: Deepwater Oil Discovery May Have Peaked; Production Peak May Follow in 10 Years," *Oil & Gas Journal* (July 26, 2004): 18–25.

25. OK, so he then broke Albertan hearts to become an LA King and then a Phoenix Coyote (sad, really . . .), and he's originally from Brantford, Ontario, but he'll always be *The Great One* and an Edmonton Oiler.

26. If you're in the mood, you can tramp into your local smelly swamp, disturb the sediment, collect the gas in an inverted bucket or bag, and light it to make a nice big bang. Known as the Volterra experiment, it's an exercise

beloved of undergraduate microbiology students, although you should think twice before you try it because it works rather well!

27. This may have happened before: the release of methane hydrate coming about as a result of continental drift, and the result being a significant extinction event. Discussed in W. F. Ruddiman, *Plows, Plagues, and Petroleum: How Humans Took Control of Climate* (Princeton, NJ: Princeton University Press, 2005).

28. A. Imam, R. A. Starzman, and M. A. Barrufet, "Hubbert Revisited #6: Multicyclic Hubbert Model Shows Global Conventional Gas Output Peaking in 2019," *Oil and Gas Journal* 16, August 2004, pp. 1–12.

29. Natural gas is highly explosive, so getting it out of the ground is a dangerous proposition. Don't believe me? Ask BP about the charred remains of the Deepwater Horizon platform in the Gulf of Mexico. It's particularly annoying when one is drilling for oil but also finds gas. The gas escapes up the well and—boom. The easiest way of dealing with this is by conducting a controlled burn of the natural gas to get rid of it in a safe way. The gas escapes from the well and then is simply burned off—flared—to avoid explosions.

30. R. Williams, "Future Energy Supply #2."

31. Imam et al., "Hubbert Revisited #6."

32. J. Goodell, *Big Coal: The Dirty Secret behind America's Energy Future* (New York: Houghton Mifflin, 2006).

33. Interview by Thomas Friedman for article in the *New York Times*, January 1, 2007.

34. W. S. Jevons, *The Coal Question* (London: Macmillan, 1865).

35. Quoted in *Time*, August 26, 2002.

36. A phrase that is beginning to weary me. Remove the word *foreign*, I say.

37. . . . and cyanobacteria and various protists.

38. A quick search threw up this website: http://journeytoforever.org/biodiesel_make.html. There seem to be lots of others. Apparently, a car run on biodiesel smells like the local fish 'n' chip shop—which has to be better than regular diesel!

39. M. Sedlak and W. M. Y. Ho, "Production of Ethanol from Cellulosic Biomass Hydrolysate Using Genetically Engineered *Saccharomyces* Yeast Capable of Co-Fermenting Glucose and Xylose," *Applied Biochemistry and Biotechnology* 113–16 (2004): 403–16.

40. Literally a brewery, but in this case just a regular old pub on the waterfront.

41. Resource Efficient Agricultural Production (http://reap-canada.com).

42. D. J. Tilman, J. Hill, and C. Lehman, "Carbon-Negative Biofuels from Low-Input, High-Diversity Grassland Biomass," *Science* 314 (2006): 1498–1600.

43. By percent, that is. France gets three-quarters of its electricity from nuclear power.

44. Excuse my rough translation of "little mushroom cloud."

45. New Zealand Police at http://www.police.govt.nz/operation/wharf (accessed January 25, 2007).

46. M. Andrews, *The Rainbow Warrior Affair*, at http://www.kauricoast.co.nz (accessed January 25, 2007).

47. BP, "Energy in Focus: The BP Statistical Review of World Energy," 2004.

48. Makes great tank-busting warheads, though. . . .

49. M. Long, "Half Life: The Legacy of America's Nuclear Waste," *National Geographic*, July 2002.

50. K. Deffeyes, I. MacGregor, and J. Kukula, "Uranium Distribution in Mined Deposits and in the Earth's Crust," report to US Department of Energy, Grand Junction, Colorado, 1978. "Towards a European Strategy for the Security of Energy Supply," European Commission Energy Green Paper, European Commission, 2001.

51. Hubbert, "Nuclear Energy and the Fossil Fuels."

52. I Mahmoud'ont believe you.

53. http://www.eia.doe.gov/.

54. Actually, when you think about it, that would certainly serve as an incentive to get the shopping over with quickly: *Kids, kids, hurry up! The car's gonna blow any minute!*

55. Hydrogen, H_2, atomic weight = 2; natural gas, CH_4, atomic weight = 16.

56. The *Hindenburg* was a zeppelin made buoyant with hydrogen. It went up in flames in Manchester, New Jersey, on May 6, 1937, killing all thirty-six onboard and crashing to the ground in a dramatic fireball, reminding the world that hydrogen is a highly flammable gas.

57. Or cyanobacterium or photosynthetic protist.

58. Actually, Photosystem II, which is a complex of various different large pigment molecules. The thylakoid membrane; chloroplasts have stacks of these things operating like little power plants inside leaf cells.

59. The Haber process is responsible for producing the millions of tons of nitrogen-based fertilizers that are essential for modern food production. The process involves multiple steps carried out under high temperature and pressure, but, briefly, natural gas is reacted with steam and oxygen over a nickel oxide catalyst to make hydrogen. The hydrogen is then reacted with nitrogen over an iron oxide catalyst to make ammonia.

60. According to my buddy Kevin Gibson, this used to be an ad for Iceland vacations. Love it. Shame, then, that Iceland has suffered so badly through the 2008–2010 financial crisis, setting back its plans.

Chapter 6. The Ecological Debt

1. M. Coffey, "The Dust Storms," *Natural History* 87 (1978): 72–83.

2. J. Steinbeck, *The Grapes of Wrath* (New York: Sundial Press, 1941).

3. The adoption of no-till agriculture has contributed much to paying back the ecological debt to the soil. Other debts are being accumulated, however, notably the drawdown of the Ogallala aquifer that waters the region.

4. The term *global commons* has been used before in reference to the few global resources that remain unexploited and common-pool: mainly Antarctica, the deep ocean, and space. See J. Vogler, *The Global Commons: A Regime Analysis* (Chichester, UK: John Wiley & Sons, 1995). The most prolific author of treatises on the global commons is Elinor Ostrom of Indiana University; see E. Ostrom, *Governing the Commons: The Evolution of Institutions for Collective Action* (Cambridge: Cambridge University Press, 1990). I apologize to these authors for using an existing term differently, but there is really no better way to express what I want to convey, and, with respect, I find their use of the term a little constricting.

5. F. Montaigne, "Still Waters: The Global Fish Crisis," *National Geographic*, April 2007.

6. They are, of course, by no means alone. The Europeans, particularly the Spanish, take large volumes of fish and also operate in the deep oceans. Europe also takes large volumes of fish from off the coast of Africa. It seems to me that African fish are needed more in Africa than in Madrid.

7. *By-catch* refers to all the unwanted species that get caught. They usually get tossed back into the ocean dismembered or dead.

8. The Holocene is the geological period from roughly 12,000 BP to present. Essentially, it is the "human era" since the last major glaciation.

9. A. Weisman, *The World without Us* (New York: Thomas Dunne Books, 2007).

10. D. Archer and V. Brovkin, "The Millennial Atmosphere Lifetime of Anthropogenic CO_2," *Climate Change* 90 (2008): 283–97.

11. Statement made at hearing about proposed Rush Creek Mine, reported in the *Charleston Gazette*, February 25, 2005.

12. See Ohio Valley Environmental Coalition's website under "Outrageous Quotes": http://www.ohvec.org/outrageous.html (accessed November 29, 2006).

13. Among plenty of other things, of course, including nucleic acids (DNA).

14. Guano is bird poop, and the deposits left in some areas (notably Chile) by seabirds were prodigious. The realization that guano could be mined and shipped to agricultural regions as nitrogen fertilizer spawned a surprisingly large bird poop industry. Alas, humans can even overexploit bird poop, and Chilean guano went into decline early in the twentieth century. Germany was cut off from access to Chilean guano at the beginning of the First World War, thanks to the inadequacy of its navy, and the scene was set for Fritz Haber to change the world in nitrate-starved Germany.

15. P. Roberts, *The End of Food* (New York: Houghton Mifflin, 2008). M. Pollan, *The Omnivore's Dilemma: A Natural History of Four Meals* (New York: Penguin, 2007). T. E. Crews and M. B. Peoples, "Legume vs. Fertilizer Sources of Nitrogen: Ecological Tradeoffs and Human Needs," *Agriculture, Ecosystems, and Environment* 102 (2004): 279–97.

16. D. A. Pfeiffer, *Eating Fossil Fuels: Oil, Food, and the Coming Crisis in Agriculture* (Gabriola Island, BC, Canada: New Society Publishers, 2006).

17. A bunch of folks have used this, and I don't know who was first. The acronym TANSTAAFL—"There ain't no such thing as a free lunch"—is used variously.

18. Reverend Thomas Robert Malthus first published his *Essay on the Principal of Population* in 1798, and it has been a lightning rod ever since.

19. United Nations Population Division, World Population Prospects, available online at http://www.esa.un.org/unpp/ (accessed December 16, 2006). US Census Bureau, Historical Estimates of World Population, available online at http://www.census.gov/ipc/www/worldhis.html. J. E. Cohen, "Human Population: The Next Half Century," *Science* 302 (2003): 1172–75.

20. G. Hardin, "Nobody Ever Dies of Overpopulation," *Science* 171 (1971): 527.

21. M. Wackernagel and W. Rees, *Our Ecological Footprint: Reducing Human Impacts on the Earth* (Gabriola Island, BC, Canada: New Society Publishers, 1996).

22. A. Lovins, *World Energy Strategies: Facts, Issues, and Opinions* (London: Friends of the Earth, 1975).

23. I can't back this up, but consider that 75 percent of Nigeria's population survives on subsistence agriculture and that its main exports are oil, oil, and oil (and some cocoa, rubber, and other agricultural commodities). Nigeria is the eighth-largest oil exporter in the world, ahead of Venezuela, Mexico, Iraq, and the United Kingdom, shifting nearly two and a half million barrels per day in 2008. Nigeria consumes roughly 13 percent of its oil and exports the rest. See the CIA World Factbook at https://www.cia.gov/library/publications/the-world-factbook/index.html.

Chapter 7. The View from Mauna Loa

1. "Very likely" in this context is code for 90 to 99 percent certain.

2. The IPCC, formed by the United Nations, has provided detailed analyses of the global warming crisis roughly every five years since 1990. Multiple detailed and summary documents describing the status of the field are available from http://www.ipcc.ch. Most of the data used in this chapter are derived from IPCC sources.

3. Average minimum temperature for West Lafayette, Indiana, on December 16 over the last fifty years is 20 degrees (−7° C).

4. A new island was recently discovered in Greenland. It had been assumed to be a nunatak (mountain surrounded by land-based ice), but as the ice melted its true nature was revealed. Its discoverer, Dennis Schmidt, named it Uunartoq Qeqertoq—Inuit for "the Warming Island."

5. Unusually warm water off the coast of Scotland? Everything is relative.

6. J. Lovelock, *Gaia: A New Look at Life on Earth* (Oxford: Oxford University Press, 1987). Also worthy of a read is Lovelock's *The Revenge of Gaia* (London: Penguin, 2006), which is one of the more interesting and compelling discussions of global warming.

7. There is a set of planetary cycles affecting the orientation of the earth relative to the sun and relative to its proximity to the sun. They are affected, among other things, by the precise shape of the earth's elliptical orbit, which changes in a predictable way. Combined, these effects do have significant impacts on the global climate, affecting the amount of incoming radiation and the regions of the planet that receive it. They were described in detail by Milutin Milankovitch and have become known as Milankovitch cycles. The balance of our understanding of these cycles, however, predicts that without human-caused global warming the earth should presently be cooling slightly and should continue to do so for another 23,000 years; see J. Imbrie and J. Z. Imbrie, "Modelling the Climatic Response to Orbital Variations," *Science* 207 (1980): 943–53.

8. Hence the term *greenhouse effect*.

9. T. R. Karl and K. E. Trenberth, "Modern Global Climate Change," *Science* 302 (2003): 1719–23.

10. With thanks to Joni Mitchell's "Both Sides Now," first released on the Reprise label.

11. Archaea in the rumen of cattle produce copious amounts of methane—even more than a baked-bean-eating Englishman! The global population of swamp-adapted Archaea presumably increased with agriculture as the cultivation of rice in flooded paddies developed in east Asia more than five thousand years ago. W. F. Ruddiman, *Plows, Plagues, and Petroleum: How*

Humans Took Control of Climate (Princeton, NJ: University of Princeton Press, 2005).

12. This, however, depends on how you look at it. Viewed another way, the atmosphere is a very thin film—like a layer of plastic wrap around an orange.

13. G. M. Woodwell, "The Role of Forests in Climatic Change," in *Managing the World's Forests*, edited by N. P. Sharmna (Dubuque, IA: Kendall/Hunt, 1992).

14. G. J. Macdonald, *The Long-Term Impacts of Increasing Atmospheric Carbon Dioxide Levels* (Cambridge, MA: Ballinger, 1982).

15. The technical term for the higher absorbance of electromagnetic energy from darker objects is a *higher albedo*.

16. A. Malthe-Sorenssen et al., "Release of Methane from a Volcanic Basin as a Mechanism for Initial Eocene Global Warming," *Nature* 429 (2004): 542–45.

17. J. D. Hughes, *Pan's Travail: Environmental Problems of the Ancient Greeks and Romans* (Baltimore: Johns Hopkins Press, 1994).

18. From melting ice caps, sea ice, increased precipitation, and influx from rivers.

19. Albeit the educated guesses of the best-informed scientists in the field. . . .

20. UK Meteorological Office, Hadley Center, http://www.metoffice .gov.uk/research/hadleycentre/ (accessed December 16, 2006).

21. K. Emanuel, "Increasing Destructiveness of Tropical Cyclones over the Past 30 Years," *Nature* 436 (2005): 686–88. T. Spencer and I. Douglas, "The Significance of Environmental Change: Diversity, Disturbance, and Tropical Ecosystems," in *Environmental Change and Tropical Geomorphology*, edited by I. Douglas and T. Spencer (London: Allen & Unwin, 1985).

22. A. Gore, *An Inconvenient Truth: The Planetary Emergency of Global Warming and What We Can Do about It* (Emmaus, PA: Rodale, 2006).

23. Carbon dioxide forms bicarbonate in water.

24. T. J. Goreau and R. L. Hayes, "Coral Bleaching and Ocean 'Hot Spots,'" *Ambio* 23 (1994): 176–80.

25. R. Lal, "Climate Change, Soil Carbon Dynamics, and Global Food

Security," in *Climate Change and Global Food Security*, edited by R. Lal, B. A. Stewart, N. Uphott, and D. O. Hansen (Boca Raton, FL: Taylor & Francis, 2005), pp. 113–43.

26. R. Darwin, S. Rosen, and S. Shashpouri, "Greenhouse Gases and Food Security in Low-Income Countries," in *Climate Change and Global Food Security*, edited by Lal, Stewart, Uphott, and Hansen (see note 25), pp. 71–111.

27. The combination of evaporation from inanimate objects such as lakes or the soil and transpiration from plants.

28. John Holdren is President Obama's adviser for science and technology, director of the White House Office of Science and Technology Policy, and co-chair of the President's Council of Advisers on Science and Technology (PCAST). He was previously the Teresa and John Heinz Professor of Environmental Policy at the Kennedy School of Government at Harvard University, director of the Science, Technology, and Public Policy Program at the Harvard's Belfer Center for Science and International Affairs, and director of the Woods Hole Research Center. He was president of the American Association for the Advancement of Science (AAAS) from 2006 to 2007.

He has actually made this statement many times, slightly modified. One example I found was the 8th John Chaffee Memorial Lecture on Science and the Environment, January 17, 2008, Washington, DC, National Council for Science and the Environment.

PART III. THE WEALTH OF NATIONS

1. J. P. Eaton and C. A. Haas, *Titanic: Destination Disaster. The Legends and the Reality*, rev. ed. (New York: W. W. Norton, 1996).

2. . . . the type of pride that cometh before a fall . . .

Chapter 8. Collision Course

1. R. Heinberg, *The Party's Over: Oil, War, and the Fate of Industrial Societies* (Gabriola Island, BC, Canada: New Society Publishers, 2003).

2. Oilitis? Fossilfuelcombustionitis?

3. This concept was expounded on by economist Simon Kuznet. The main outcome of his theory is generally referred to as the Kuznet Curve. Plotting some kind of social or environmental outcome (e.g., Amount of Pollution Caused) (y axis) against some measure of economic prosperity (e.g., per Capita GDP) (x axis), the curve tends to form some derivative of an inverted U shape (an *n*, I guess). The synthesis is that the poorest nations cause relatively little pollution because they are too poor for much economic activity; rapidly developing nations have high productivity without remediation and are the worst polluters; whereas developed nations, having traveled the farthest along the Kuznet Curve, have high levels of production and consumption but are also able to conduct significant steps toward remediation.

4. Bbl = blue barrel, per the color of paint used by Rockefeller's Standard Oil. A barrel is 42 gallons.

5. J. H. Kunstler, *The Long Emergency: Surviving the End of Oil, Climate Change, and Other Converging Catastrophes of the Twenty-First Century* (New York: Grove Press, 2005). I wanted this title and was annoyed when I came across Kunstler's book and found that he had already used it. As a result, I use the term "the great recession," but I'll admit that I prefer "the long emergency." It means essentially the same thing. Sigh.

6. The oil companies themselves will actually do rather well in the early days of the great recession. They will be selling smaller volumes of a more valuable commodity (while it lasts) at a much higher price.

7. Speech at the Uruguay Round (8th round) negotiations of the Multilateral Trade Negotiations (MTN) under the General Agreement on Tariffs and Trade (GATT), which would eventually lead to the formation of the World Trade Organization (WTO), Punta del Este, Uruguay, September 1986.

8. It was interesting that Uncle Deryck used the very phrase "the sun will never set," first uttered by John Wilson in *Noctes Ambrosianae* in 1829, and used repeatedly thereafter . . . until nightfall finally came to said empire.

9. Speech at the Lord Mayor's Luncheon, Mansion House, London, November 1, 1942.

10. This subtitle comes from a seminar given at Purdue University by Stanford emeritus professor Amos Nur.

11. T. Shelley, *Oil, Politics, Poverty and the Planet* (London: Zed Books, 2005).

12. W. S. Churchill, *The Second World War, Vol. IV: The Hinge of Fate* (London: Published in association with the Cooperation Publishing Company [by] Houghton Mifflin, 1950).

13. W. D. Smith, "Price Quadruples for Iranian Crude Oil at Auction," *New York Times*, December 12, 1973.

14. Heinberg, *The Party's Over*. Ahmed Zaki Yamani was the Saudi Minister of Petroleum and Mineral Resources from 1962 to 1986 and longtime OPEC minister.

15. This is also the stated motivation of Osama bin Laden's terrorist attacks against the United States.

16. F. E. Clements, *Plant Succession: An Analysis of the Development of Vegetation* (Chicago: University of Chicago Press, 1916).

17. H. A. Gleason, "The Individualistic Concept of Plant Association," *American Midland Naturalist* 21 (1939): 92–110.

18. Ecological concept, intuitively named. A species that has significant "ecological value." Remove a keystone species, and the ecosystem will see significant change . . . an oak tree in an English woodland . . . lichens from a Scandinavian forest (the reindeer all die, etc., etc.).

19. . . . just for kicks.

20. There is a wide range of what is normal. Grasslands may have a natural fire frequency of five to twenty-five years. Forests may have a fire frequency of twenty-five to two-hundred-plus years. Fire ecology is a fascinating subject. As an example, consider the Australian mountain ash tree (*Eucalyptus regnans*), whose seed will only germinate after a fire. This seems to be an adaptation that ensures that the seed will lie dormant in the ground until the undergrowth is cleared of competition. It just so happens (well, no, I doubt it's a coincidence) that the mature mountain ash tree is laden with inflammable oils that promote a good, hot burn. As the parents die in a wildfire, it seems as if they go out in a blaze of glory that will ensure that their offspring have the best possible start in life. If the forest fails to burn for more than a few hundred years, it is doomed: the mature trees will eventually die of old age as their seeds rot in the deep shade of the underbrush.

21. Holling was the pioneer of "resiliency thinking," an area now studied by a number of researchers. Two of the most important/accesible texts are: L. H. Gunderson and C. S. Holling, *Panarchy: Understanding Transformations in Human and Natural Systems* (Washington, DC: Island Press, 2002), and B. H. Walker and D. Salt, *Resiliency Thinking: Sustaining Ecosystems and People in a Changing World* (Washington, DC: Island Press, 2006).

22. First (Neil Armstrong) and last (Gene Cernan) people on the moon were both graduates of Purdue University . . . Go, Boilers!

23. Eldon Joersz in SR-71 Blackbird; Andy Green in Thrust SSC; Ken Warby in Spirit of Australia.

Chapter 9. Around the World in Eighty Depressions

1. A. K. Ellis, *Teaching and Learning Elementary Social Studies* (Upper Saddle River, NJ: Allyn & Bacon, 1997). This may be misattributed, but the quote is attributed to Bohr in this source.

2. Speech in London, December 16, 1970, as quoted in the *Times* (London), December 17, 1970.

3. Afghanistan, Kazakhstan, Kyrgyzstan, Tajikistan, Turkmenistan, Uzbekistan.

4. The obvious exception to this is Dubai, which is attempting to invest in non-oil businesses. I still don't see how they will manage beyond oil. The luxurious condos and playgrounds will be hard to maintain without oil revenues. Freshwater is entirely from desalinization, and I expect Dubai will go the way of Las Vegas . . . a glittering anomaly of an oil age with a sudden and rapid collapse waiting around the corner. The investments of Dubai businessmen may save their families—but for futures elsewhere, not in Dubai.

5. Big questions as to the legitimacy of the 2009 elections.

6. With the obvious exception of Kazakhstan.

7. If you prefer "Palestinian Territory," go for it.

8. J. M. Sharp, "US Foreign Aid to Israel," Congressional Research Service Report, January 2, 2008.

9. I'll bet you a dime to a dollar, he'll be the next president of Russia.

10. A quick note on Dmitry Medvedev. Former chair of the board of

directors of Gazprom and current Russian president. I'm rather cheekily considering Putin as the likely long-term figurehead of Russia, and I am assuming he will spend a term as PM and then recover the presidency.

11. A recent tragedy at a hydro plant at Cheryomushky in southern Siberia, however, highlights the fact that much of Russia's old Soviet-era infrastructure is in poor condition. Sixty-two workers were killed when the plant failed (not the dam), and they were drowned, which also reminds us that no energy source is completely safe. In fact, many more people have suffered and died in accidents at hydro plants than in nuclear plants.

12. World Nuclear Association, "Nuclear Power in Russia," http://www .world-nuclear.org/info/inf45.html (accessed December 27, 2010).

13. J. M. Diamond, *Guns, Germs, and Steel: The Fates of Human Societies* (New York: Houghton Mifflin, 1997).

14. Plans are in discussion to bring water to Vegas from aquifers under the Nevada-Utah border area a few hundred miles to the north. This would likely have a huge impact on the farmers of that region. It's also a sign of desperation.

15. I prefer the names Bosnywash, Boswash, or Boshington that have variously been used.

16. . . . and comedian—now Hollywood writer among other things; see his humor blog Kung Fu Monkey, at http://kfmonkey.blogspot.com/.

17. The replacement of W with Barack, however, has changed things significantly. Fingers crossed.

18. OK, so the dissolution of the Canadian Parliament (December 2008) does not support this claim. Canadian politics are not perfect.

19. He convinced Japan to open its borders to trade with the United States during the Edo period. The "Harris Treaty" is named after him.

20. Vague enough? I know, but do you count San Marino, Guernsey, and so on, bringing the total up to forty-nine, or do you stick to the basics and call it forty-two? Also, I do not include Russia as part of Europe here, as others often do.

21. . . . also illustrating the massive size of the US economy.

22. Old Peculier, a barley wine (strong beer). Don't have too many, especially if you're playing darts with Steve Humphreys.

23. "An Energy Policy for Europe," communication from the Commis-

sion to the European Council and the European Parliament, Brussels, January 10, 2007.

24. Xinhua News Agency, November 28 and 29, 2006.

25. M. K. Gandhi, *An Autobiography: The Story of My Experiments with Truth*, translated by M. H. Desai (Boston: Beacon Press, 1993).

26. E. Luce, *In Spite of the Gods: The Strange Rise of Modern India* (New York: Random House, 2007).

27. World Health Organization, http://www.who.int/.

28. P. Ehrlich, *The Population Bomb* (New York: Ballantine Books, 1968).

29. Interestingly, a pipeline through the Sahara to the Mediterranean Sea would probably have been significantly cheaper to construct, but it would have put the outlet point closer to Europe and would have had to pass through Libya.

Chapter 10. End of Empire

1. A. L. Miller, "China as an Emerging Superpower?" *Stanford Journal of International Relations* 6 (2005).

2. A. Negri and M. Hardt, *Empire* (Cambridge, MA: Harvard University Press, 2000).

3. I. Asimov, *Foundation* (New York: Doubleday, 1951; Bantam Dell, 2004). Some deletions from the original text.

PART IV. A GENERAL THEORY

Chapter 11. Ecology Is the Foundation of Economics

1. R. Heinlein, *The Notebooks of Lazarus Long* (New York: Ace Books, 1978).

2. J. K. Rowling, *Harry Potter and the Chamber of Secrets* (New York: Arthur A. Levine, 1999).

3. Cheeky of me, I know, to use a quote from Milton Friedman as I open

my critique of capitalism and suggest major changes to its underpinnings. I'll tell you what, though: I bet he wouldn't mind.

4. After William Stanley Jevons, who predicted the demise of the British coal industry in the nineteenth century.

5. A classic—and very depressing—example of the way in which a technological solution to reduce one source of pollution (here, carbon emissions from driving) can increase others. The credentials of the Prius lose some of their green tinge when you consider that the reduced carbon dioxide emissions from driving a Prius are offset, at least partially, because: (1) The Prius is more energy-intensive to manufacture than similar cars such as the Corolla and has a shorter lifetime, (2) The batteries contain nickel, which has to be mined—an environmental problem—and discarded at the end of their life—another environmental problem. The biggest disaster, however, is probably that the Prius fools people into thinking they are being green when they are not. A good start point for data on the whole life-cycle environmental costs of the Pius is from CNW Marketing Research, Inc. *The Energy Cost of New Vehicles from Concept to Disposal. The Non-Technical Report* (colloquially termed the "dust to dust" report). http://www.enwmr.com (accessed December 27, 2010).

6. P. Barta, B. Lamonde, L. Miranda-Morales, and N. Boucher, "Traveled Distance, Stock, and Fuel Efficiency of Private Vehicles in Canada: Price Elasticities and Rebound Effect," *Transportation* 36 (2009): 389–402. M. Frondel, J. Peters, and C. Vance, "Identifying the Rebound: Evidence from a German Household Panel," *Energy Journal* 29 (2008):145–63.

7. It's actually not all that efficient in real terms, but it uses very little gas because it is so small.

8. G. Hardin, *Filters against Folly: How to Survive Despite Economists, Ecologists, and the Merely Eloquent* (New York: Penguin, 1985).

9. Right, so if you're on the ball, you can apply the "you can never do one thing" thing easily here. The Jevons paradox still operates, but less directly. More health can result in an aging population that can add certain environmental stresses. Also, the overuse of antibiotics can lead to resistance issues.

10. Again, another Jevons paradox. Better communications can lead fairly directly to more efficient coordination of resource extraction, etc.

Chapter 12. A New Foundation

1. M. Friedman, *Capitalism and Freedom* (Chicago: University of Chicago Press, 1962).

2. Corporate Average Fuel Efficiency.

3. J. Rifkin, *The Hydrogen Economy: The Creation of the Worldwide Energy Web and the Redistribution of Power on Earth* (New York: JP Tarcher/Penguin, 2002).

4. P. Hoffman, *Tomorrow's Energy: Hydrogen, Fuel Cells, and the Prospects for a Cleaner Planet* (Cambridge, MA: MIT Press, 2001).

5. Reese was also an activist in the Welsh nationalist movement and editor of *Barn* (Opinion), a Welsh language magazine.

6. D. Jensen, *The Problem of Civilization: Volume 1 of Endgame* (New York: Seven Stories Press, 2006).

7. I first heard this quote from Alan Watson, a weed science professor at McGill University. It has been well used and seems to be rather old, but I cannot turn up its origins.

8. With sandstorms from the north, coal dust from the south, and a mess of homegrown pollution from a city of twelve million people, Beijing is getting a tad icky. The 2008 Olympics would have been the phlegmiest in history were it not for the closing of many factories and power plants in the Beijing area and fortuitously mild weather.

9. M. Pollan, *The Omnivore's Dilemma: A Natural History of Four Meals* (New York: Penguin, 2007).

10. Aldo Leopold (1887–1948) was one of the most important early American environmental writers, and he is most revered for his simple, elegant, no-nonsense chapter "The Land Ethic" in his seminal work *A Sand County Almanac*, first published soon after his death, in 1949. A. Leopold, *A Sand County Almanac: With Essays on Conservations from Round River* (New York: Random House, 1970).

11. Better known as the Iroquois Federation, made up of the Mohawk, Oneida, Onondaga, Cayuga, Seneca, and Tuscarora tribes. *Iroquois* is sometimes considered a derogatory name.

12. Everything is relative: The first few hundred generations of Ameri-

cans, arriving in a new continent with sharp stone hunting tools and advanced techniques, probably caused the extinction of the North American megafauna (also discussed in chapter 1).

13. At a panel discussion with musician Bono and others at the 2002 World Economic Forum, New York, February 2, 2002.

14. A. Huxley, *Brave New World* (London: Chatto & Windus, 1932), L. Lowry, *The Giver* (New York: Bantam Books, 1993). Another favorite is G. Orwell, *1984* (London: Secker & Warburg, 1949). The earliest I know of is A. Trollope, *The Fixed Period* (London: Blackwood & Sons, 1882).

15. Just a few examples of different types: B. Aldiss, *Earthworks* (London: Faber & Faber, 1965); I. Asimov, *The Caves of Steel* (New York: Doubleday, 1954); R. Bradbury, *The Martian Chronicles* (New York: Doubleday, 1950); H. G. Wells, *The Time Machine* (London: William Heinemann, 1895).

16. W. Churchill, *A Little Matter of Genocide: Holocaust and Denial in the Americas: 1942–Present* (San Francisco: City Lights Books, 1997).

17. With some exceptions allowed for some rural couples, couples without siblings, couples of some ethnic minorities, and so forth.

18. S. C. B. S., as named by S. G. H.

19. The southeast: Norfolk, Suffolk.

20. Now the Isthmus of Panama.

21. Ronald Ross was an eclectic fellow of a million interests, at which he mostly failed. He never considered himself a scientist but struggled away in dusty labs in India and eventually came up with the solution to yellow fever and malaria, largely by determining its epidemiology and mosquito transmission; then went on to win the second Nobel Prize for medicine in 1902. The quotation is from his acceptance speech.

22. Ah, the cultural difference between the Brits and the Yanks: the Brits disguised the taste in gin & tonic!

23. I have taken two of these. Lariam messed with my head, made me nutty and paranoid, and gave me the craziest hallucinations, including a nasty "bad trip" with rabid dogs and monster-sized cockroaches. Not funny. Malarone was much more expensive but was not psychotropic in the slightest.

24. G. Hardin, "Lifeboat Ethics: The Case against Helping the Poor," *Psychology Today*, September 1979.

Chapter 13. Reconnecting

1. Renaissance humanist Francesco Petrarca, writing in the early fourteenth century, is generally considered to be the first to coin the term "Dark Ages" for the early medieval period following the fall of the Roman Empire.

2. N. Klein, *Fences and Windows: Dispatches from the Front Lines of the Globalization Debate* (New York: Picador, 2005).

3. G. Wearden, "BP Profits Jump after Oil Price Rise," *Guardian*, April 27, 2010.

4. G. Hardin, "The Tragedy of the Commons," *Science* 162 (1968): 1243–48.

5. Pollution operates in the same way: the tiny amount of pollution released by an individual seems insignificant, but everyone's small contribution can create a mess.

6. Hardin, "The Tragedy of the Commons."

7. In fairness to Hardin, he never really used the medieval commons as his backdrop. That image was an embellishment added gradually by the many writers following in his footsteps. It was used often enough that it became accepted as truth. The most important studies of the medieval English commons and the explanation of their nontragedy status comes from Susan Buck at the University of North Carolina. For her most comprehensive contribution, see S. Buck, *The Global Commons: An Introduction* (Washington, DC: Island Press, 1998).

8. E. Ostrom, *Governing the Commons: The Evolution of Institutions for Collective Action* (Cambridge: Cambridge University Press, 1993). Ostrom was the first woman to win this prize—a significant breakthrough. The award of an economic prize for a student of collective action and social systems who has provided an analysis criticizing the accepted capitalist norms is perhaps an even bigger breakthrough.

9. *When We Were Kings*, 1996, directed by Leon Gast. The film won an Academy Award for Best Documentary, Feature, in 1997.

10. Hey, now that I think about it . . . what were you and Dad up to that weekend?

11. I wonder if this is where the Aussies got their classic descriptor for hot, dry weather: "Drier than a Pommie's bathmat!"

12. Grandpa was too old to fight in the Second World War. In any case, he had paid his debt in the First World War, fighting in Mesopotamia (Iraq) and Afghanistan. In the end he died of malaria in Manchester.

13. N. Longmate, *How We Lived Then* (London: Hutchinson, 2002). W. K. Hancock and M. M. Gowing, *The British War Economy* (London: HMSO, 1949).

INDEX

Numbers presented in italics indicate images.

EAGLE VALLEY LIBRARY DISTRICT
P.O. BOX 240 600 BROADWAY
EAGLE, CO 81631 / 328-8800